Recomposing Ecopoetics

Under the Sign of Nature: Explorations in Ecocriticism
Michael P. Branch, Kate Rigby, John Tallmadge, *Editors*

Recomposing Ecopoetics

NORTH AMERICAN POETRY OF THE SELF-CONSCIOUS ANTHROPOCENE

Lynn Keller

UNIVERSITY OF VIRGINIA PRESS

CHARLOTTESVILLE AND LONDON

University of Virginia Press
© 2017 by the Rector and Visitors of the University of Virginia
All rights reserved
Printed in the United States of America on acid-free paper

First published 2017

9 8 7 6 5 4 3 2 1

Library of Congress Cataloging-in-Publication Data

Names: Keller, Lynn, [date] author.
Title: Recomposing ecopoetics : North American poetry of the self-conscious
    anthropocene / Lynn Keller.
Other titles: North American poetry of the self-conscious anthropocene
Description: Charlottesville : University of Virginia Press, 2017. | Series: Under the sign of
    nature : explorations in ecocriticism | Includes bibliographical references and index.
Identifiers: LCCN 2017025188 | ISBN 9780813940618 (cloth : alk. paper) | ISBN
    9780813940625 (pbk. : alk. paper) | ISBN 9780813940632 (ebook)
Subjects: LCSH: Ecocriticism. | Philosophy of nature in literature. | Place (Philosophy)
    in literature. | Ecology in literature. | Human-animal relationships in literature.
    | Environmentalism in literature. | American poetry—21st century—History and
    criticism. | Canadian poetry—21st century—History and criticism.
Classification: LCC PN98.E36 K45 2017 | DDC 809/.9336—dc23
LC record available at https://lccn.loc.gov/2017025188

Cover art: Cut-Bank (Kikait), Jeremy Herndl, 2013. (Collection of the Surrey Art Gallery;
photo by Scott Massey)

For Caroline and Joe

A poetics that can operate in the interrogative, with epistemological curiosity and ethical concern, is not so much language as instrument to peer through as instrument of investigative engagement. As such it takes part in the recomposing of contemporary consciousness, contemporary sensibilities.
—Joan Retallack, "What Is Experimental Poetry & Why Do We Need It?"

Contents

Illustrations

Acknowledgments

Two communities have been crucial to the development of this book. The first is the Center for Culture, History, and Environment (CHE) in the Nelson Institute for Environmental Studies at the University of Wisconsin–Madison. When I turned my scholarship toward environmental inquiry, I started attending the regular CHE colloquia in order to learn how scholars in multiple disciplines were discussing environmental issues. I gained a great deal more—most rewardingly, an extraordinarily interesting and caring group of faculty and graduate student colleagues outside my home department of English. My particular thanks to Bill Cronon and Gregg Mitman, founding leaders of CHE, who pulled me in and have continued to support me.

The second is the English Department at Stockholm University, where I was a visiting professor in the first half of 2014. Claudia Egerer, then department chair, generously invited me to give a series of lectures for graduate students and faculty in lieu of one of my courses. Those lectures, which enabled me to gather the thinking I had been doing in recent years, provided the backbone for this book. I am grateful for the warm welcome I received from all the members of that department through Sweden's dark winter months, and especially to Claudia, Bo Ekeland, and Paul Schreiber for their valuable feedback in response to my lectures.

Without composing the Stockholm lectures, I could never have written a proposal that would have convinced the John Simon Guggenheim Memorial Foundation to award me a fellowship. I am honored and grateful for the Guggenheim Fellowship in 2015–2016 that enabled me to write this book with the speed its timely subject warrants. Also formative was the interdisciplinary fall 2013 Faculty Development Seminar "Environmental Studies in the Time of the Anthropocene," organized by Rob Nixon and sponsored by the Center for the Humanities, the Institute for Research in the Humanities, and the College of Letters and Science at the University of Wisconsin–Madison. I am grateful to Rob for his thoughtful leadership and to the other participants: Samer Alatout, Monique Allewaert, Anna Andrzejewski, Joshua Calhoun, Kata Beilin, Will Brockliss, Mark Johnson, Rick Keller, Gregg Mitman, Larry Nesper, Sai Suryanarayanan, Alberto Vargas, and Lydia Zepeda.

Many other wonderful friends and colleagues have also provided valuable assistance, among them Stephen Brick, Michael Davidson, Alan Golding, Caroline Levine, Angela Hume, Dee Morris, Jed Rasula, Joan Retallack, Jack W. Williams, and David Zimmerman. By inviting me to give talks in the spring of 2014, Marco Armiero, Evy Varsamopoulou, and Caitlin DeSilvey—all generous hosts—enabled me to get additional responses to ideas I was developing. Special thanks to the members of the stimulating ACLA seminar that Angela Hume and I organized in 2015, "The Opening of the Field: New Approaches to Ecopoetics": Angie and Joan again, Rob Halpern, Matt Hooley, Michelle Niemann, Gillian Osborne, Sonya Posmentier, Margaret Ronda, Joshua Schuster, and Jonathan Skinner. I am deeply thankful for the powerful and courageous writing of all the poets discussed here; several of them deserve additional thanks for answering questions or providing resources. The person who has most helped me bring this book into the world is my former doctoral student Michelle Niemann, whom I hired initially so that I could have an informed and insightful reader responding to my chapters as I produced them during my fellowship year. Her comments prompted revisions that have significantly sharpened the arguments in this book. As she began to establish a business in academic editing, her responsibilities expanded: she commented on the revised chapters; helped me trim the manuscript; shifted the style to suit the press's stipulations; and properly formatted the notes along with the rest of the manuscript. Always prompt, efficient, and careful, as well as marvelously intelligent and sensible, she relieved me of a huge amount of labor and stress. A thousand thanks to Michelle.

I wish to acknowledge the poets, photographers, and presses who generously granted permission to reprint images from the books discussed here: Ian Teh and Coffee House Press; Jonathan Skinner and BlazeVOX; Evelyn Reilly, James Sherry, and Roof Books; Forrest Gander, Raymond Meeks, Lucas Foglia, and New Directions; Angela Rawlings, Matt Ceolin, and Coach House Books; Jody Gladding and Milkweed Editions. I am also grateful to the editors who published articles that overlap with material published here:

"21st-Century Ecopoetry and the Scalar Challenges of the Anthropocene," in *The News from Poems: Essays on the 21st-Century American Poetry of Engagement*, edited by Jeffrey Gray and Ann Keniston; "The Ecopoetics of Hyperobjects: Evelyn Reilly's *Styrofoam*," in *Interdisciplinary Studies in Literature and Environment*; and "a.rawlings: Ecopoetic Intersubjectivity," in *Jacket2*. "Making Art 'under these apo-calypso rays': Crisis, Apocalypse, and Contemporary Ecopoetics," an abbreviated version of chapter 3, is forthcoming in a collection currently titled *Ecopoetics: A Critical Anthology*, edited by Angela Hume and Gillian Osborne.

My thanks to Boyd Zenner at the University of Virginia Press, to the manuscript's anonymous readers, and to the editors of the series Under the Sign of Nature, Michael Branch, SueEllen Campbell, Kate Rigby, and John Tallmadge, for their faith in this book. Thanks to the press staff, and especially to Ellen Satrom and Cecilia Sorochin, and to freelance editor Sue Breckenridge, for their skillful work on its production.

Finally, endless thanks to my amazing children, Caroline and Joe Carlsmith, whose love and energy support all that I do. However dark our time, they ground the hope that sustains me.

Recomposing Ecopoetics

Introduction

Beyond Nature Poetry

The Anthropocene. Dozens of books published in the last few years include the word in their titles: from *The Birth of the Anthropocene* to *Learning to Die in the Anthropocene*, from *Art in the Anthropocene* to *Geomorphology in the Anthropocene*, from *Eating Anthropocene* to *Minimal Ethics for the Anthropocene*. Artists and museums in multiple nations are using the term to name their exhibits; for instance, *Placing the Golden Spike: Landscapes of the Anthropocene* (Milwaukee Art Museum), *Earth Works: Mapping the Anthropocene* (Norton Museum of Art, West Palm Beach), *Ark of the Anthropocene* (Weisman Art Museum, Duluth), and *Welcome to the Anthropocene: The Earth in Our Hands* (Deutsches Museum, Munich). Academic conferences concerning the Anthropocene involving diverse disciplines, such as "Big History Anthropocene" and "Democracy and Resilience in the Anthropocene," have recently been organized in Canberra, Santa Barbara, Milwaukee, Stockholm, Paris, and Sydney, among other cities. There's now even a magazine titled *Anthropocene: Innovation in the Human Age* as well as a transdisciplinary journal, *The Anthropocene Review*. Although the term may or may not be formally adopted by the International Commission on Stratigraphy to designate the current geological epoch, the awareness that humans have come to be the dominant force affecting planetary systems now pervades our culture; it is registered in the most recent Papal encyclical, in a range of academic fields as well as in public discourses, and by artists working in all kinds of media.[1]

I have coined the phrase "self-conscious Anthropocene" to provide a term, distinct from the label for the geological era that may have begun centuries ago, that foregrounds this very recent awareness. It identifies the period since the term Anthropocene was introduced when, whether or not people use that word, there is extensive "recognition that human actions are driving far-reaching changes to the life-supporting infrastructure of Earth."[2] The phrase acknowledges that, whatever the status of the Anthropocene as a geological category and regardless of whether that epoch is deemed to have begun half a century or many centuries ago, the broad appeal of the term Anthropocene signals a powerful cultural phenomenon tied to reflexive, critical, and often anxious awareness of the scale and severity of human effects on the planet. Although recognition of human planetary impact on the atmosphere, oceans, land, and ecosystems has been developing for at least a century, only very recently has this awareness become truly widespread.

It was in the year 2000 that Nobel Prize–winning atmospheric chemist Paul Crutzen and biologist Eugene Stoermer proposed that humankind has so transformed the planet that we have entered a new geological epoch they named after humans, the Anthropocene. Momentarily I will outline the debates surrounding the term and its dating that have taken place primarily among geologists and other natural scientists, but those debates are only background for this study, which concerns poetry that responds to contemporary environmental changes and challenges—that is, poetry of the self-conscious Anthropocene. As Tobias Boes and Kate Marshall observe, "Regardless of when the Anthropocene is agreed to have begun, what is different now is that it is being recognized or named as such." Going further, Nigel Clark asserts, "The awareness that humankind has grown into a preeminent force in planetary nature—and all the associated questions about how to deal with this situation—is undoubtedly one of the most momentous events our species has ever had to cope with."[3] The designation "self-conscious Anthropocene" enables us to name this period of *changed recognition* when the responsibility humans bear for the condition of the planet and for the fates of Holocene species is widely understood. While "the Anthropocene" is a term of geological reference that may reach back centuries, "the self-conscious Anthropocene" identifies a cultural reality more than a scientific one. I date it from the year of Crutzen and Stoermer's publication, since that registers transformations not simply in the environment but also in awareness, though that awareness is not tied only to the term's dissemination. Conveniently, the date corresponds with the turn of a century and the beginning of a new millennium.

Boes and Marshall also note that "*knowing* and *articulating* species-being within a reflexively produced era of geologic time requires . . . novel modes of articulation that are appropriate to these complex forms of mediation."[4] The literature examined in this book is North American writing produced in the twenty-first century whose often experimental or novel "modes of of tectonic plates, that continue to shape earth's life systems. To be sure, humans—especially the wealthiest of us—possess planet-altering powers, but we do not exercise those powers in isolation from other forces." A further complication, as Nixon and others have noted, is that while humankind may appropriately be viewed as a single entity when considered through the lens of geological time, when seen at smaller scales, human societies vary greatly in how and how much they contribute to anthropogenic environmental change, as well as in the nature and degree of environmental degradation they immediately face. There's consequent concern that focus on the Anthropocene may obscure pressing issues of environmental justice. As Nixon sees it, the challenge is to tell two stories at once, one a convergent narrative that treats the species as a single power, the other a divergent story that recognizes "We may all be in the Anthropocene but we're not all in it in the same way."[13]

The term Anthropocene generates as much wariness among ecocritics as among geologists. Having worked over recent decades to make people's thinking and reading practices less anthropocentric, some ecocritics worry that the term recenters the human and that it separates the human from the environment, as if humans were having an impact from outside. Some prefer nomenclature that does not call attention to humankind. Donna Haraway, for instance, argues that the Anthropocene is too tied up in "efforts to find ways of thinking about, theorizing, modeling, and managing a Big Thing called Globalization," too focused on "Species Man," too little focused on ongoingness, and insufficiently attentive to thinking with other planetary organisms. Wanting to convey the tentacular interconnectedness of our multispecies landscapes, she has proposed the term Chthulucene as a forward-looking alternative to Anthropocene. Others have proposed as more appropriate labels the Plantationocene, to link mass extinction of nonhuman species to the killing off of indigenous peoples that resulted from colonialism, or the Capitalocene, to stress the role capitalism has played in resource extraction, energy consumption, and development that have damaged the planet.[14] Ecocritics worry, too, about cooptation of the term Anthropocene, whereby what was originally intended as a wake-up call and a plea for difficult but urgently needed collaboration becomes just another piece of trendy and vague green-speech—as arguably has happened with sustainability.

Despite such risks, I employ the term because it is drawing the environmental humanities and the sciences together in conversations of broad social, ethical, and political importance. Science and technology cannot address the environmental challenges of our era alone; effective responses will require action by citizens and governments or the work of psychologists, urban planners, ethicists, historians, economists, sociologists, and many others, including the artists and writers who prompt the human heart and imagination and the critics who illuminate their work. At the same time, environmental literary criticism, if it is going to be socially and politically relevant, needs to be genuinely interdisciplinary; the current scientific debates around the environmental issues of the Anthropocene, including those around the so-called "good Anthropocene" (a view of the epoch as an opportunity for humans to use technology to develop less destructive ways of living on the planet) are crucial ones for contemporary creative writers and ecocritics alike to register and address. By using the Anthropocene as a conceptual framework, I show how contemporary ecopoetics can contribute to important exchanges in and among a number of fields both within and beyond the environmental humanities.

At least since the Industrial Revolution, some segment of the population has been conscious that humankind was transforming the earth's atmosphere, bodies of water, ecosystems, and landscapes; nonetheless, a truly pervasive (and often anxious) consciousness of really radical anthropogenic planetary change is a recent phenomenon. Perhaps it began with the explosion of the first atom bomb; J. Robert Oppenheimer's pronouncement at the Alamogordo test site, "now I am become death, the destroyer of worlds," spoke for humanity, not just one brilliant physicist. Or perhaps this widespread awareness might be tied to the publication of Rachel Carson's *Silent Spring* in 1962, revealing to the public that the new synthetic chemicals coming into widespread use threatened to eradicate multiple species. Or perhaps one might point to 1988, when James Hansen testified before the U.S. Congress about anthropogenic climate change. However, each of those landmarks involves a particular form of planetary modification by humans; in contrast, Crutzen and Stoermer's announcement of the Anthropocene in 2000 stands out in its deliberate inclusiveness, encompassing the addition of radioactivity to the earth's surface, the increasing numbers of toxic chemicals being released into the environment, the warming of the atmosphere and of the oceans, the runaway rates of extinction, the vast alteration of planetary surfaces (and of water quality) by resource extraction, and more. I therefore date the pervasive cultural awareness of anthropogenic planetary transformation that distinguishes the self-conscious Anthropocene from 2000.

NATURE POETRY AND EVOLVING ECOPOETICS

The writing of the self-conscious Anthropocene examined in this study is not traditional nature poetry, although that genre has been the focus of most ecocritical work on anglophone poetry, from John Elder's *Imagining the Earth* (1985)—which treats poetry by Gary Snyder, Wendell Berry, A. R. Ammons, Denise Levertov, William Everson, and, in a later edition, Mary Oliver—through Leonard M. Scigaj's *Sustainable Poetry* (1999)—on Snyder, Berry, Ammons, and W. S. Merwin—to Jonathan Bate's brilliant study of the British Romantics, *The Song of the Earth* (2000), and beyond. Poetry had a place in early ecocritical conversations because of the distinguished Romantic tradition developed by writers such as William Wordsworth, Samuel Taylor Coleridge, John Clare, and, across the Atlantic, Ralph Waldo Emerson and his Transcendentalist circle—which included Henry David Thoreau, whose prose was central to early ecocriticism in the United States.[15] The preeminence of this material for environmental critics makes sense in view of the correspondence of the Romantic period with the rise of industrialism and the beginning of such distinctively Anthropocene problems as severe urban air pollution. Raymond Williams, when tracing the history of Western "Ideas of Nature," observed that industrialization changed not just the conditions of the natural environment but people's ways of thinking about and interacting with it: "it is just at this time . . . that nature is decisively seen as separate from men. . . . [N]ow nature, increasingly, was 'out there' and it was natural to reshape it to a dominant need. . . . Nature in any other sense than that of the improvers [the industrial entrepreneurs and the philosophers whose ideas supported their exploitations of the environment] indeed fled to the margins: to the remote, the inaccessible, the relatively barren areas. Nature was where industry was not." New feelings for landscape emerged in Romantic art, expressing a growing sense of "nature as a refuge, a refuge from man; a place of healing, a solace, a retreat." Williams notes, too, that unequal distributions of costs and benefits to different social groups were immediately evident: "As the exploitation of nature continued, on a vast scale, and especially in the new extractive and industrial processes, the people who drew most profit from it went back, where they could find

it . . . to an unspoilt nature, to the purchased estates and the country retreats." He points to the irony that these very industrialists who "invest[ed]
in the smoke and the spoil" but could afford to enjoy their weekends where
the air was clear and the hillsides green were often champions of conservation of this now removed nature and of nature reserves.[16] That the cultural
and ideological contexts of Romanticism are the contexts of the early Anthropocene readily explains the attention environmental critics have given
to its versions of nature writing.

The tenacity of Romantic perspectives on nature and the human relation to it fostered an ongoing sympathy among early ecocritics for the ideas
and feelings expressed in poetry from that tradition. Environmental critics
writing in the late decades of the twentieth century responded to what was
perceived as the continually increasing separation of industrialized humanity from nature much as the Romantic poets themselves did nearly two
centuries earlier: by lamenting that split and by treating poetry as a means
of transcending it. They saw poems about nature as returning readers to a
sense of being at home on earth, sometimes conceived in terms of Heideggerian dwelling, and as allowing at least momentary solace and escape from
what Wordsworth in "Tintern Abbey" (1798) called "the din / Of towns and
cities."[17] Thus, the first sustained work of environmental criticism on Romantic poetry (along with some twentieth-century works), Bate's *The Song
of the Earth,* explores a tradition that, in the face of "a severance of mankind
from nature," "declares allegiance to what Wordsworth in the preface to
Lyrical Ballads called 'the beautiful and permanent forms of nature.'" Romanticism as an ecopoetic, Bate says, "proposes that when we commune
with those forms we live with a particular intensity, and conversely that
our lives are diminished when technology and industrialization alienate us
from those forms. It regards poetic language as a special kind of expression
which may effect an imaginative reunification of mind and nature, though
it also has a melancholy awareness of the illusoriness of its own utopian
vision." In sympathy, Bate characterizes his own study as an "experiment in
ecopoetics" (the first use of that term I know of) in which the experiment
is "to see what happens when we regard poems as imaginary parks in which
we may breathe an air that is not toxic and accommodate ourselves to a
mode of dwelling that is not alienated." Avoiding dominant critical paradigms of skepticism and constructivism, his version of ecopoetics affirms
"the sacredness . . . of the things-of-nature-in-themselves."[18]

This study's focal poets, in contrast, create poems that are more analogous to landfills scavenged by gulls or city boulevards awash in diesel fumes. Their poetry resists being approached as an escape from the problems of a warming, toxified world. Even their often fractured or partially asyntactic forms do not offer a restful parklike experience. The differences between my aims and those of Bate and other early ecocritics, and between the poems he treats and those I examine, reflect changes that have taken place in at least two intellectual realms. First, ecocriticism has been evolving in its response to debates among literary critics and in poetry circles concerning language, referentiality, accessibility, and poetic form. Secondly, ecocriticism has responded to further changes in views of nature itself. To contextualize the poetry on which this book focuses and the growing interest it holds for environmental scholars, I'll briefly review both these developments.

When ecocriticism was first developing in the late decades of the twentieth century, environmental critics sought to be scientifically informed and tended to be wary of poststructuralist thought. Then, as now, ecocriticism was a politically charged discourse; for its practitioners, environmental issues possessed political urgency, and acknowledging the phenomenological reality of the environment consequently seemed crucial. During what Lawrence Buell has labeled the "first wave" of environmental criticism, this orientation generated resistance or outright hostility toward the constructionist thinking evident in poststructuralist theory. Scigaj, for instance, in *Sustainable Poetry*, depicted poststructuralism as another mode of anthropocentric domination of nature and complained that contemporary poetry criticism is "moving far away from a poet's originary experience in nature and in real communities struggling to survive." Such attitudes determined not just what critical lenses ecocritics employed but also which recent poets and what kind of poetics gained ecocritical attention. North American experimental poets of the late twentieth century, most notably the Language writers, were not merely extending the experimental impulses and techniques of high modernism; they were also developing their poetics in explicit conversation with poststructuralist theory. Their postmodern forms of contemporary poetic experimentalism were widely (and, to my mind, mistakenly) seen as occupying what Scigaj called a "hermetically sealed textuality" that runs counter to environmentalist engagement.[19]

Ecocritical concerns about environmental politics easily mapped themselves onto ongoing contests within the poetry scene, contests that pitted experimental poetry, particularly Language poetry, against the so-called "mainstream" expressive lyric. There was a strong interest among early environmental critics in integrating frankly autobiographical discourse into their criticism, a politically motivated departure from then-dominant conventions of literary criticism. This more personal mode of criticism—demonstrated, for example, in Elder's *Imagining the Earth: Poetry and the Vision of Nature*—seems to have recognized its poetic corollary in the personal lyric. Language writers, meanwhile, were critiquing the reliance on the "pseudo-intimacy" of personal "voice" in mainstream poetics, asserting, "the self as the central and final term of creative practice is being challenged and exploded in our writing in a number of ways."[20] In addition, both because of a desire to reach a broad audience and because of an ethical value placed on simplicity by environmentalists at least since Thoreau, environmental critics gravitated toward poetry in an "accessible" plain style. In attending primarily to straightforwardly representational writing, ecocritics aligned themselves with the poetic mainstream.

Jonathan Skinner began bridging these divides by launching the journal *ecopoetics* in 2001. Reflecting the self-conscious Anthropocene, the journal, as Skinner announced in the inaugural editor's statement, "takes on the 'eco' frame, in recognition that human impact on the earth and its other species, is without a doubt the historical watershed of our generation." Observing that "'environmentalist' culture has ignored most developments in poetics since Ezra Pound," Skinner asserted that "the environmental movement stands to be criticized for the extent to which it has protected a fairly received notion of 'eco' from the proddings and complications, and enrichments, of an investigative poetics." He added, however, that the avant-gardes of the late twentieth century, "noted for linguistically sophisticated approaches to difficult issues, stand to be criticized for their overall silence on a comparable approach to environmental questions." The journal was founded on the "hunch" that there was in fact a good deal of poetry being produced that addressed environmental concerns and that did so in ways that "subvert the endless debates about 'language' vs. lyric, margin vs. mainstream, performed vs. written, innovative vs. academic, or, now, digitized vs. printed approaches to poetry." That hunch has been borne out not only by the diversity of material in the issues of *ecopoetics* but also by the massive anthology *The Arcadia Project: North American Postmodern Pastoral* (2012), edited by Joshua Corey and G. C. Waldrep, which highlights those previously overlooked experimental or investigative poetics, by *The Ecopoetry Anthology*, a huge tome of varied work edited by Ann Fisher-Wirth and Laura-Gray Street (2013), and by Camille T. Dungy's *Black Nature* (2009).

Jed Rasula's *This Compost* (2002) drew attention to little-recognized forms of environmental focus in the work of Black Mountain poets and their antecedents, while the developing interest among environmental critics of poetry in more experimental forms was at once registered and reinforced by the small-press publication in 2010 of Brenda Ijiima's *Eco Language Reader.* This is the context in which most of the ecopoetic work to be discussed in this book has become visible.[21]

Meanwhile, ideas of nature themselves have been changing. Whether explicit or implicit, affirmation of nature's sacredness by early ecocritics and the poets they attended to follows the intellectual currents that environmental historian William Cronon charts and challenges in his landmark essay from 1995, "The Trouble with Wilderness; or, Getting Back to the Wrong Nature." Like Williams, Cronon stresses that "nature" and "wilderness" are evolving cultural constructions, so that wilderness, once seen as "the antithesis of all that was orderly and good," had by the end of the nineteenth century become sacred. He argues that the Romantic doctrine of the sublime, according to which the divine is manifest in nature's most awe-inspiring landscapes, combined in the United States with nostalgia for the vanishing frontier to produce a sense of nature as something apart from human civilization, a sacred and vanishing space offering escape from industrialized modernity, a treasured refuge for human and nonhuman species alike. This sense remained predominant in both environmentally oriented poetry and criticism until very recently, and such work attempted to offer readers the beauties and consolations of undisturbed nature, even if mourning its diminishment. Cronon argues, however, that such thinking is deeply problematic: its dualistic vision of humans as separate from nature "poses a serious threat to responsible environmentalism" because it does not encourage people to live sustainably and respectfully *in* nature. Wanting contemporary Americans to take care not just of distant and supposedly unspoiled wilderness protected from human impact, but also of the landscapes we use and the places we inhabit, Cronon calls for a rethinking of nature and the wild that escapes the dualism between humanity and nature so fundamental to Romanticism's legacy.[22]

Critiques of the ideas of nature on which traditional nature writing rests have appeared with increasing frequency in the self-conscious Anthropocene. Precisely because Anthropocene self-consciousness recognizes the pervasive impact of humankind on the entire planet and challenges notions of any place being pristine or untouched by people, it has contributed significantly to changes in environmentalist thinking about nature. Writing in 2011 Crutzen and Christian Schwägerl have this to say about nature now: "Geographers Erle Ellis and Navin Ramankutty argue we are no longer disturbing natural ecosystems. Instead, we now live in 'human systems with natural ecosystems embedded within them.' The long-held barriers between nature and culture are breaking down. It's no longer us against 'Nature.' Instead, it's we who decide what nature is and what it will be." Similarly, Jed Purdy asserts, "It doesn't make sense anymore to try to honor and preserve *nature,* a natural world that is outside of us, a nature that is defined partly by being *not human,* a nature that is purest in wilderness, rain forests, and the ocean. Instead, in a world we can't help shaping, the question is what kind of world we will shape."[23] In the twenty-first century, environmentalist organizations previously devoted to wilderness preservation have been expanding their purview to embrace issues of environmental pollution affecting residents of cities and environmentally degraded regions, as well as energy issues tied to global warming, and they have increasingly modified their strategies for preserving what had earlier been imagined as pristine lands to take into account the people who live on or make their living from those lands.

Responding to comparable pressures, ecocriticism has increasingly understood nature as thoroughly intertwined with culture, and has expanded the body of texts studied to include works that depict urban environments or landscapes of extraction, or that explore chemical spills, global warming, and other Anthropocene issues. Timothy Morton has been a particularly audible critic of received ideas of nature, announcing in *Ecology without Nature* that "the idea of nature is getting in the way of properly ecological forms of culture, philosophy, politics, and art." In its place he champions what he calls "the ecological thought," "a practice and a process of becoming fully aware of how human beings are connected with other beings—animal, vegetable, or mineral." Morton's ecological thought involves encountering much more than Wordsworth's beautiful and permanent forms of nature that Bate invites readers to attend to: it requires contemplating human interconnection even with beings that are not strictly natural, including cyborgs or forms of artificial intelligence, and thinking about such unsettling topics as where our toilet waste goes and how we regularly drink recycled waste water. It involves losing "our sense of Nature as pristine and nonartificial." Such understandings have come to be so widespread that Ursula Heise could accurately observe in reviewing

Morton's 2013 book *Hyperobjects* that "recent environmentalist thought, from Stacy Alaimo and Richard White to Richard Hobbs and Peter Kareiva, has already moved well beyond this separation [of humans from a nature conceived of as 'over yonder'] in ways that don't tally with the strawman environmentalism Morton attacks."[24]

Resisting a focus on Romantic pastoral and the wild, numerous scholars in the environmental humanities have recently been pushing beyond narrow understandings of what counts as environmental and beyond traditional Western understandings of the human place in the natural world. No longer thinking of nature or even ecological processes as separable from culture, ecocriticism has turned increasingly toward the methodologies of cultural studies and has drawn on an ever more diverse body of theoretical literature, escaping what Buell termed "first-wave ecocriticism's naively pre-theoretical valorization of experiential contact with the natural world."[25] Attention has been shifting toward issues of environmental justice in the context of global literatures, thereby linking ecocritical with postcolonial as well as queer and race studies. All these developments, along with the dramatic changes earth systems have been undergoing in the twenty-first century, have opened the door to poetry and poetics that fit the conventions of "nature writing" in neither form nor content.

Nonetheless, ecocriticism concerning anglophone poetry in particular has continued to focus largely on nature poetry, just as the most popular poetry associated with environmental concern has continued to be work depicting solitary experiences in wild or rural settings. Because this study does not treat such poetry, and in some ways pushes back against it, I want also to acknowledge its power in generating a sense of connection to non-urban environments and an appreciation of their value. Careful attention to the "beautiful forms of nature"—that phrase Bate took from Wordsworth—provides one motivation for protecting the environment from further degradation. Moreover, some well-known nature poets have, through their prose writing, offered important conceptions of how societies should be organized and how political change might take place. For example, Wendell Berry has championed local networks of agrarianism, nonindustrial eating, and sustainable agriculture, and Gary Snyder has articulated a bioregionalism in which watersheds define areas of shared environmental interests and potential activism.

Looking briefly at a couple samples of late twentieth-century nature poetry by celebrated senior poets, born in the mid-1930s, will demonstrate both the strengths of the genre as it has been generally practiced, as well as its limitations in relation to our present moment. My first example is a poem by Wendell Berry that I have loved—a poem I chose to read at the informal memorial where my family and I scattered my mother's ashes by a pond in an area of restored prairie just outside Madison, Wisconsin. Titled "The Peace of Wild Things," it comes from Berry's volume *Openings,* published in 1968, at the height of America's war in Vietnam:

> When despair for the world grows in me
> and I wake in the night at the least sound
> in fear of what my life and my children's lives may be,
> I go and lie down where the wood drake
> rests in his beauty on the water, and the great heron feeds.
> I come into the peace of wild things
> who do not tax their lives with forethought
> of grief. I come into the presence of still water.
> And I feel above me the day-blind stars
> waiting with their light. For a time
> I rest in the grace of the world, and am free.[26]

Neither my mother nor I share Berry's explicitly Christian faith, so his allusion to the Twenty-Third Psalm—"He maketh me to lie down in green pastures: He leadeth me beside the still waters"—is not the source of the comfort I find in this poem. I take pleasure simply in thinking of my mother's ashes strewn where she would have appreciated the peacefulness and quiet freedom that I savor when I visit the spot. Berry's vision of resting in "the grace of the world," rendered with the graceful closing of three anapestic feet, is profoundly appealing, and it has obvious continuity with Wordsworth's message in his "Lines Composed a Few Miles above Tintern Abbey": that being in or even recalling having been in places of natural beauty and tranquility provides a soul-soothing reprieve from "the fretful stir / Unprofitable, and the fever of the world." (Even Berry's punning allusion to taxing aligns with Wordsworth's invocation of finance in the word "unprofitable," as both gesture toward capitalism's contribution to what disturbs them.) The repetition of a pattern fundamental to Romantic poetry enacted in the late twentieth-century speaker's desire to escape from a world "too much with us," in Wordsworth's phrase, into the habitat of wild birds demonstrates the durability of the perspectives and longings that accompanied the rise of industrialism.[27] And yet now, fifty years after

Berry composed "The Peace of Wild Things," when more than 80 percent of Americans are living in urban areas, awareness of how few people in the developed world know the colorful plumage of the male wood duck (though its range includes much of the United States) or have access to such undeveloped landscapes makes this lovely vision of taking comfort in nature feel anachronistic and nostalgic. Nostalgia seems an insufficient response to current environmental problems.

Where Berry's speaker, whose "rest" echoes that of the wood drake, seems able to feel a part of nature "for a time," my second representative example of recent nature poetry places greater emphasis on the gap between the human and nonhuman nature. It's a poem by Mary Oliver, who is literally America's most popular living poet, a best-selling writer whose public readings may draw crowds of thousands. Winner of a Pulitzer Prize and a National Book Award, she is widely appreciated as an "indefatigable guide to the natural world."[28] Rarely depicting humans other than her speaker and rarely acknowledging human impact on the natural world, Oliver's poems describe with wonder animals and sometimes plants associated with the wild. Where exactly these encounters with deer, fox, owls, water lilies, herons, and so forth take place is not disclosed—perhaps in fact they occurred in suburban spaces—but they create the impression of a speaker privileged to observe life in the wild. The observed life forms serve as prompts for conscious love of this world or as examples humans would do well to imitate.

Here, then, is another poem in which water fowl appear, Oliver's "The Kingfisher" from her 1990 volume *House of Light*:

> The kingfisher rises out of the black wave
> like a blue flower, in his beak
> he carries a silver leaf. I think that this is
> the prettiest world—so long as you don't mind
> a little dying, how could there be a day in your whole life
> that doesn't have its splash of happiness?
> There are more fish than there are leaves
> on a thousand trees, and anyway the kingfisher
> wasn't born to think about it, or anything else.
> When the wave snaps shut over his blue head, the water
> remains water—hunger is the only story
> he has every heard in his life that he could believe.
> I don't say he's right. Neither
> do I say he's wrong. Religiously he swallows the silver leaf

with its broken red river, and with a rough and easy cry
I couldn't rouse out of my thoughtful body
if my life depended on it, he swings back
over the bright sea to do the same thing, to do it
(As I long to do something, anything) perfectly.[29]

Where the peace of wild things offered Berry escape from what troubled him, Oliver in "The Kingfisher" finds the world of nonhuman nature itself troubled by death and predation so that awareness of "a little dying" impinges on the speaker's aestheticizing appreciation of this as the "prettiest world." However, the speaker refuses to weigh in on the ethics of the kingfisher's killing of the fish (euphemistically introduced as a silver leaf), regarding such debates as irrelevant to animal behavior. She is confident that the predatory bird is incapable of abstract thought; its behavior is governed by one simple desire: to eat so as to live. And while she says she won't judge the bird's behavior, her description of his consumption of the fish elevates that act to a form of communion; her metaphorical language ("the silver leaf / with its broken red river") aestheticizes the gore of slaughter, while the bird's "religious" behavior suggests innately reverent observance. Nonhuman nature, the poem announces, is capable of a perfection that inevitably eludes the inescapably "thoughtful" (fallen) human. "The Kingfisher," then, demonstrates the attitudes Williams and Cronon observe in connection with our Romantic inheritance: the sacralization of nonhuman nature and the assumption that there is a stark gap between the human being with her rational mind and the other inhabitants of the planet. These produce a longing to be fully part of "rough and easy" nature, alongside a melancholy awareness that even language can't accomplish that unification. Oliver's gestures toward personification perform lightly playful, self-consciously anthropocentric attempts at bridging the gap, but the dualistic sense of the human divided from nonhuman nature that Cronon, Morton, and other environmental scholars regard as problematic governs "The Kingfisher."

Although Berry, a farmer and committed agrarian, often presents landscapes more obviously used by humans than Oliver's, the nature that both poets turn to is not evidently a diminished one; perhaps because both are Christian writers who link nature to divinity and perfection, in their work the natural world and its cycles are imagined as essentially unchanging and timeless, as is the consolation nature offers. Again, however, from the perspective of the self-conscious Anthropocene, we might note that the kind of nature both poems depict is unavailable as first-hand experience to a great many people on this planet, who inhabit degraded landscapes or live in urban centers. The world of the twenty-first century is full of urban dwellers who have no experience of wood drakes or kingfishers or the comparable native species of their regions. If brought to rural Kentucky, where Berry works his organic farm with horses rather than machines in an area where his family has farmed for generations, they might well feel more frightened than calmed. Ill at ease in the quiet of that place without traffic and anxious about disease-carrying ticks and mosquitoes or possible snakes, they might well take no pleasure in lying on the rough ground by a lake's edge.

Yet the tremendous popularity of both poets' work suggests that poems like these help readers in very different situations from the poets' imagine themselves as taking solace and finding wonder or delight even where they might not actually do so. In providing this imagined experience, the poems may foster values associated with environmental conservation. As Scott Slovic observes, "nature writing is a 'literature of hope' in its assumption that the elevation of consciousness may lead to wholesome political change."[30] And even if conservation is, appropriately, no longer the sole focus of environmentalism, it nonetheless remains crucial in the immediate Anthropocene; we desperately need the carbon sequestration provided by the world's forests, for example (currently about 20 percent of the world's oxygen is released by rainforests), and many scientific arguments can be offered for the importance of preserving not just individual species but entire ecosystems with the biodiversity they contain. Poems like these, then, can support ends valued by a range of environmentalists.[31] Yet nature poetry alone, especially work like Oliver's that presents nature's "true gift" as lying in its unchanging patterns,[32] is an insufficient poetic response to the radical instabilities of the environmental mess in which we find ourselves.

ECOPOETICS OF THE SELF-CONSCIOUS ANTHROPOCENE: "WING/SPAN/SCREW/CLUSTER (AVES)"

This book will therefore focus on writing, often more or less experimental, that moves beyond or transforms the conventions of nature poetry. As an example, I will now introduce another poem that takes birds as its subject. In the poems by Berry and Oliver just discussed, watching or being near birds in the wild reminded the speakers of the perfections of nonhuman wild creatures or of the sublime peacefulness of the natural realm they inhabit. This third poem, however, represents birds quite differently, as it offers a critique of the kinds of transcendence, long associated with birds' flight, of which Cronon is wary. Using disjunctive construction and asyntactic language, often derived from the Internet and formatted to evoke domain names, this poem from Evelyn Reilly's volume *Styrofoam* (2009), titled "Wing/Span/Screw/Cluster (Aves)," attends to anthropogenic planetary change while it adapts collage poetics indebted to the techniques of high modernism to an ecological model of interconnection. Both formally and semantically, it encourages readers to think in terms of a vast net of interconnection in which birds and other wild creatures cannot be associated with escape from human strife or human limitation, for those now shape all planetary experience in the Anthropocene. Where nature poetry has tended, as Juliana Spahr notes, "to show the beautiful bird but not so often the bulldozer off to the side that was destroying the bird's habitat," Reilly's poetry—and that of the other writers treated here, including Spahr herself—acknowledges the beauty of nature within an exploration of unfolding ecological catastrophe. And while, as Spahr goes on to observe, nature poetry "wasn't talking about how the bird, often a bird which had arrived recently from somewhere else, interacted with and changed the larger system of this small part of the world we live in and on," Reilly and the other focal poets in this study examine interrelation, interaction, and environmental change.[33] Birds in Reilly's poem dramatize the current impact of humans on other species, an impact that involves careless destruction of individual creatures as well as the extinction or threatened extinction of entire species. In addition, birds in the poem are among a number of entities associated with flight—from angels and levitating saints to space trash—all of which are associated in the poem with the environmentally problematic human longing for transcendence.

The verbal text of "Wing/Span/Screw/Cluster (Aves)," too long to present in full here, is preceded by two black-and-white images that serve as visual epigraphs announcing major themes. The first displays a partially mangled bird carcass on a dirt surface, captioned "One of about 51,900 Google image search results for 'roadkill+bird.'"[34] The second also comes from the Internet and is a cropped photo of Giovanni Bernini's seventeenth-century marble sculpture the *Ecstasy of Saint Teresa*. The former provides an image of humans' destructive impact on other species, and the latter, as I'll show, offers an explanation for that destruction.

The opening point made by the verbal text is that killing birds is now a commonplace activity for industrialized humans:

much the usual mangle
at www.roadkill.com

flaps down/ *quiet*

here.incold[35]

Spatially isolated below this appears a biblical-sounding imperative, "'lo,'" which might also be letters from the elided "blood" we can't help but hear after "incold"; this call to attention introduces a section of text concerned with Bernini's sensuous sculpture. As a figure *"in thrall"* to the ecstasy of spiritual transport, one whose desire is directed upward toward the golden rays that pour from heaven, Saint Teresa represents the longing for transcendence of one's earthly condition—a focus that distracts human attention and care from this world on which the survival of human and nonhuman animals depends. What Reilly elsewhere calls "the mesmerizing spell of the transcendent,"[36] she regards as an important determinant of humankind's damaging impact on real birds; it is key to "the actual.entangle / man (sic) to aves (sick)." The juxtapositional structure of the poem presents that upward-reaching impulse as expressed also in humans' exploration of outer space, which has yielded "a poly.fix.styx.fury.flurry.slurry / of extra-terrain garbage // Some 15,000 pieces ranging from fingernail-sized paint flecks / to 10-ton rocket stages hurtling through the Earth's orbit" (*S* 28–29). Ironically, human fascination with the space "above" us has resulted in the production of space debris that proves dangerous to our own space missions. What the poem presents as truly miraculous is not something out of this world, like the angel descended from heaven in Bernini's sculpture, but creatures threatened within it: hummingbirds with their astonishingly rapid heartbeats and wing rotation rates as well as their incandescent plumage. However, many hummingbird species are extinct or nearing extinction, mostly due to anthropogenic habitat loss, and some of these are listed in italics in the poem:

Yet still.humming in fastest ::: 1200/ min (heartbeat) 50/ sec (wingbeat)

skirts hemmed
intonalwitness.artistry

Heliangelus regalis
Eriocnemis mirabilis

ofthe entrance
en*trance*

[please install dimmer]   (*S* 29)

I understand the bracketed words as a plea, perhaps directed especially toward writers and other artists, to dim the glowing rays from the heavens that so enrapture us and in Reilly's view (as in Cronon's) maladjust our eyes to a quotidian earthly focus. Subsequent lines, in concert with a visual triptych showing the similarities of bone structure among "protoavian dinosaur," "bird," and "middle-aged human with / osteoporotic disintegration," suggest that humans could easily share the fate of the dinosaurs or of the endangered hummingbirds, particularly if we don't pay more attention to "the real real world" in all its gritty impurity. The outward and upward focus of "ekstasis: exteriosis" is linked in the poem to species extermination; "Wing/Span/Screw/Cluster (Aves)" closes by naming three additional endangered or possibly extinct species of hummingbirds, the earth's jewels we humans have failed to value truly and have carelessly destroyed:

Calzadito Turquesa
Colibrí de Esmeraldas
Metalura Iracunda

(smallest death ladders

(cheapest cosmos jewelry

XXX   (*S* 30–31)

As much as Berry or Oliver, Reilly appreciates the beauty of birds (the hummingbirds' iridescent "skirts hemmed / intonalwitness.artistry") and the pleasure of their "lovely.metallic.names," but, feeling the weight of the self-conscious Anthropocene, she refuses to depict nonhuman animals apart from human impact—impact not only on the birds themselves but on the larger planetary environment, including distant levels of the atmosphere where our trash floats. In contrast to the poems by the older poets, Berry and Oliver, "nature" here doesn't offer escape or solace; nor does it exemplify lofty perfection. Instead, entities in nature reveal intertwined networks of anthropogenic change.

In this poem, meaning emerges not from the unspooling of logically sequential sentences or the repetition of images, but from proliferating links generated through parataxis. Page space becomes a plastic medium within which to arrange pieces of information and perception, and, as is generally true in collage art, juxtaposition invites attention to connection. We are invited to contemplate the relation between apparently contrasting human activities directed upward, or between the X's that sound in *ecstasy*, *extra* (meaning beyond or outside, as in "extra-terrain garbage"), *ex*tinction and *ex*termination. Reilly's digitally inflected punctuation—the dots replacing spaces between words, as in domain names—evokes the nonlinear modes of information organization and transmission we depend on in this era of globalized commerce and consumption. Reilly has usefully commented on her sense of what will be required formally to generate an ecopoetics in which poets "participate in realizing the full implications of our position as language-using animals in a world composed of interconnection." She does not advocate writing that extends the techniques of conventional nature lyric, "that simply expands the arena of natural description to include landfills and polluted streams, or that devises yet more astute metaphors based on carbon cycles and energy flows." She continues, "While these tactics might have their uses, I think that ecopoetics must be a matter of finding formal strategies that effect a larger paradigm shift and that actually participate in the task of abolishing the aesthetic use of nature as mirror for human narcissism."[37]

It will not surprise a reader who has seen the arrangements of *Styrofoam*'s space-filled pages that Reilly finds useful precedent in the formal strategies of Charles Olson. Again summoning the informational and structural resources of the Internet, she describes the contribution to ecopoetics of his open field poetics as "the opening of the page both topo- and typographically as a surface for juxtapositions, transforming it into a kind of MapQuest program, capable of being manipulated to investigate adjacencies in any direction, and in which any apparently peripheral element can be moved to a central position. In addition, his use of open parentheses made it possible to turn a poem into a theoretically endless branching diagram, in which any word or phrase can become the jumping-off point for an entirely new set of diagrammed relationships."[38] Reilly's description of Olson's projectivist page, from an essay published in 2010, sounds much like Morton's description of "the mesh" in *The Ecological Thought,* published the same year. The mesh is Morton's term for "the interconnectedness of all living and non-living things." It designates a form of connectedness in which there can be no definite background or foreground: "Each point of the mesh is both the center and edge of a system of points, so there is no absolute center or edge." Ecological instability reigns in the mesh, where everything is interdependent, connected, potentially significant to everything else—hence the "disorienting openness" Morton attributes to "the ecological thought."[39] Reilly's and Morton's shared emphasis on endlessly branching connections even among apparently disparate things, and on open, relational forms in which no element is inherently or lastingly central, points to dimensions of environmental thinking emerging in the self-conscious Anthropocene that differ meaningfully from the perspectives inherited from the early era of industrialization.

Not all the poets on whom I will focus are exploring branching forms or collage as a kind of (inter)netted fabric. However, recognizing the scale and complexity of the environmental problems we humans face and the responsibilities we in the industrialized world must assume, they all embrace the challenge of trying to imagine the state of the world as it really is. They aspire not to represent beautiful scenes of nature without humans, but instead to sustain what Joan Retallack calls "a complex realism."[40] Through their poetry they seek to better understand the nature and scope of the changes humans have wrought in the Anthropocene, and the impact of those changes on human and nonhuman bodies and lives; they are interested in exploring how current environmental problems are rooted in received ways of thinking and speaking, in our ways of relating to human and nonhuman others, as well as in our social, political, and material cultures. Using a range of formal strategies, they try to imagine how already evident anthropogenic environmental changes will continue to affect the planet through geological as well as human time, how the vast human population might live on earth sustainably and justly into the future, and what will happen if we fail to do so.

None of these writers imagines that poetry will save the world. But their writing suggests a belief that poets have significant responsibilities and a meaningful role to play in both considering and determining "what kind of world we will shape."[41] Jorie Graham, whose *Sea Change* is discussed in chapter 3, says this about the current functions of the artistic imagination in a 2010 interview titled "Instructions for Building the Arc":

> Scientists can provide all the information in the world, but if the human soul of the listeners only seizes it as "information" it does not necessarily awaken them to a genuine physical belief that the outcomes being described are in a world co-extensive with this very one in which they are living, with this very time in which their children are growing. It is easy to "capture" information and then shove it to one side of one's life. The conceptual intellect is great at that. It is in a way the primary job of the imagination to connect the world in which you are, to one in which you have not yet been, or cannot imagine being. And if that connection occurs, it allows one to hope one can be roused to action, or at least to the change of world view which we need in order to envision, and undertake, genuine action.[42]

In a more recent interview Graham explains the artist's role slightly differently, suggesting that scientists are actively seeking the help of artists so that the broader public may better grasp scientific perspectives, think in expanded temporalities, and respond appropriately to the probably unwelcome implications of new information:

> What is being sought by scientists, in artists' practical use of the Imagination, is how to make the 'deep future'—seven to ten generations hence—feel actually 'connected' to us, right down to this very minute of our lives, this choice we make to use this Styrofoam cup, this plastic bag. . . . How can you expect a person to find, let alone feel, and act upon, the fine thread that truly connects their very next choice to a life 1,000 years hence which might not in any way resemble what we know of as human life? How do we make sacrifices—ones that will affect our entire way of life in our only life—for those who we do not even know will exist, that they might have a planet still livable, a biome still conducive to human habitation. This is a very hard task indeed. One cannot imagine many requests that have ever been made of the human Imagination that exceed it.[43]

Far from regarding their poems as "imaginary parks in which we may breathe an air that is not toxic,"[44] the writers on whose work I focus use the resources of the imagination to help readers recognize in the air they are breathing toxins that might otherwise go unregistered, even while doing somatic damage; or, they may remind readers that in the lands set aside as parks, once home to now exiled indigenous peoples, the lives of the myriad interdependent species currently at home there are rendered precarious by the cascading effects of changing climate. These poets' work, then, does not fill the role the Romantic poet John Keats assigned to poetry, "To soothe the cares, and lift the thoughts of man."

Importantly, however, this work of the self-conscious Anthropocene aspires to more than grim consciousness-raising, though that may be among its goals. The poets treated in this study try to contribute to the development of new ways of thinking, of new paradigms alternative to those that brought us to current crises and stalemates, and for most of them formal or linguistic experimentalism is a key resource in this quest. On this topic Joan Retallack's essay "What Is Experimental Poetry & Why Do We Need It?" is particularly pertinent. After quoting Wittgenstein when he explains that the lack of progress in philosophy is "because our language has remained the same and keeps seducing us into asking the same questions," she notes, "What we long for is implanted in our grammatical structures as much as it is in our vocabularies." Change in either one—our desires or our linguistic structures—could prompt change in the other. Every formal experiment, in Retallack's view, is "a move away from the present state of things" that may "enact interrogations into [the contemporary moment's] most problematic structures." When approached as an instrument of genuinely "investigative engagement," language "takes part in the recomposing of contemporary consciousness, contemporary sensibilities." Consequently, Retallack endorses "the poet as radical epistemologist" who investigates, interrogates, and transforms the ways of knowing that take form in written language, who enacts a belief that "it matters to find new ways of being among one and others in the world via poetic forms." Having endorsed John Dewey's vision of art's "use being a new training of modes of perception," she calls attention to "a radical reconception of 'nature poetry' [that] is currently taking place, so radical that, like Stein's invention of new modes of description, it's hardly recognizable as the genre."[45] That radical reconception is the subject of this study.

THE CHAPTERS AHEAD

Each subsequent chapter focuses on an issue or conceptual challenge crucial to the self-conscious Anthropocene as it is addressed by two or three poets. Chapter 1 attends to scale and its perception—that is, to the challenges of grasping the overwhelming size and complexity as well as the rapidity of

Anthropocene planetary change—an issue that shadows all the chapters to follow. It examines poetic responses to the collision of discrepant scales of time and space encountered when one tries to think the Anthropocene and the place of humankind or the human individual within it. For while the few hundred years since the Industrial Revolution constitute a minuscule unit in geological time, the transformations wrought by our single species in those few years will affect the planet for an unfathomably deep future. The three poets whose work is discussed pursue different strategies in response to what I term "scalar dissonance." In "Unnamed Dragonfly Species," from *Well Then There Now* (2011), a text that interweaves a narrative about people who obsessively track glacial melting on the Internet with species names from a New York state list of endangered or extinct species, Juliana Spahr exposes the psychological and affective dynamics of a dissonance that she treats as insuperable. In "The Carboniferous and Ecopoetics," from *Redstart* (2012), Forrest Gander focuses not on affective but on perceptual challenges. Gander attempts to make geological time imaginable through highly sensuous renderings of earlier epochs, thereby bringing home the disproportion of human consumption within three hundred years of virtually all the carbon that accumulated underground over more than 300 million years. Ed Roberson, who, like Gander, has scientific as well as arts training, presents scalar shifting as part of the human perceptual toolkit, evident in our accommodation to the perspective gained from airplanes or spacecraft, and also in our ability to tune into minute natural phenomena in our immediate surroundings. That we will use this tool to our advantage before it's too late remains, in his work, unlikely, but his lines that constantly shift direction to explore divergent aspects of the phenomenological world suggest the value of behaving so that one may, as his volume's title has it, "see the earth before the end of the world."

Problematics of scale remain evident in chapters 2 and 3, the former treating a material issue—the vast accumulation of plastics as ineradicable toxic "hyperobjects" (Morton's term)—and the latter the conceptual and rhetorical dilemmas shaping apocalyptic discourse in a time of continual crisis and diminished individual agency. Chapter 2 examines Reilly's *Styrofoam* and Adam Dickinson's *The Polymers* (2013), volumes that engage with the wonders and the environmental horrors of plastic. Plastics, which do not biodegrade and are leaching endocrine-disrupting chemicals into the biosphere, exist on a temporal scale virtually beyond human conception with distributions that challenge conventional understandings of space.

Plastics also point to the Anthropocene's dissolution of the division between the natural and the artificial or manufactured, and to the dissolution of the boundaries between inside and outside, particularly those of the human body. These are crucial issues in both volumes, where playful procedures delighting in the plasticity of the artistic imagination and in the inexhaustible plenitude of plastic polymers—what Dickinson calls "the chemical language of polymers"—coexist with grim awareness of plastic's inescapable toxicity.

While Lawrence Buell, in the mid-1990s, identified apocalyptic rhetoric as "the single most powerful metaphor that the contemporary environmental imagination has at its disposal," twenty years later people are experiencing "apocalypse fatigue" even as environmental apocalypse looms as an all too likely nonmetaphoric reality. Chapter 3 draws on Frederick Buell's thinking about "dwelling in crisis" and about awareness of being embedded and embodied in damaged ecosystems in considering how two poets with very different aesthetics—Jorie Graham in *Sea Change* (2008) and Evelyn Reilly in *Apocalypso* (2012)—use differing modes of poetic pleasure to renew the force of apocalyptic writing and render apocalyptic awareness more bearable.[46]

The next two chapters examine how poets of the self-conscious Anthropocene are reenvisioning topics that have been central to ecocriticism since its beginnings in the early 1980s: human–animal relations and a sense of place. Chapter 4 explores poetic attempts to better understand nonhuman modes of intelligence, perception, and communication, so as to correct anthropocentric biases and better reflect the interdependence of human and nonhuman species. In visually and aurally inventive work, a.rawlings, Jody Gladding, and Jonathan Skinner employ varied "grammars of animacy" (a term adopted from Robin Wall Kimmerer's ruminations on her people's Anishanaabe language) to imaginatively transcribe, translate, and transmute animal languages into human tongue. In so doing, they modify the English language in ways that undermine the divide on which human exceptionalism depends. These poets focus their curiosity about animal expression, interspecies communication, and the possibility for intersubjectivity between humans and animals on nonmammalian species: butterflies, birds, and beetles. In so doing they minimize risks of anthropomorphizing while they explore a more mutualistic understanding of the human being as, in Val Plumwood's terms, a "self-in-relationship with nature." Their poetry, which exemplifies what Gander calls "a reorientation from objectivity toward intersubjectivity," heightens readers' awareness of the potential agency and intentionality of earth-others.⁴⁷

Chapter 5 explores the globalized sense of place evident in twenty-first-century ecopoetics, demonstrating the relevance to ecocriticism of geographical theory, especially Doreen Massey's call for a more socially contextualized understanding of space, in which any locality can be understood in terms of its dynamic links to a wider world. I examine several of Juliana Spahr's poems from *Well Then There Now* that, sometimes by putting text through multiple translation machines, explore the complex interactions in Hawai'i of multiple cultures and species from different ecosystems, as well as the dependency of one's sense of place on one's cultural positioning. Forrest Gander's *Core Samples from the World* (2012) reconsiders what is meant by "the foreign" and "the foreigner" in a time when global travel is commonplace and environmental degradation is homogenizing landscapes. The chapter concludes with analysis of Jena Osman's "Mercury Rising" from *The Network* (2011), which intermingles imagination of the planet Mercury with considerations of mercury poisoning and of the town Mercury in the Nevada Test Site. Osman's powerful revelation of environmental toxicity rests on a keen sense of interacting imaginary, locally specific, and planetary places.

The final chapter, on environmental justice poetry, comes full circle to show how writing that pushes "beyond" nature poetry need not be severed from it. Ed Roberson's *City Eclogue,* Mark Nowak's *Coal Mountain Elementary,* and Myung Mi Kim's *Penury* bring together, as Nixon has urged, consideration of the Great Acceleration of the Anthropocene with the Great Divide between the world's wealthy and poor, the powerful and the disenfranchised. Although the discourses of urbanism and environmental justice have often been at odds with those of nature and conservation, they, too, are brought together in these volumes. While this work rejects traditional visions of nature as something apart from human habitation and use, and while it critiques hierarchies that value wild and rural over urban or industrial environments, it nonetheless incorporates into its exposure of the human costs of environmental disruption a concern for the nonhuman, nonbuilt nature that is valued by conservationists. Roberson's syntactically complex representations of the racialization of space, Nowak's documentary "remix poetry" depicting coal mining disasters across the globe, and Kim's minimalist space-filled representations of the experience of refugees fleeing from war all capitalize on and modify the resources of traditional discourses of nature, particularly the pastoral, in drawing attention to environmental justice issues. In bringing together the discourses of nature and environmental justice, these poets enhance the reach and power of both.

If it rarely provides the uplift that many people since Keats have sought in poetry, the work examined in this book offers its own kinds of aesthetic, intellectual, and emotional pleasures. These include the comfort of implied hope—a hope that need not seem entirely delusional. That these poets believe it's worth using the time of their precious lives to produce this environmentally engaged work in which they seek to give linguistic form to constructive ways of interacting with the rest of the biosphere in itself conveys a heartening belief in the real-world importance of language in all its amazing flexibility. It conveys, moreover, faith in the potentially formative power of the malleable ways of thinking language can encourage or encode. In a 2005 article Hans Joachim Schellnhuber, Paul J. Crutzen, William C. Clark, and Julian Hunt wryly define the Anthropocene as "a new geological epoch in which humankind has emerged as a globally significant (and potentially intelligent) force capable of reshaping the face of the Earth past all recognition."[48] These American and Canadian poets are doing what they can to cultivate that intelligence, with hope that their visions can help us use our collective capabilities to make scientifically governed choices that are ethical in relation to humans and nonhumans across the globe and that hold in view the systems that have sustained myriad species as well as the qualities that have given human lives value.

CHAPTER 1

"In Deep Time into Deepsong"

Writing the Scalar Challenges of the Anthropocene

Early in 2014 I attended a talk by the noted American environmental historian Donald Worster, titled "Second Earth: Thinking about Environmental History on a Planetary Scale," in which Worster considered the implications of several chronologically distinct maps of the globe. He identified a 1587 Mercator map of what he called "Second Earth" as the founding document of an era in which Europeans, inhabiting a world where many of the natural resources were depleted, turned to pursuing the seemingly infinite abundance of the New World. That age of abundance, he observed, is now coming to an end. Resource depletion is undermining the foundations for manufactured abundance. The Second Earth is shrinking, and we humans are entering "the age of limits," in which we face unprecedented resource constraints. At the end of the talk, Worster introduced photos of the earth taken from space—going from the iconic "blue marble" image taken from a distance of forty-five thousand kilometers from the earth by the crew of Apollo 17 on their way to the moon in 1972, to the "pale blue dot," taken less than twenty years later, in 1990, by the Voyager 1 spacecraft as it exited the solar system, at about 6 billion kilometers from the earth. In these representations, the earth's size diminishes dramatically as advancing space exploration enables views from increasingly vast distances. Worster used these images to demonstrate both that our conception of the earth, which expanded with the discovery of "Second Earth," is now contracting, and also that our understanding of the earth's boundaries now comes not from cartographers but from scientists. The sciences tell us not just of the depletion of specific resources but of the perturbation of whole systems on which human survival and the survival of myriad other life forms depend. Following a rhetorical pattern common in recent environmental writing, he turned from describing recent changes to calling for corresponding changes in thinking and behavior that might enable human survival. We need, he proposed, a post-Mercator revolution of the mind to deal with the perceptual, moral, and economic transformation that is under way.[1]

Worster's presentation exemplifies an emergent environmental discourse that emphasizes currently changing or divergent scales of phenomena and of perception, and that stresses the importance of learning to think across multiple scales. Although Worster didn't mention the Anthropocene, he was participating in the current discourse of Anthropocene scales and the challenges they pose. For fundamental to the concept of the Anthropocene is its bringing together—and even into collision—vastly discrepant scales, especially of time and space, but also of technology. The scales involved are at once material and conceptual, including concepts of the human and of human agency. Multiple types of scales are often intertwined. The very rapidity of current environmental alterations, evident, for instance, in a rate of extinction known to have precedent only five times in planetary history, suggests that environmental change itself is occurring on scales that are, for humans, unprecedented and verging on unimaginable.

In the poems to be examined here, Juliana Spahr, Forrest Gander, and Ed Roberson grapple with the challenges of thinking in scalar terms appropriate to the Anthropocene as they attempt to help readers grasp what is happening to nonhuman nature and to planetary systems on nearly unimaginable scales, both vast and minute. Their different strategies imply differing visions of poetry's role in fostering conceptual and cultural change, while the poetry of all three reveals an instability, a dance between the desire to locate in poetry useful resources for changing perception and understanding, and a counter-recognition of the limited powers of both language and the human mind, particularly in the face of environmental disruption of a scale and complexity previously unknown.

While Spahr in "Unnamed Dragonfly Species" approaches Anthropocene awareness as a largely emotional challenge, one that produces an affective confounding that is also an ethical, conceptual, and political quandary, the works I will consider by Gander and Roberson treat the challenges of scale as more perceptual than emotional. Perhaps because their early training in the natural sciences makes imagination at extreme scales come more easily, they find scalar dissonance less problematic, and their poems model possible strategies for apprehending processes and phenomena at suprahuman scales. Both imply that poetry's ability to help us grasp the colliding scales of the Anthropocene could prove a crucial resource for humans now, although even with that resource in place, hopes for meaningful change remain tentative. Being able to grasp scalar challenges—something that Gander guides his readers to do and that Roberson presents as already among their perceptual resources—lays the groundwork for the complex processes of identifying and instituting changes that would be effective in responding to the planet's energy needs and in minimizing global warming.

THE COLLIDING SCALES OF THE SELF-CONSCIOUS ANTHROPOCENE

In the self-conscious Anthropocene, *Homo sapiens* not only emerges as the planet's dominant species, but also acquires the status of an immensely powerful geological force. The very name Anthropocene points to how very big humans have come to seem, as our vastly expanded population transforms earth's surfaces through agriculture, mining, and urbanization, as we take control of the global nitrogen cycle through manufactured fertilizers, as we alter the carbon dioxide levels in the atmosphere and acidify the oceans by burning fossil fuels. Our impact and technological powers seem immense. But humankind also appears very small, as humans do not control the effects of anthropogenic changes, many of which have been unintentional. Ultimately, human powers are dwarfed by the nonhuman laws and powers of nature, whose inexorable effects could, at elusive but perhaps imminent tipping points, emerge in full force, perhaps eliminating the human species and many other species that humans have not already managed to destroy.

Just as humans now seem at once vastly more significant and more insignificant than ever before,[2] we are now challenged to understand the world at both much larger and much smaller scales than before. Recognizing the significance of current planetary changes requires us to extend our restricted anthropocentric vision to think in scales of deep time and space. Simultaneously, we must shrink our gaze to attend to the surprisingly grand significance of microbes and microfauna and small pollinating or disease-carrying insects, of energy released by subatomic particles, of the health effects of minute amounts of toxic chemicals, or the vast significance of what might seem small changes in the composition of the earth's atmosphere. Moreover, we feel called upon somehow to address as individual consumers and private citizens of distinct nations complex global problems that can be solved only by political, scientific, and corporate collaboration on an international scale.

Different scalar perspectives often exist in tension or conflict with one another. Thus, while we may regard the time period since the beginning of the Industrial Revolution as a substantial one, and the period since humans began killing nonhuman animals as very long indeed, in the scale of geological time human habitation of the planet occupies a tiny blip. Thinking in terms of geological time encourages us to acknowledge the planet's indifference to the survival of *Homo sapiens* and to the maintenance of the atmospheric conditions on which the survival of many Holocene species depends. As such, it may encourage species humility (though perhaps not for those who place all their faith in our technological powers). Yet humankind's impact on the planet, however carelessly enacted, promises to extend into the vast temporal distance of the planetary future. Our minds, moreover, have difficulty grasping either that vast future our behavior is altering or the past of deep time before we evolved, let alone thinking those together with our familiarly scaled present. Paleontologist and evolutionary biologist Henry Gee, who speaks of the "poignant contrast between time as we experience it in our everyday lives and the incomprehensibly greater scale of Deep Time," describes the latter as "like an endless, dark corridor, with no landmarks to give it scale."[3]

Thinking about the Anthropocene with an eye to addressing its problems demands that we bring these discrepant time scales together—or that we focus clearly on their discrepancies and the impact of those discrepancies. Among those concerned that our thinking take into account the Anthropocene challenges of scale, I discern two positions: the first, an aspirational one, calls for us to somehow think through the incomprehensible and bring the varied scales together; the other, a skeptical position, emphasizes scale variants and scale effects to suggest that we cannot meet current environmental challenges simply by trying to scale up or scale down our thinking, just as we cannot scale up many of what we might want to regard as problem-solving technologies.

The aspirational camp, with which I suspect Worster aligns, calls for extending our thinking to include scales beyond those of everyday human experience in order to conceptualize "human agency over multiple and incommensurable scales at once."[4] The quoted words are Derek Woods's characterization of the position of historian Dipesh Chakrabarty, whose influential article "The Climate of History: Four Theses" advances this way of thinking with the aim of bringing reason fully to bear in responding to climate change. Chakrabarty proposes that "anthropogenic explanations of climate change spell the collapse of the age-old humanist distinction between natural history and human history." Historians have previously assumed that, beyond its repetitive changes associated with cycles like the seasons, the natural environment changed so slowly "as to make the history of man's relation to his environment almost timeless and thus not a subject of historiography at all." This would correspond with the sense of timeless nature that I noted in poems by Wendell Berry and Mary Oliver in my introduction. Even environmental historians, Chakrabarty claims, "looked upon human beings as biological agents," a very different kind of agency from the geological agency proposed by climate scientists. "To call human beings geological agents is to scale up our imagination of the human," he observes: "There was no point in human history when humans were not biological agents. But we can become geological agents only historically and collectively, that is, when we have reached numbers and invented technologies that are on a scale large enough to have an impact on the planet itself." He claims that historical understanding of the crisis of climate change "requires us to bring together intellectual formations that are somewhat in tension with each other: the planetary and the global; deep and recorded histories; species thinking and critiques of capital."[5]

Historians are wary of thinking in the monolithic terms of species, and Chakrabarty raises the question of whether such generalizing talk simply obscures "the reality of capitalist production and the logic of imperial . . . domination that it fosters." He acknowledges that much responsibility for the current crisis lies with the rich nations and rich classes rather than all of humankind. (Chakrabarty is pointing to a common critique of the Anthropocene concept—to be explored in chapter 6—that, in framing humans as a species, it elides issues of environmental justice.) He nonetheless argues that the history of capital alone is insufficient to explain climate change. He proposes that the combined resources of geology, archeology, and history are needed to explain the current catastrophe—that is, the combined resources of disciplines that work in divergent time scales. We are called upon "to mix together the immiscible chronologies of capital and species history."[6] Precisely because he believes an (otherwise unlikely) awareness of pan-human collectivity arises from the shared sense of catastrophe prompted by climate change, Chakrabarty does not dismiss this as impossible, though it requires working at the limits of historical understanding. In a more recent essay, "Climate and Capital: On Conjoined Histories," he has elaborated on three of the "rifts" that he sees us necessarily straddling as we think or speak about climate change. These inject, he acknowledges, "a certain degree of contradictoriness in our thinking, for we are being asked to think about different scales simultaneously,"[7] but he embraces those tensions as sites of productive possibility.[8] The essay explains why it's necessary to bring together different scales—for instance, why economists, politicians, and others thinking in terms of risk management need to understand scientists' uncertainties about exact climatic tipping points and "safe" levels of greenhouse gases.

In Chakrabarty's view, the climate crisis requires us to meet the challenge of "mov[ing] back and forth between thinking on these different scales all at once," bringing human-centered thinking into play with a planetary perspective.[9] Given that paleoclimatologists, evolutionary biologists, and other natural historians think in terms of far larger time scales than historians, Chakrabarty positions himself as championing a kind of thinking that is unfamiliar to historians and humanists, but by no means ungraspable. He concludes another essay on essentially the same issues by advocating "multiple-track narratives so that the story of the ontologically-endowed, justice-driven human can be told alongside the other agency that we also are—a species that has now acquired the potency of a geophysical force, and thus is blind, at this level, to its own perennial concerns with justice that otherwise forms the staple of humanist narratives."[10]

If Chakrabarty articulates an aspirational approach to the problem of scale in the Anthropocene, Derek Woods's critique of Chakrabarty represents the second, skeptical position on this issue. Woods does not believe that we can in fact "scale up our imagination of the human," as Chakrabarty proposes, because of what are called scale variants, which create scale effects. As Woods explains in "Scale Critique for the Anthropocene," "at its most general, scale variance means that the observation and the operation of systems are subject to different constraints at different scales due to real discontinuities." For example, while insects can walk on the ceiling and fall from it without damage, because surface forces have more impact on them than the force of gravity, insect bodies could not be dramatically scaled up and have that remain true. Insects "inhabit a different regime of scale constraint from that of larger vertebrates."[11] Global climate change, he asserts, does not operate like the familiar cartographic scale where one can smoothly zoom in and out (think Google Maps). Non-cartographic concepts of scale introduce discontinuities, and scaling up or down may introduce contradictions or failures.

In relation to current global climate change, nature's response to multiple anthropogenic changes of the Anthropocene, this has powerful implications for human agency and responsibility. Timothy Clark, on whose work Woods draws, points out that "with climate change . . . we have a map, its scale includes the whole earth but when it comes to relating the threat to daily questions of politics, ethics or specific interpretations of history, culture, etc., the map is often almost mockingly useless." Clark explains:

> Scale effects in relation to climate change are confusing because they take the easy, daily equations of moral and political accounting and drop into them both a zero and an infinity: the greater the number of people engaged in modern forms of consumption then the less the relative influence or responsibility of each but the worse the cumulative impact of their insignificance. As a result of scale effects what is self-evident or rational at one scale may well be destructive or unjust at another. Hence, progressive social and economic policies designed to disseminate Western levels of prosperity may even resemble, on another scale, an insane plan to destroy the biosphere. Yet, for any individual household, motorist, etc., a scale effect in their actions is invisible. It is not present in any phenomenon in itself (no eidetic reduction will flush it out); but only in the contingency of how many other such phenomena there are, have been and will be, at even vast distances in space or time. Human agency becomes, as it were, displaced from within by its own act, a kind of demonic iterability.[12]

Woods and Clark emphasize the agency of the nonhuman, which, along with scale effects themselves, they see as insufficiently recognized. Woods argues that "the scale-critical subject of the Anthropocene is not 'our species' but the sum of terraforming assemblages composed of humans, non-human species, and technics. . . . 'Anthropocene,' ironically, names the disempowerment of human beings in relation to terraforming assemblages that draw much of their agency from nonhumans."[13] As the environmental crisis erodes boundaries between intellectual disciplines so that people attempt to "think 'everything at once,'" Clark sees "an implosion of scales, implicating seemingly trivial or small actions with enormous stakes while intellectual boundaries and lines of demarcation fold in upon each other."[14]

Rather than advocating, as Chakrabarty did, multitrack narratives that bring together in tension-filled amalgamation the different scale perspectives of different disciplines, Clark proposes a metacritical analysis that separates out different scales. He proposes examining assumptions about scale in different kinds of readings of literary texts—the personal scale, the scale of a national culture, the scale of the entire earth and its inhabitants over a time scale of (in his example) six hundred years—to clarify the inadequacy of familiar critical assumptions and highlight nonhuman agency. His approach, then, is also multitrack, but emphasizes disjunctive scale effects and does not aim for synthesis. Clark advocates a way of reading that would make clear the need for change in methods of thinking and analysis but is not itself a means to that change. Woods similarly announces, "the point is not to think human agency across scale domains, as Chakrabarty argues, but to recognize that (what earth-science calls) humanity as geophysical force is the emergent property of operations in discontinuous scale domains."[15]

As I understand them, these two positions represent different assessments of human capability. Chakrabarty and his ilk believe that by pushing the limits of current forms of thinking, we may straddle scalar rifts sufficiently to use reason to address climate change, while Woods and company believe that the mind is itself like the nonscaling phenomena in nature that they call to our attention. The human mind cannot scale up and down without failure or error, and therefore it is best used now to recognize the disjunctions of scalar effects. The three poets to whose work I now turn demonstrate comparably differing emphases and different assessments of human perceptual and conceptual limits.

Juliana Spahr's emphasis in "Unnamed Dragonfly Species" is on a psychological dimension of Anthropocene scalar challenges that I call "scalar dissonance": the cognitive and affective dissonance between minute individual agency and enormous collective impact. As we collectively lurch toward one tipping point after another, each of which has cascading consequences we can barely comprehend, the individual feels tiny and helpless.[16] One's conscientious choices—not to travel by airplane, say, to eat locally and organically grown produce, or to purchase clothes only for necessity rather than fashion—seem completely without impact. Yet on a collective scale, our unconscientious, wasteful behaviors cause significant environmental damage. Ruling political, corporate, and economic systems, which seem responsible for continuing and dangerous environmental degradation, are evidently beyond the individual's control, even as the individual cannot avoid participating in them. The mental and emotional costs of maintaining an awareness of these scale variants as part of one's moral and political consciousness—the awareness Clark and Woods want to cultivate—can be high. Spahr's poem illuminates what it feels like to try to live one's daily life with the sense of imploding scales that Clark identifies. Her work exposes the disjunction of scalar effects as she struggles with the agonizing impossibility of bringing divergent scales into alignment. I will also suggest, however—here's the dance—that Spahr's poem points indirectly to other possible avenues through which individuals in the self-conscious Anthropocene might legitimately feel less disempowered.

In the poems I'll examine by Forrest Gander and Ed Roberson—both of whom have had substantial training in natural sciences—psychological struggles are not a focal interest; instead, like Chakrabarty, these two take interest in what their writing implies are attainable ways of stretching our thinking to meet the scalar challenges of the Anthropocene. That does not mean they suggest that we will manage to apply that thinking pervasively and promptly enough to avert disaster. Even so, we might see them as attempting to participate in Worster's revolution of the mind—what Evelyn Reilly talks about as a paradigm shift—in order to respond to current environmental crises. They model fresh ways of deploying traditional resources of the literary imagination, such as storytelling, lyricism, and metaphor, along with the human gifts of attention and sensory perception, to foster thinking that might straddle divergent Anthropocene scales.

SCALAR DISSONANCE AND JULIANA SPAHR'S "UNNAMED DRAGONFLY SPECIES"

Spahr's "Unnamed Dragonfly Species," from her 2011 collection *Well Then There Now,* explores how daunted people feel when they try to grasp the suprahuman scale of the human-generated transformations taking place in the Anthropocene. It effectively exposes scalar dissonance and its accompanying aggregate of emotions and intellectual responses, drawing the reader into that experience through its rhetoric and construction. "Unnamed Dragonfly Species" presents information about two huge and complex environmental issues, global warming and species extinction, but its focus is less on the data than on the difficulties nonscientists from the U.S. experience trying to process the reality of global warming and respond meaningfully to it.

The piece is woven of two strands. One is a narrative concerning an unspecified but socially cohesive "they" who, in a year when hot temperatures came so early in April that their city's daffodils all died almost as soon as they bloomed, became preoccupied with the melting of glaciers, which they learned about and observed on the Internet. Spahr's pronoun, "they," functions inclusively to embrace an unclosed group to which the reader might belong. Inserted between each of the sentences in that narrative about "they" is the bold-faced name of a plant or animal species. These names, which constitute the second strand, are alphabetically organized entries from a list of approximately 150 "endangered, threatened and special concern plant, fish, and wildlife species of New York State" found on a state government website.[17]

Spahr's presentation of the experience of the people learning about glacial melting positions the reader not just as audience to their story but also as participant in the analogous experience provided not by the Internet but by the poem. While each of the work's eleven sections begins with a sentence and ends with a species name, their content varies, so that some sections report the struggles "they" went through as they grew increasingly preoccupied with and informed about the geological evidence of rapid global warming, while others provide enough of the factual information "they" were trying to process that the reader has to struggle as "they" did to confront the mind-boggling scale of this global transformation. On the one hand, the reader is being invited to process information that is difficult to absorb; on the other, the reader is prompted to examine the conceptual and psychological drama this information produces both by reading about others who confronted this information and by examining his or her own responses to it.

Like all the poems in *Well Then There Now,* this one is preceded by a map showing its place of composition, for which the specific address (in Brooklyn) appears in the book's "Acknowledgments and Other Information," as well as by that location's geographical coordinates. This emphasis on specific location suggests that Spahr values attention to local particularities within a consciously global context. Yet the place where "they" are experiencing the Anthropocene is most immediately the indeterminate space of the information-overloaded World Wide Web, an unfathomably vast realm of data that can be difficult to connect to one's non-Internet reality in some specific locale. "On the internet they realized," begins an early section, as one might say "on the boat to Dubrovnik they realized" or "on the plateau near Santa Fe," but without any comparable sense of locatedness, orientation, or perspective. Spahr does not announce how difficult it is to grasp the actual scale, let alone the significance, of the facts about glacial melting that follow. She simply lists what "they" were learning, using "that" as an anaphoric base and saying nothing about how "they" reacted to this digitally obtained information: (For now I will attend only to the sentences that follow "they"'s experience, delaying attention to the text's other strand.)

> On the internet they realized that Iceland's Vatnajokull glacier is melting by about three feet a year. **Common Loon** That the Bering Glacier in Alaska recently lost as much as seven and a half miles in a sixty day period. **Common Nighthawk** That the European Alps lost half their ice over the last century and that many of the rivers of Europe were likely to be gone in twenty to thirty years time. **Common Sanddragon** That the Columbia Glacier in Alaska will continue to recede, possibly at a rate of as much as ten miles in ten years. **Common Tern** That thirty-six cubic miles of ice had melted from glaciers in West Antarctica in the past decade and that alone had raised sea levels worldwide by about one-sixtieth of an inch. (*WTTN* 78)

Various units of measure for both space and time appear here—miles and cubic miles, feet, inches, a half century, thirty years, a decade, a year, sixty days—scalar options in familiar and readily imagined units, but applied to objects that were created and exist on scales far more difficult to apprehend. Did such accumulating knowledge bring home to "they" the scalar reality of this planetary transformation? Or did this wash of data prove too much to absorb? Similar uncertainties apply to the poem's readers. Will Spahr awaken her readers with the startling facts and, with their multiplication, open dulled eyes to the severity of the situation? Or is she recreating the dulling mesmerization that "they" may have experienced? Might the repetitive anaphoric lists, as Judith Butler suggests is the case with the repetitions involved in performing gender identity, serve a normalizing function?[18] By suspending the narrative of "they" while providing factual data, Spahr allows her readers to have, and reflect on, their independent experience of this information.

This section identifies 1988 as a turning point year in the history of global warming, and in the next section Spahr explores how oblivious the younger "they" had been to climate change at that time. Spahr's narrative of an ordinary "they" helps readers acknowledge how little people generally think of anything outside their own immediate context and personal needs—unless, like that year's explosion of Pan Am Flight 103 over Lockerbie, Scotland, the event is particularly dramatic or spectacular. The scale of human attention tends to be small and self-centered, and not attuned to what Rob Nixon has called "slow violence."[19] Even changes that geologists, oceanographers, or climatologists recognize as alarmingly rapid or dramatic can, because of their geographical distance and their suprahuman scale, remain abstracted from ordinary lives. Only when the daffodils in one's own city suddenly die as early spring temperatures weirdly spike into the nineties does one take note: "This happened right where they were living" (*WTTN* 75). Readers may well recognize themselves in the younger "they" who spent their time thinking about finishing college and getting jobs or hitting baseballs or ridding themselves of drunk boyfriends rather than pondering locally imperceptible changes in global climate.

In the present time of "Unnamed Dragonfly Species," however, "they" have been drawn into an obsessive quest for more information, drawing the reader, too, into more engagement. The next section begins, "After the piece of the Antarctic Pine Island glacier broke off, they could not stop thinking about glaciers and the way they thought about glaciers the most was by reading about them on the internet late at night, their eyes blurring and their shoulders tight" (*WTTN* 82). Now Spahr recounts not just the facts but the shifting responses "they" have to the accumulating data and the scale of change it cumulatively suggests. At one point, "they" try to take comfort in a statistic "liked by oil drillers" that the melting away of the entire Antarctic Pine Island Glacier wouldn't "matter much because it would only raise sea levels by a quarter of an inch." But questions that "surface through this blurry comfort of small amounts of rising ocean" make them relinquish such false reassurance. They can't avoid seeing that the oil drillers haven't grasped how scale works in this scenario: the statistics offered for one melting glacier have to be added to the many others, so the amount of sea-level rise won't be limited to a quarter inch. Moreover, a quarter inch of water in the ocean is not like a quarter inch of oil in a can with vertical sides; a rise of one foot of ocean level, they learn, "typically means that shorelines end up one hundred feet or more inland." So much for attempts to minimize the hard-to-grasp scale of the ongoing changes. The section ends by identifying four island nations that, because of rising seas, "will most certainly be entirely displaced in the next thirty years," a clear dismissal of the oil drillers' perspective. The next begins with "they" recognizing themselves as island dwellers (on Long Island, presumably) for whom what's happening to Pine Island Glacier has a "scary relevance." Despite desires to minimize worry, the collapse of spatial or temporal distances taking place in the self-conscious Anthropocene undermines attempts to consider environmental changes associated with global warming as insignificantly small or "far away."

The remaining sections of "Unnamed Dragonfly Species" offer a compelling portrayal of the psychology of "they," with whose mental states Spahr's readers are likely to identify. By matter-of-factly recording their thoughts and behaviors, Spahr effectively registers the difficulties most Americans are apt to face in trying to maintain awareness of alterations that are overwhelmingly vast, complexly interrelated, and dire but as yet, they tell themselves, "far away from them." Hypocrisy, inconsistency, and self-deluding fantasy are all part of the picture. Still seeking some mode of comfort, "they" try out positive ways of viewing these incipient transformations: trying "to see climate change as just one more tendency of life towards change" (WTTN 84–85); trying to look forward to having more fjords to visit or to new plants evolving; or latching onto theories about anthropogenic warming counteracting the earth's movement into an already overdue ice age. Although more reading only increases their confusion, they continue to seek out more information, even while trying to insure that neither excessive information nor guilt will paralyze them.

Profound contradictions emerge in their sense of agency with the disjunction between their negligible impact as individuals who would like to reduce their carbon footprint and their unavoidable participation in the immensely consequential energy and resource consumption of global capitalism:

> they knew that they were in part responsible for it, whatever it was that was causing this, because they lived in the place that used the largest amount of the stuff most likely to cause this warming. **Northern Wild Monk's-hood** They lived among those who used the most stuff up, who burned the most stuff, who produced the most stuff, and other things like that. **Olympia Marble** And even if they tried to live their lives with less stuff than others, they still benefited and were a part of the system that produced all this stuff and because of this they had a hard time figuring out how to move beyond their own personal renewed commitment to denial of stuff and yet their awareness of how they benefited daily from being a part of the system that used up the most stuff. **Osprey** (WTTN 86–87)

The passage reflects exactly the conflicting scales and the scale effects emphasized by Clark, who observes that "the greater the number of people engaged in modern forms of consumption then the less the relative influence or responsibility of each but the worse the cumulative impact of their insignificance."[20] In addition to being unable to reconcile the scale of individual action with that of collective impact, "they" are struggling to alter their sense of the interrelations between the human and nonhuman realms as they gain a clearer sense of the consequences of species agency. In the time before they had begun to "enter the word 'glacier' into Google over and over," they had not "thought about their relationship with things big and cold and full of fresh water" with which they had no "actual contact" (*WTTN* 88–89).

All the unsettling insight they gain into the enormous and rapid scale of anthropogenic environmental change and the inconsequence of individual ethical choice produces huge anxiety. So "they tried to balance out all their anxiety with loud attempts at celebrations of life" (*WTTN* 92). The work's longest sentence lists some of those attempts, all of which aimed at convincing themselves that their lives were good enough that the melting didn't matter. In this final section, their—and our—dissonant fix emerges starkly: it seems impossible to sustain such self-delusion and equally impossible to face reality in the full scale of its terrifying transformation—the rapidity and vastness of the changes taking place; their cascading and inconceivably varied, frightening consequences; and "their" (our) complicity in it all. After the fifteen-line sentence cataloging the various ways in which they try loudly to savor the social, intellectual, and sensual pleasures in their lives, Spahr concludes the poem with the following scale-conscious passage:

> **Unnamed Dragonfly Species** They were anxious and they were paralyzed by the largeness and the connectedness of systems, a largeness of relation that they liked to think about and often celebrated but now seemed unbearably tragic. **Upland Sandpiper** The connected relationship between water and land seemed deeply damaged, perhaps beyond repair in numerous places. **Vesper Sparrow** The systems of relation between living things of all sorts seemed to have become in recent centuries so hierarchically human that things not human were dying at an unprecedented rate. **Wavy-rayed Lampmussel** And the systems of human governments and corporations felt so large and unchangeable and so distant from them yet the effects of their actions felt so connected and so immediate to what was happening. **Whip-poor-will** They knew this but didn't know what else to do. **Wood Turtle** And so they just went on living while talking loudly. **Worm Snake** Living and watching on a screen things far away from them melting. **Yellow-breasted Chat** (*WTTN* 92–3)

The work ends there, with Spahr having recreated the agonizing dynamics of scalar dissonance and exposed problematic scale effects but offering no program or model for "what else to do." On the contrary, she has presented the reader with a further challenge, explicitly identified only here at the work's end with the line "things not human were dying at an unprecedented rate." She adds to the challenge of facing global warming the challenge of thinking about mass extinction, a key aspect of the Anthropocene.

The title phrase, "Unnamed Dragonfly Species," highlights the limits of human knowledge in this context. The other species on the New York State list have names, often carefully descriptive ones like "Leatherback Sea Turtle" or "Brook Floater Buffalo Pebble Snail." However, this one species that is disappearing or has disappeared before it has even been named signals that we are losing life forms in our immediate environments before we even recognize them—or in this case, after we learn to recognize them, but before we can add them to our taxonomies. Science has identified about 1.2 million species on earth, but that is thought to be only about 15 percent of the life forms in existence; a major study published in 2011 estimated a total of 8.7 million species on the planet. Many of the yet-to-be-identified are smaller creatures such as beetles or the microfauna (bacteria, fungi, viruses) so crucial to soil and plant life; many others are plants and animals whose habitats in the tropics are now under extreme threat. It's no wonder people find it difficult to know "what else to do": as we go on living in ways that are unintentionally destroying habitats and blindly eliminating species, as well as melting the planet's glaciers, it seems we don't know in the most literal ways what we are doing. Our impact is huge, but while we may imagine our knowledge and our control to be large, they appear in fact small and extremely partial.[21]

The primary aim of "Unnamed Dragonfly Species" seems to be to expose and explore the stymying dilemmas of Anthropocene scalar dissonance. Yet I detect a countercurrent, generated by the species list, that may point readers in a particular direction of political engagement as an alternative. Admittedly, there are multiple ways to interpret those names that relentlessly interrupt the narrative. They might be heard as a grimly memorializing gesture, like reading the names of the war dead at an antiwar rally. Or this list might be solely an elegiac gesture.[22] But these creatures are endangered or threatened as well as extinct, and those still extant survive in a specific place that is not distant and not in the cloud: the state of New York, where Spahr was writing and where "they" were living their embodied lives. (In addition, not all the species listed as threatened or endangered in New York are so on a broader geographic scale.) The list, then, brings to a local level a global problem that is often connected to global warming and that is certainly part of the Anthropocene. By not putting punctuation between each species name and the sentence that follows, Spahr invites readers to think of the two strands of the work as part of one thing. Maybe a reader in New York can barely imagine what it means "that Kilimanjaro in East Africa has lost eighty-two percent of its area in eighty-eight years" and has no idea what she might do about it, but perhaps she can imagine what her world would be without whippoorwills, peregrine falcons, or red-headed woodpeckers, and perhaps there is something she could do to help prevent that. It's true, of course, that readers would be unfamiliar with many of the species listed, but at least some, such as the cougar or the nation's emblem, the bald eagle, are guaranteed to be recognizable. So it may be that Spahr, by interweaving the two threads of this work, directs her reader to the possibilities of local action when globally effective action is beyond conception.

Spahr's thinking might be fruitfully linked to Jonathan Franzen's controversial essay "Carbon Capture," which warns that awareness of global warming as the supreme environmental issue of our time is short-circuiting other, still valuable environmental projects. (I am not suggesting that Spahr propounds what Franzen's critics see as a false dichotomy emerging from his essay, setting concern about climate change and big energy issues against conservation and concern with biodiversity. Rather, she shares his recognition that awareness of climate change can generate paralyzing guilt and that climate change is easy to deplore but difficult to respond to. She may well share his counterbalancing sense of the importance of "an appreciation of nature as a collection of specific threatened habitats.") Considering birds and their future adaptation to a warmer world, Franzen notes that "the larger and healthier and more diverse our bird populations are, the greater the chances that many species will survive, even thrive. To prevent extinctions in the future, it's not enough to curb our carbon emissions. *We also have to keep a whole lot of wild birds alive right now.*" Drawing on the philosopher Dale Jamieson, Franzen invokes the discourse of Anthropocene scales:

> Jamieson's larger contention is that climate change is different in category from any other problem the world has ever faced. For one thing, it deeply confuses the human brain, which evolved to focus on the present, not the

far future, and on readily perceivable movement, not slow and probabilistic developments. . . . The great hope of the Enlightenment—that human rationality would enable us to transcend our evolutionary limitations—has taken a beating from wars and genocides, but only now, on the problem of climate change, has it foundered altogether.[23]

That sense of foundering, evident in how stuck Spahr's "they" seem, brings to mind Clark's perspective. Just as Franzen turns to the impressive example of what a small institution, the Amazon Conservation Association, has been able to accomplish on behalf of local human and nonhuman communities, it seems to me that Spahr points to a focus on local habitat preservation and local activism more generally as "what else to do." The poem's unrelenting tolling of one endangered species after another casts a shadow of self-indulgence on the emotional struggles of "they." Clearly, it's delusory to imagine that the "things far away from them melting" will have no impact close at hand, but as Spahr encourages readers to examine their own perhaps near-paralyzing dilemmas in the presence of dramatically discrepant scales of global events and personal comprehension or agency, her interweaving of two (not unrelated) threads within this work suggests that potentially more manageable issues may be addressed nearby.

IMAGINING DEEP TIME IN FORREST GANDER'S "THE CARBONIFEROUS AND ECOPOETICS"

Gander's poetic prose in "The Carboniferous and Ecopoetics" (2012) deploys the observational skills and knowledge that he cultivated partly through undergraduate training in geology, along with the expressive resources of a sensuous lyricism, to draw readers imaginatively into a non-anthropocentrically scaled understanding of planetary history. "The Carboniferous and Ecopoetics" is collected in *Redstart: An Ecological Poetics,* which Gander wrote with Australian poet John Kinsella; part I of "The Carboniferous and Ecopoetics" seems to be "The Carboniferous," and I will refer to it as such. This section makes deep evolutionary time imaginable to the nonscientist without trivializing or shrinking it—without making it fit accustomed scales. Inviting readers into the distant past in ways that draw on familiar references and literary conventions without rendering the scene itself familiar, he translates scientific understandings so that his readers will grasp the brevity of human planetary habitation as well as the limits of the planet's current carbon resources. (Gander is an accomplished translator of poetry from foreign languages, especially Spanish. I use the word "translation" with that achievement in mind, since he similarly translates into compelling lyricism scientific languages nonscientists find hard to process.) Only after that is accomplished does he introduce more straightforward data, like that Spahr provided, to convey a collision of scales currently occurring as human habitation, which occupies a miniscule segment of geological time, suddenly overwhelms planetary space, consuming resources whose effectively imagined history makes evident that they cannot be replaced in a time scale relevant to the human species. The extremity of Worster's "age of limits" gains vivid immediacy.

"The Carboniferous" begins by echoing the opening of countless origin stories, though here instead of "in the beginning" we have a phrase that suggests an extended historical awareness of cycles or of endings followed by new developments: "In one of the beginnings." Having drawn in readers with a version of one of the most familiar and inviting narrative devices, Gander then tells his story in the present tense, with each paragraph making a colossal leap forward in time, so that the reader is immersed in an always changing now that traverses hundreds of millions of years. The first two paragraphs are representative:

> In one of the beginnings, below the fluff- and leaf-encrusted surface of a wide, shallow body of water, microscopic spores swirl with bat-winged algae. A cloudy soup of exertions and excretions, the sea drizzles its grit into rich mud.
>
> Trilobites are dying off. (Miles Davis could have been quoting nature when he said, "I listen to what I can leave out.") Brachiopods, mollusks, and corals cluster in wide, shallow seas riven by sharks. Thick fish with lungs and lobes are giving way to a new species, the lung reconfigured as a swim bladder. Like surreal, underwater candelabra, crinoids effloresce; on long branching stems they stretch up toward the waves, each arm filtering small animals and plants through the calyx where a mouth is hidden.[24]

The alien richness of this temporally removed world is conveyed as much by an aural density of thickly alliterating consonants and echoing vowels ("drizzles its grit into rich mud," "thick fish with lungs and lobes," "shallow seas riven by sharks") and by a striking, sometimes scientific vocabulary (riven, effloresce, calyx, crinoids) as it is by the strange visual phenomena depicted (surreally waving underwater candelabra). Yet as he makes the alien geological past vivid to the senses, Gander's interjection of a reference to a celebrated musician—one of several references to artists in "The Carboniferous"—acknowledges that one inevitably brings one's mediating cultural perspective to one's understanding of nature. Additionally, Miles Davis's intuition of nature's principles indicates that artists' insights may have transtemporal relevance adequate even to prehuman worlds.

Frequently, Gander draws on familiar perspectives to assist his readers' process of imagining: carboniferous bugs "hover over bouquet-size spiders and a sort of millipede that grows five feet long." Yet the scale of what's described is decidedly not that of our familiar world, unless in its horror movies. Sometimes his technique is cinematic, zooming in for a close-up and a moment suspended in time before drawing back for more panoramic vistas, while descriptions insistently involve senses of smell and touch, as well as sound and sight:

> Below, in the umbratile interval between one step and another, a tetrapod resembling a large newt freezes and blinks into the sound of the world, the chirp and whirr of insects and the high frequency mutter of its own species. Fronds brush fronds in a light breeze. (And what, eons later, does the Kreutzer Sonata, which Tolstoy will deem dangerous for its capacity to arouse erotic feelings, what does that music have over this sound?) The animal blinks again, its hydraulic limbs holding it above smudged tracks that mark where others of its kind mated, their mouths popping, cheek muscles bulging. Five tumescent digits on each foot channel ground vibrations into neural impulses. It takes stock and goes on. ("I am still alive then. That may come in useful," Beckett's Molloy quips.) (RS 6)

References tying the scene to modern works of art interrupt the illusion of presence, but only to diminish illusions of human specialness. They do not diminish the reader's vivid immersion in this evolutionary drama as he or she witnesses as, for instance, "Ferns luxuriate across wetlands: dragonfly seed ferns, rhizomatic ferns, ferns spoked like the dorsal fin of a swordfish, each loosing into the air millions of spores coated with oil and chlorophyll" (RS 6–7). As if present, readers follow the transformations of organic materials during a radically distant time in which layers of plant life are laid down so thickly and so rapidly that "they don't have time to decay" and instead are pressed into coal, our legacy from the Carboniferous. That period, the time covered by Gander's astonishing creation story, lasted from approximately

395 to 299 million years ago. By the point in the text where Gander identifies coal as a form of sunlight, readers are prepared to accept that startling vision as nonmetaphoric: "When we pick up a piece of coal, it is the fossil residue of photosynthesis, a condensation of Paleozoic sunlight that we hold in our hands" (RS 7). By exerting imaginative pressure to extend ordinary sense perceptions so that near-mythic marvel and factual particularity merge in depictions of the phenomenal world, Gander generates understanding of otherwise mind-boggling geological processes and time scales.

With the arrival of the human, Gander's narrative accelerates and he begins to introduce statistics, but still as part of a story, which readers now understand to have been all along the story of coal. He moves through the Industrial Revolution and up to the Great Acceleration:

> and then, about three decades ago, mountaintop removal mining. In West Virginia alone, more than 350,000 acres of forested mountains are lopped off, and 1,200 miles of streams are buried. The overburden or leftover rock fills adjacent valleys. One of the by-products of excavation is slurry, a pool of chemical waste and toxic metals. Postexcavation by-products like ash and poisonous gases are released in the next phase: the burning of coal in power plants. (RS 8)

The narrative ends as Gander shifts from the current unprecedented consumption of coal to its imminent exhaustion:

> In China, where more than 6,000 men died in mines in 2004, where coal seams in the north hiss in unstoppable fires started by small-scale mining operators, and where the deserts are yawning wider at an alarming rate, coal is powering unprecedented industrialization. Some scientists estimate that coal will provide half the world's energy by the year 2100. And a hundred years after that, all the exploitable reserves of coal in the earth will be exhausted. (RS 9)

What took nearly a hundred million years to create more than three hundred million years ago will have been consumed by one species in less than three hundred years; "the relation between those two sets of numbers," Gander notes, "represents six orders of magnitude." A reader who has taken the journey of this story of coal from its enchanting beginnings to its sudden end can't avoid registering the significance of this shocking scalar disproportion. While rapid consumption of fossil fuels by the developed world has had benefits as well as costs, its recklessness could hardly be more clear.

Yet the section is not quite over. Or perhaps what appears after the dividing line following the passage just quoted should be thought of as the "and" linking "The Carboniferous" with "Ecopoetics" in the work's title. On a new page, with a horizontal line at the top, the final passage before section II reads: "A poem, even excavated from its context and the time of its writing, is a curiously renewable form of energy. It's hard to be sure whether it is from the future or the past that the poet Henry Vaughan writes, 'They are all gone into the world of light! / And I alone sit ling'ring here'" (*RS* 10). At this point, as past and future blur—and again the transtemporal quality of artistic insight emerges—questions of scale fade into the background. Rather than dwelling further on the horror of coal's planet-poisoning consumption, or on the straits in which that leaves us, Gander turns to considering the powers of art, inviting readers to light their lives with the energy to be discovered in poems. What I find startling here is the use of metaphor. The preceding pages of "The Carboniferous" contain a number of similes (e.g., "Beneath hundreds of thousands of meters of overlying rot, the peat beds contract like a frog's iris into thin horizontal lines") and an occasional metaphor (e.g., "At full throttle, technologies advance") that help the reader envision the planetary changes depicted. Here, however, there's a striking disjunction between the very literal problems of the combustion of nonrenewable, polluting coal that Gander has been emphasizing and the claim that poems are a form of "renewable energy." For however much poems may speak with renewed relevance to different eras, and however much they may warm our hearts or illuminate our minds, poems cannot warm our homes or power our industries unless through the burning of the paper they are printed on. They cannot in any direct way solve our energy problems or slow climate change.

I suspect Gander intends this abrupt shift to highlight a problem pervasive in ecopoetics: the disjunction between the perhaps quixotic hope many poets, including himself, place in poetry, on the one hand, and the limited agency of any writing that relies on shifts in consciousness and awareness to generate social or political change, on the other. Part II, "Ecopoetics," written in a more scholarly mode, wrestles with the claims made for ecopoetics and what should be expected from it, still pondering whether, as Auden announced, "poetry makes nothing happen" (*RS* 14). Although much of this section takes the form of questions, cautions, and qualifications, Gander ultimately gives weight to several recent anthropological studies as "register[ing] support for the argument that language, perception, and conception are irrevocably connected" (*RS* 15), with changed conception opening the way for changed behavior. (This echoes Joan Retallack's argument mentioned in the introduction, and it is a literary version of the hope of historians Worster and Chakrabarty.) Yet he carefully qualifies his claims:

> If language does affect the way we think about being in the world, poetry *can* make something happen. I would suggest that it does. Certainly, I feel it has profoundly influenced the way I experience the world. But it probably doesn't affect perception nearly as directly as poets might wish. Getting rid of the capital I, eliminating pronouns altogether, deconstructing normative syntax, making the word "wordy"—these techniques, all more than a century old, impact the reader. But the effects are complex and subtle and may not correspond to a writer's intentions at all. (*RS* 16–17)

Gander goes on to offer the possibility that "poems might be seen to take responsibility for certain ways of thinking and writing, as Charles Altieri notes, 'precisely by inviting audiences to see what powers they take on as they adapt themselves to how the texts ask to be read'" (*RS* 17). Part I of "The Carboniferous and Ecopoetics" constitutes such an invitation. It employs several of the techniques he lists, such as eliminating the "I" and stressing the materiality of language—which, he notes, "look a lot like innovative poetic strategies championed for the last hundred years" (*RS* 11)— to provide his audience with powers of vision less focused on the human subject and human scale. By enabling readers to imagine unaccustomed realms and time scales in richly sensuous ways, "The Carboniferous" conveys a somatically based understanding of anthropogenic environmental damage and of the planetary limits humans are up against. Yet in "Ecopoetics" the question of whether taking on those perceptual powers will translate into "ways of *being* in the world that might lead to less exploitative and destructive histories" remains (*RS* 15). In putting the two parts, with the unsettling "and," together into one work, Gander demonstrates his own impassioned investment in and hopes for the powers of language and their connection to perception or apprehension. At the same time, he exposes his uncertainties and discomforts around claims that have been made by avant-gardes throughout the twentieth and into the twenty-first-century—claims he himself longs to make—that link linguistic experimentation to social or political transformation.

MULTISCALAR PERCEPTION IN ED ROBERSON'S *TO SEE THE EARTH BEFORE THE END OF THE WORLD*

If Gander in "The Carboniferous" works to cultivate in his readers a sensorily perceptive imagination that will enable them to grasp unfamiliar Anthropocene scales, Roberson highlights the perceptual range and flexibility that our minds and senses already have. His writing in *To See the Earth Before the End of the World* (2010) conveys an awareness that humans have adapted before to shifting perspectival scales, for instance in the aerial views made available by plane flight and more recently by photos from space exploration.[25] His poems suggest that humans move through the world perceiving in a kind of constantly shifting scalar kaleidoscope. Roberson—who has studied both painting and limnology and whose writing over four decades has demonstrated an intensive interest in perspective and perception—implies that apprehending Anthropocene scales is only an extension of an adjustment that, however astonishing, has long been part of the human tool kit. Despite this hopeful vision of human perceptual flexibility, however, his title poem seems to reject any hope that this ability, or the poet's calling attention to it, will prove helpful in averting environmental disaster. At the same time, he sounds less anxious than Spahr or Gander, as his work enacts and advocates an attention to one's immediate sensory environment that refuses absorption in abstract guilt, fear, or concerns about language's limited power.

Roberson ponders the adaptability of human scalar perception in "Topoi," whose speaker describes the geography observed from a plane descending into Newark and then wonders,

at

what point did we become so familiar with

such long perspective we could look down
and recognize the pile of Denver by the drop off
and crumble of the plate up   into the Rockies,
or say   That's Detroit!   by the link of lakes by

Lake St. Clair some thirty-thousand feet
above Lake Erie while just barely spotting Huron
on the horizon?   (*TSEB* 11)

Roberson's speaker goes on to note that people in earlier civilizations who survived by hunting had similar maps in their heads, though limited to terrain traversed on foot. He notes, too, that we have lost the hunter's vision and that we are now in a situation of extreme precarity, figured with a cartoonlike image of humankind as a dancing bear suddenly realizing the ball on which it dances is hanging over the abyss: "Like trained bear / dancing on a circus ball, we look down, our feet in a step / from which there is no step off" (*TSEB* 11). The scale has shifted; the earth itself is tiny. Yet it's also the size of all life throughout evolutionary time; in Roberson's play with the notion of footprint as "the surface over which / a phenomenon exists," the earth becomes "this footprint of all step ever taken," "the footprint of life." At once large and small, it's all we've got, "the ball that all our ways are woven from."

Repeatedly in the volume, Roberson places human experience within a context of astronomical space and deep time that challenges anthropocentrism in its dwarfing of the human. "The oceans of the time men don't exist," he notes, "include only a drop that we do / and see / above them another ocean's spray of stars"—rendering the human an infinitesimal part of a gorgeous pattern (*TSEB* 21). He incorporates mention that the sun's light travels for 93 million miles or that stars whose light we see may have burnt out long ago. But rather than making such perspectives daunting, he suggests, sometimes subtly, the many shifting scales we regularly accommodate. "Deep Time," for instance, begins with the familiar tree canopy assuming the scale of the entire sky with leaves as its clouds and its Milky Way; from that tree world, Roberson renders the return of the seventeen-year cicadas (itself an oddly scaled life cycle from a human perspective) as the generation of distant stars. The arrival of the cicada's music merges with the arrival of starlight delayed by its travel through space. Through metaphor, scales of time and space shift repeatedly, and sound partially substitutes for visible light ("heard but unseen / insect star births"), though sunlight coming through the trees also is scaled up as "explosions of nova":

> Where trees are a sky
>   whose spider web
>   radio antennas'
>   search receives
>   the rhythmic static
>   of cicadas,
>
> a song arrives
>   that died leaving
>   seventeen years ago.

                    Deep

cumulus leaves—
            whose cloud and Milky Way
      are green,
                    and heard but unseen
            insect star   births
                    have yet to reach us from—

refract the sun
            -light filtered
      through to brilliant spike
                    explosions of nova   (*TSEB* 7)

The poem concludes by noting "that one / day our own / insect sun" will explode, hissing "in deep time into deepsong" (*TSEB* 7). That vision of our puny sun disappearing into deep time is no more of a scalar wonder than the tree skies and cicadas' radio transmissions with which the poem opens. Weaving through the twists of what Roberson calls his "polyphonic syntax" as well as the scalar and perceptual shifts of his descriptions may be dizzying (are these literal spiderwebs, or have the outermost twigs of the trees assumed the delicate proportion of spiderwebs, which in turn act as antennas receiving the cicadas' song?).[26] But such writing invites readers to embrace the challenge of planetary scalar transformation as a manageable operation—one particularly familiar to poets and poetry readers via the action of metaphor. Readers of poetry are accustomed to phrases like "insect sun," and Roberson's writing implies that such imaginative practice prepares people to see humankind in varying scales—here, in its geological insignificance.

   As in "Topoi," where the modern speaker possessed an internal map analogous to the mental map of a primitive hunter, Roberson often presents continuities between past, present, and possible future adaptations in ways that make clear what is, on a human scale, calamitously at stake now, while also suggesting that shifts that might counteract current risks are within our grasp because grounded in earlier human patterns. While acknowledging losses, he also suggests the possibility of nondeclensionist environmental narratives.

   Even though its title "Old Dependency" emphasizes a continuity in human experience, and although the poem involves a profound loss, it embraces compensating gains in technology—here, the satellite-dependent technology of the digital watch. The title alludes to the lines from Wallace Stevens's "Sunday Morning": "We live in an old chaos of the sun, / Or old dependency of day and night."[27] Roberson's poem compares the time-keeping of a watch adjusted by satellite signal with the human body's now diminished sense of time. His body has forgotten "how the sunrise set / men's cycles," an adjustment once made through a close "melanin-melatonin connection." Consequently, he needs a piece of "inorganic / jewelry // connecting a crystal oscillation through / a radio wave in orbit" as a cyborgian prosthesis, an intravenous feed supplying time and rhythm to his being. Toward the poem's end, the speaker offers a kind of prayer for a realignment through that "gemstone cut music on [his] arm" that would reconnect him not only with the rhythm of natural cycles but with an intense sensitivity to ecosystemic relationality:

> let this renew an old interpretation
> how we could talk
>
> to rock, listen to plants explain
> in the stomach what membranous
> exchange
>
> is the dawn star with ear of corn;   (*TSEB* 17)

But rather than closing with this atavistic longing alone (an example of what Noah Heringman critiques as evolutionary nostalgia),[28] he turns toward his present reality, which is characterized by a compromised responsiveness to biological cycles and by the body's imbrication with the machine. All along he has presented the watch in anthropomorphizing metaphors that blur the boundary between machine and human and align their disparate scales. "My watch sits meditating, on the sill, / faces out the window at tonight's / radio sky," he writes, before presenting the watch's clasp as its "knees . . . folded underneath" in a posture of prayer, the watch "a timing sun's worshipper" (the signal-sending satellite was introduced as "Sun-like"). At the same time, he describes the human body as having a (watchlike) "band to the watched face of the sun," through the "melanin-melatonin connection" operating via the skin. Modern humanity no longer responds sensitively to that mechanism that "tells the wake and sleep"; it is no longer functioning in the ways it evolved to function. Accepting humans' new dependency on the watch and the sunlike satellite as contiguous with the old dependency on the sun, the speaker continues on from the prayer-like passage quoted above to close the poem as follows: "the watch, its passage, and waking flesh / working to live in time" (*TSEB* 17). Planetary cycles, biological processes, and human technology—however different their scales—are seen as functioning in harmony.

"Waking flesh." The phrase captures something both Gander and Roberson value for living in the self-conscious Anthropocene: a turning toward what our senses can teach us. While calling attention to humankind's ultimate insignificance, shrinking us in our own eyes (as Gander does too, in "The Carboniferous"), Roberson asks his readers also to see through enlarging lenses—to "widen . . . the tube of that measure // of sight we are given"—so as "to see ourselves / in the brief moment / that we are / of the earth" (*TSEB* 127, 22). Thus, his title poem, which concerns global warming, challenges us to be fully present to our current crisis, not in an anxious way, but in an attentive one, and to live in that awareness.[29]

The opening of "To See the Earth Before the End of the World" emphasizes the scalar discrepancies of the Anthropocene: the world is dying piece by piece, and each of those pieces is "longer than we," not just longer than a human lifetime, but longer than multiple generations or perhaps than the existence of humankind.

> People are grabbing at the chance to see
> the earth before the end of the world,
> the world's death piece by piece each longer than we.
>
> Some endings of the world overlap our lived
> time, skidding for generations
> to the crash scene of species extinction
> the five minutes it takes for the plane to fall,
> the mile ago it takes to stop the train,
> the small bay   to coast the liner into the ground,
>
> the line of title to a nation   until the land dies,
> the continent uninhabitable. (*TSEB* 3)

Because some of those endings of monumental phenomena overlap with our lifetimes or with recent generations, we're able to witness their final moments—comparable, on another scale, to someone's witnessing the last five minutes in the flight of a crashing plane or to being present at the small bay where a sinking ocean liner comes to rest. The names of ocean liners like the SS *Norway* or the *Queen Mary* invoke the imagined sturdy might of nations, but nations themselves last only as long as the land is habitable. As today's climate refugees from small island nations are discovering, land itself can die; soon, whole continents could well become uninhabitable. (Indeed, recent studies predict that by this century's end, many population centers on the Persian Gulf Coast are likely to experience temperatures that humans cannot survive without air conditioning.) In the first half of the poem, Roberson works to give his readers a feeling for the almost un-imaginable coming together of discrepant large and small scales, or what he calls "the very subtlety of time between // large and small," which finds us witnessing, in a revision of that formulation, "a subtle collapse of time between large // and our small human extinction."

After that important line underscoring human insignificance in the scale of deep time, the poem shifts focus, as the poet meditates first on his individual situation and then on how humankind got to this point. "If I have a table / at this event, mine bears an ice sculpture." While others are "grabbing" at last chances and "chasing" after glaciers, he imagines himself sitting still before a small segment of one of the pieces "longer than we" that he can contemplate and observe. It is, moreover, a sculpture, a work of art (bringing to mind Gander's turning to poetry at the close of "The Carboniferous"). "Of whatever loss it is," Roberson observes, "it lasts as long as ice / does until it disappears." He expresses no obvious anxiety or mourning; rather than focusing on regret for loss, he focuses on present duration. There's an attitude of acceptance; the time he has is the time he has, what he has to observe is what he has to observe, and, as ice sculpture, his bit of the earth is not only fascinating in its constant change but also implicitly beautiful.

In saying that the sculpture of glacial ice that adorns the speaker's table will melt into air, Roberson alludes to Marx and Engels's critique of capi-talism, perhaps pointing to capitalism's responsibility for the climate change described in the poem.[30] Yet his closing lines make clear that he regards the disappearance and loss we are witnessing, whether or not their proximate cause is capitalism, as consequences of irreversible choices made much earlier:

> All that once chased us and we
> chased to a balance chasing back, tooth for spear,
> knife for claw,

> locks us in this grip
> we just now see
> our own lives taken by
> taking them out.   Hunting the bear,
> we hunt the glacier with the changes come
> of that choice.

Again thinking in terms of human continuities across eras, Roberson locates the origin of our climate crisis with the earliest human hunters, who devised spears and knives to gain advantage over other species. In assuming dominion over nature, we humans initiated the process of killing the glacier as well; our own lives are being taken by our "taking out" the lives of other species. This is something "we just now see"—that is, we only now see clearly what we have done, and it's something we'll only see for a momentary now, before we, too, situated on a rapidly warming planet, melt into vapor and air. Prospero's lines from *The Tempest,* which lie behind the English translation of Marx's phrase, come to mind. Prospero anticipates that "the great globe itself, / yea, all which it inherit, shall dissolve," and perhaps there's some comfort here; in the Anthropocene as before it, each being on earth still has one life and one death.[31] Roberson's assessment of the power of poetry, like that of Spahr and Gander, is shifting and unstable. In the deterministic vision that closes "To See the Earth Before the End of the World," Roberson denies that the human ability to flexibly perceive in shifting scales can help in averting or delaying eco-catastrophe, though other poems in the same volume highlight human perceptual abilities more hopefully.

Recognizing the importance of scale-variant perception to environmental problem-solving in the self-conscious Anthropocene, Spahr, Gander, and Roberson resourcefully employ varied formal and linguistic strategies to bring emotional and sensory immediacy to issues of scale. Whether or not they believe that the human mind is capable of bridging the scalar discrepancies and meeting the scalar challenges we face, the claims they make for poetry's contributions to environmental problem-solving remain modest and heavily qualified. Nonetheless, scientists or politicians proposing to address global environmental problems through lifestyle changes or policies that require them will need to take into account the profound psychological challenges posed by the scalar dissonance Spahr dramatizes. Those who, like Chakrabarty, hope to foster thinking on several scales simultaneously, keeping in view the needs of human individuals and societies alongside the large impact of *anthropos* as a geological force, might learn from what Roberson and Gander reveal about lending sensory power to multitrack narrative and about metaphor's access to multiscalar imagination. Appropriately, none of the three poets seems willing to relinquish all hope that imaginative or experimental uses of language—or the unflinching attentiveness that makes such language possible—may contribute to positive ecopolitical change, whether by highlighting particular perceptual abilities with eco-ethical implications, cultivating particular ways of conceptualizing the relations of nature and culture or human interrelations with natural processes, or suggesting small-scale avenues for environmental activism.

CHAPTER 2

Toxicity, Nets, and Polymeric Chains
The Ecopoetics of Plastic

One consequential way in which humans are altering the planetary environment is through the production of synthetic chemicals, many of which imperil human and animal health. This chapter explores examples of what I call the *poetics of interconnection* that two poets, one Canadian and one American, have experimentally devised in response to one set of such materials, plastics. Adam Dickinson in *The Polymers* and Evelyn Reilly in *Styrofoam* approach poetic form and composition in radically different ways, but both have devised formal models that reflect the environmental problems plastics produce and that metaphorically enact the environmental relations plastics highlight. The chained forms of *The Polymers* and the collage nets woven in *Styrofoam* enact the imbrication of nature and culture or the natural and the artificial; the permeability between what has conventionally been considered the bounded inside and outside; and the thorough interrelation of living things with one another and with substances in their environments, including human-devised toxins. These works illustrate Reilly's proposition that ecopoetics "attempts to trace kinetics of whole systems, and to enact connections rather than to mark distinctions."[1]

Two concepts useful for understanding the environmental interconnections plastic reveals, as well as the ecopoetry that responds to plastic and its toxicity, are *risk society* and *trans-corporeality*. The former was introduced by sociologist Ulrich Beck in the mid-1980s and has proved influential in multiple disciplines. Following from industrialization, the risk society is "a phase of development of modern society in which the social, political, ecological and individual risks created by the momentum of innovation increasingly elude the control and protective institutions of industrial society."[2] Created through the "logics of unintended and unknown side-effects," "it arises through the automatic operation of autonomous modernisation processes which are blind and deaf to consequences and dangers."[3] The potential dangers involved, moreover, cannot be delimited in space or time: they cannot be contained by national borders, and they may manifest in subsequent generations rather than present ones. They "not only elude sensory perception and the powers of the imagination, but also scientific determination" and tend to be incalculable. Paradoxically, while science is "involved in the origin and deepening of risk situations," the threats we face *require the sensory organs of science—theories, experiments, measuring instruments—in order to become visible and interpretable as threats at all."*[4] The threats to human and animal health posed by xenobiotic chemicals from plastics fit the unsettling patterns of the risk society: they are unintended side-effects of scientific and industrial innovation; they flow throughout the biosphere over time and space and affect bodies in ways that are consequential, even if invisible or not immediately evident; they pose significant yet incalculable ongoing risks that pervade our lives and those of other animals.

Building partly on Beck's ideas, Stacy Alaimo in *Bodily Natures* develops the concept of trans-corporeality to acknowledge the "interconnections, interchanges, and transits between human bodies and nonhuman natures"; her notion of the trans-corporeal subject "underlines the extent to which the substance of the human is ultimately inseparable from 'the environment.'" Toxic bodies—bodies that have absorbed industrial pollutants— demonstrate the interconnection Alaimo highlights, with potentially significant ethical consequences: "The traffic in toxins [that is, a toxic chemical's ability to poison various bodies and places in the course of its production, consumption, and disposal] may render it nearly impossible for humans to imagine that our own well-being is disconnected from that of the rest of the planet or to imagine that it is possible to protect 'nature' by merely creating separate, distinct areas in which it is 'preserved.'"[5] As I will demonstrate, through the content of their poems as well as their netted and chained forms, both Reilly and Dickinson convey the body's material interconnection with the wider environment and highlight how, in the polluted industrialized world of the Anthropocene, that entanglement puts both human and nonhuman lives at risk.

Dickinson and Reilly would agree with Alaimo that "an understanding of the material interchanges between bodies (both human and nonhuman) and the wider environment often requires the mediation of scientific information."[6] Their poems engage with the molecular scale of chemistry and more broadly with the language, sign systems, and methods of science.

Besides indicating the importance of scientific literacy, this broadens the linguistic and visual resources of their art, and each poet responds with playful exuberance to that expansion of possibilities; the porosity between the playful and the serious becomes yet another form of interconnectedness their poetics explore. *The Polymers* and *Styrofoam* bring art and science together, while displaying how art may illuminate science for a broader public, how art may be complicit with science's failures, and how art may offer valuably different ways of knowing the world that can complement those of science or counter science's limitations. Neither poet simply idealizes art or simply criticizes science. We'll see, for instance, that Reilly presents contemporary art as being just as subject to corporate cooptation as science is. She reveals that art can foster or sustain environmentally destructive ideologies, just as science can act in accordance with them. Both poets align the experimentalism of art with the experimental spirit of science. Yet they also enact critiques of science's pretensions to a more objective knowledge and more reliable truth than those that art proffers. Their distinctive ways of translating the language of science into the language of poetry manifest a shared desire to generate alternative understandings of the world, what Reilly speaks of as a "paradigm shift" sought through the formal strategies of ecopoetics.[7]

Although scale is no longer my analytic focus as it was in chapter 1, both the material and conceptual challenges of scale remain crucial here, as the opening of *Styrofoam*'s first poem readily demonstrates. The first line is: "Answer: Styrofoam deathlessness." What immediately follows, "Question: How long does it take?" seems off the mark as a response, as if the questioner were unable to grasp what has just been asserted.[8] The query suggests how incomprehensible people find the timescale of Styrofoam's nonbiodegradable permanence. In the context of that time-twisting and mind-bending consciousness of anthropogenic transformation of natural materials, Reilly attempts an invocation of the muse who seems also a modern version of one of the Fates: a "little dead Greek lady" accessorized with synthetic polymers and holding as her emblem not a tool for writing nor for spinning, measuring, or cutting the thread of individuals' lives but a vial of, it seems, liquid thermoplastic polymers. Describing her as "dead" in her "eternity.saddle" perhaps undercuts any immortality sustained solely by the human imagination, in contrast with the actual deathlessness of thermoplastics:

& all the time singing in my throat

little dead Greek lady
in your eternity.saddle

[hat: 59% Acrylic 41% Modacrylic]
[ornamental trim: 24% Polyvinyl 76% Polyamide]

holding a vial

    enwrapped

Enter: 8,9,13,14,17-ethynyl-13-methyl-
7,8,9,11,12,14,15,16-octahydro-cyclopenta-diol

(aka environmental sources of hormonal activity   (*S* 9)

When the poet/speaker tries to engage in the traditional poetic invitation
to an immortal power to sing through her, she finds herself possessed by
something more likely to induce illness, hormonal disruption, and despair
than inspiration. This volume's muse hails the entrance into the environment of the ever-expanding multitude of plastic polymers and the incredibly enduring threats they pose to environmental health.

Subsequent "answers" in this poem reemphasize the altered sense of
time required to grasp the impact of the nonbiodegradable materials we
are now producing and discarding in such vast quantities:

Answer: It is a misconception that materials
biodegrade in a meaningful timeframe

Answer: Thought to be composters landfills
are actually vast mummifiers

        of waste   (*S* 10)

Many kinds of plastic will decay only in the scale of deep time. The rate
of plastic breakdown (not to be confused with biodegradation) varies according to the kind of plastic and the conditions, such as temperature and
exposure to sunlight. A plastic grocery bag may degrade in five hundred

years if exposed to ultraviolet light but may last indefinitely underground. Some kinds of plastic break down in less than a decade, some in millennia, while some are considered permanently chemically bonded: they will never break down. Even when broken down by photo degradation, plastics retain their polymeric forms. In a far more material way than our gods and muses, they are immortal.

Plastics are being invented ("Enter: 8,9,13,14,17-ethynyl-13-methyl-. . ."), produced, and discarded in astonishing quantities and at an accelerating rate. According to Susan Freinkel, "We've produced nearly as much plastic in the first decade of this millennium as we did in the entire twentieth century." Globally, the Worldwatch Institute reports, some 299 million tons of plastic were produced in 2013, an increase of nearly 4 percent over the preceding year. Given its durability, this massive production, which accounts for about 4 percent of petroleum use worldwide in plastic produced and another 4 percent to power its manufacture, generates a huge material problem of waste. (Much plastic is used once and discarded; a small percentage is recycled.) Right now somewhere between 22 and 43 percent of plastics end up in ever-growing landfills, while between 10 and 20 million tons each year go into the ocean, where pieces are consumed by marine animals and sea birds, often with fatal results. *National Geographic* reports that 269,000 tons of plastic debris float in the oceans, and "some four billion plastic microfibers per square kilometer litter the deep sea." Earth's oceans are rapidly becoming a plastic soup.[9]

As garbage, plastic is problematic not only in its volume and persistence but crucially as a source of toxic pollution; plastics leach carcinogenic, mutagenic, and endocrine-disrupting chemicals into the air, water, and soil and into the tissues of plants and of nonhuman and human animals. (A few words about endocrine disruptors: these substances mimic naturally occurring hormones and thus may activate, deactivate, or modify signals our hormones carry. A large body of research on wildlife and lab animals suggests that endocrine disruptors cause reductions in fertility; abnormalities in reproductive organs; increases in mammalian, ovarian, and prostate cancer; increases in immune and autoimmune disorders and in some neurodegenerative diseases. Some research on humans suggests that these chemicals—including PCBs, phthalates, plasticizers such as BPA and DEHP, the pesticide DDT, BBDEs in fire retardants, and PFCs in nonstick cookware—are reducing human fertility and increasing the incidence of obesity, diabetes, endometriosis, some cancers, and neurodegenerative diseases such as Parkinson's.

Endocrine-disrupting chemicals pose the greatest risk to prenatal and early postnatal beings; their damage may be passed on to future generations.) Ironically, plastic may do more harm when broken down than when intact, since its small pellets, called nurdles or, more poetically, mermaid's tears, are ingested by aquatic organisms, including zooplankton, and can accumulate through the food chain; those same tiny pellets, while leaching chemicals introduced in their own manufacture, also act as sponges to which other chemical pollutants and toxins, such as DDT and heavy metals, attach, making the plastic in the sea far more deadly than that on land.[10]

The chemical toxicity of plastics points to another scalar problem: we are accustomed to understanding toxicity as correlated to dosage; that is the premise behind all sorts of EPA or FDA regulations of acceptable levels of consumption or exposure. But while natural toxins tend to do more damage at high doses, the effects of endocrine disruptors are often not dose-dependent. As Nancy Langston explains in *Toxic Bodies,* unlike natural toxins, synthetic endocrine disruptors often lack a threshold below which they produce no adverse effects; their "biological effects occur at doses that are orders of magnitude lower than current dose limits for other toxins."[11] This produces a regulatory problem (or lapse) intensified by the fact that these effects may not be apparent immediately after exposure; exemplifying what Rob Nixon has called slow violence, the effects may be delayed, invisible until manifest in subsequent generations.

While keenly aware of plastic as a multifaceted environmental problem—as accumulating nonbiodegradable waste; as a danger to environmental, human, and animal health; as an industry that contributes significantly to global warming; and so forth—these poets do not interact with plastics in solely negative terms.[12] The richness of their work lies in its unsimplifying ambivalence. Plastic is a wondrous material that has been attractive to artists and designers since its invention, and it is bound up with beneficial or intriguing as well as troubling aspects of our petrochemical era. It has come to be essential to the world we inhabit, defining our material culture, making possible medical as well as military advances, even determining our modes of digital communication. As is suggested by his title, *The Polymers,* Dickinson's interest in plastics is part of the volume's larger nonjudgmental interest in "giant molecules composed of numerous repeating parts," long chains of recurring forms that are the basis of natural as well as synthetic materials—of "the human brain, skin, hair, as well as DNA"—and which he finds metaphorically may describe all sorts of cultural practices involving obsessive conduct, linguistic or social repetition, memory, intimacy, and interrelation. In his volume he sometimes explores the toxic effects of plastic, but more frequently he exposes the cultural polymers that determine people's behavior and bind people together. The structure of the volume and of poems within it, moreover, conveys Dickinson's interest in how the molecular structure and categorizations of plastic might generate "an organizing principle (a poetics)" for his own writing. For Reilly, it is not so much polymeric forms as their trait of plasticity that generates the positive side of her ambivalence. In her work, plastics speak to the flexible resourcefulness of the human brain demonstrated in their very invention; to the malleability of language and form that is so crucial to the poet's craft; and to the plasticity of artistic materials more generally that fosters invention and rewards human creativity, enabling new formations. The intriguing characteristics of plastic, then, feed Dickinson's and Reilly's experimentalism, which each hopes may open possibilities for ways of thinking alternative to those that brought us to our present environmental crises.

CHAINS OF INTERCONNECTION IN ADAM DICKINSON'S *THE POLYMERS*

The Canadian poet Adam Dickinson has explicitly located poetic experiments like his as pataphysical projects (more on that momentarily) that "constitute a form of resistance to the colossal science project that the industrialized world is currently performing on the bodies of its citizens without consent." In an interview he similarly observed that "pollution is fundamentally a matter of experimental writing—we are creating chemicals that affect the endocrine system in our bodies, interfering with how hormonal messages are sent and received."[13] The huge unethical and uncontrolled scientific experiment in which we are caught calls for a responding, ethical literary experiment. Yet, as Dickinson observes, the contributions poetic experimentalism might make to environmentalism have rarely been recognized. While he earnestly acknowledges the importance of scientific insights into the nature of materiality, in several essays Dickinson has lamented that "the ecocritical emphasis on scientifically established realism has resulted in suspicion of experimental poetics"; "the argument that environmentally focused literature sufficiently represents reality by reflecting scientific stories about the world undermines the importance of alternate forms of thought expressed in the metaphorical and paratactic poetics of experimental writing." Moreover, the prevalent equation of realism (as what is desired in ecocriticism) and materialism (as what science offers) is, he believes, reductive; Dickinson cites Daniel Tiffany, who points out in *Toy Medium* that "the crisis of representation in quantum physics, for example, exposes the fact that '*materialism is not inherently realistic.*'" He quotes Tiffany: "materialism in its most rigorous forms descends unavoidably into language, to a place where matter is mostly not matter, where matter cannot be distinguished from the tropes and analogies that make it intelligible (and hence secure the equation of materialism and realism)."[14] In Dickinson's view, we need to recognize the semiotic nature of science as well as the contributions experimental poetics can make to understanding of the world science explores by expanding the current field of signification. This is where pataphysics comes in. "The playful poetics of pataphysics," he writes, "represent a serious attempt to think of art as an alternative form of science in its own right capable of expanding what matters in semiotic and material environments by interrogating the distinctions between culture and nature, and between human and nonhuman."[15]

So what is pataphysics? Invented in the early twentieth century by the French writer Alfred Jarry (perhaps best known as the author of *Ubu Roi* and as the inspiration for the later Oulipo), it "is 'the science of imaginary solutions'; it studies the particulars and exceptions that ultimately inhabit and subvert the generalizing assumptions of traditional scientific systems." Dickinson sees pataphysical texts, which explore unconventional perspectives, as contributing to ecocriticism by "conducting research at the complex and controversial thresholds between nature and culture"; the methodological constraints employed in their construction are analogous to experimental controls in a scientific laboratory.[16]

The varied compositional constraints Dickinson employs in *The Polymers* are based on either the specific molecular make-up of polymers (the number of carbon, hydrogen, oxygen, or chlorine atoms) or the repetition and recombination essential to their chainlike forms. The volume's poems are preceded by a page of translucent plastic headed "Cellophane," containing text that defines polymers, notes their prevalence, and points to some of the significance plastic holds—for example, "plastic marks both the presence and the absence of natural objects, embodying tension between the literal and the metaphorical, as it recreates the world as an alternate or translated reality." On the back side of that plastic page Dickinson explains the book's project in terms that make it comparable to contemporary genetic science:

"This book directs its attention to sequencing the seven principal synthetic resins that predominate in Western petroleum culture." That sequencing produces the volume's broadest constraint: the poems are arranged in seven sections corresponding to the seven most common categories of plastic resins, familiar to readers through recycling codes, with each poem constituting an atom in the molecular formula for that section's polymer; this determines the number of poems in the book. A drawing of its plastic resin molecule functions as each section's table of contents; the section's poem titles take the place of symbols for chemical elements in the usual diagram of the molecule. As a further development of this constraint, the titles begin with the initial letter of that atom's abbreviation (H for hydrogen, C for carbon, etc.). The poems, Dickinson states in an interview, "attempt to map the social expression of these resins, replacing each constituent atom with a specific behaviour or phenomena." The final section, "Other"— corresponding to the number 7 resin identification code with that same name—introduces two imaginary polymer molecules that potentially could exist, generated by Dickinson's search for "the repeating chemical units at the heart of some controversial, culturally influential texts that have been subjected to their own forms of historical repetition and obsession."[17] The texts he chose, and for which he created striking molecular models, are Darwin's *Origin of Species* and the Canadian Charter of Rights and Freedoms.

The volume's poems are constructed following a range of polymeric constraints; some of those "experimental protocols" are spelled out, or at least suggested, in the "Materials and Methods" section at the back of the book. Describing a few of these polymeric experiments will convey the flavor of this conceptual project: a couple of poems record remarks overheard in line—a human chain—for museums; one arranges names of coalition military operations in the Iraq War, while another makes a polymer of states' license plate slogans. Several present only drawings of polymers and give them titles that imaginatively interpret the designs made by those drawings; one interpreted as a police phalanx is titled, "Honed Security Procedures Following the G-20 Toronto Summit Protests," for instance, while another containing two pairs of hexagons interprets them as T-shirted breasts with the title, "Che Guevara Delighted to See His Face on the Breasts of So Many Beautiful Women." One poem is composed of "the immediate words on either side of all occurrences of the word 'and' in the 'Nature' section of [Emerson's] 'Nature.'" "Halter Top" is made entirely of words devised anagrammatically from the letters in "polyethylene terephthalate." Another anagrammatically constructed poem consists of alphabetically arranged "constituent elements" derived from section 64 of the Canadian Environmental Protection Act—the section that defines the conditions for identifying a substance as environmentally toxic. "Historical Accident" recalls a story from the history of plastics concerning a contest in the 1860s for devising a material to substitute for the ivory of billiard balls. "Corporatocracy," playing with the fairy tale of Pinocchio, imagines various resins for lies; in successively lengthening lines analogous to Pinocchio's nose that grows longer with each lie he tells, it describes "resins respon- / sible for the accu- / mulation of un- / truths in the human / nose."[18]

A simple demonstration of the way in which Dickinson's formal constraints speak to the impact of plastics is offered by the first poem in the first section—organized according to the chemical construction of polyester (resin code number 1)—titled "Hail." As these opening lines demonstrate, a chain is generated through the familiar repetitive device of anaphora (repetition of constitutive parts being a key trait of polymeric molecules):

> Hello from inside
> the albatross
> with a windproof lighter
> and Japanese police tape.
> Hello from staghorn
> coral beds
> waving at the beaked whale's
> mistake,
> all six square metres
> of fertilizer bags.
> Hello from can-opened
> delta gators,
> taxidermied
> with twenty-five grocery sacks
> and a Halloween Hulk mask.
> Hello from the zipped-up
> leatherback
> who shat bits of rope for a month.
> Hello from bacteria
> making their germinal way
> to the poles in the pockets
> of packing foam.   (*TP* 7)

Marine animals such as beaked whales and leatherback sea turtles are, like the albatrosses of Midway Island made famous by Chris Jordan's photography, among the creatures that frequently consume plastic detritus that blocks their intestines and often kills them. Hailing the reader later in the poem, alongside animals threatened by inland plastic waste ("desiccated, / bowel-obstructed camels") and some of the discarded plastic objects that trap, choke, or otherwise threaten nonhuman animals ("six-pack rings" or "fishnet thigh-highs"), are bodily fluids key to mammalian reproduction: "breast milk," "cord blood," "sperm." These, too, are infiltrated with dangerous chemicals from plastic. The poem catalogs grizzly manifestations of Anthropocene trans-corporeality involving plastics, while its mention of coral beds gestures toward other, equally deadly anthropogenic environmental changes. That all the damaged bodies offer the same greeting, "Hello from . . . ," speaks to their environmental interconnection and our common vulnerability to the same human-produced materials.

Like "Hail," most of the poems in the volume are composed in complete sentences, chains of words linked in accordance with the rules of syntax. Often, however, the sentences are skewed by the punning or homophonic substitution of unexpected words or letters—as in the poem made largely of twisted verbal formulae that begins, "For all intensive purposes, the fire distinguishers / are pigments of the imagination" (TP 23).[19] A different kind of verbal torquing in the poem "Hormones" gives the impression of an elegant example of Mad Libs, a fill-in-the-blank word game in which players start with a phrasal template and insert words of the correct grammatical category that they believe will surprise and amuse when read aloud. The overall structure of the syntactic chain is not modified, but the unexpected words are like substituted atoms whose unanticipated chemical bonds shift the properties of the molecule or sentence. "Hormones" opens:

None of the customs officers
can read the receipts new chemists
wave at the border.
Passports gullwing on the counter
as guards ringbill signatures
in stiff-lip service to regs
and rebar. Checkpoints
are the flagships of chalk lines
and compromised eggs.

> Nucleotides full of acid rain
> slick capital letters
> asleep in their holsters
> and mess up the paragraph
> as a small arms insurgent
> of epidermal composition.   (*TP* 50)

Unlike Mad Libs, Dickinson's surprising sentences often have serious implications. Here, sentences apparently about crossing national borders that involve customs officers, checkpoints, officials with guns, and the showing of
passports are infiltrated with terms invoking various kinds of chemical pollution that do not respect man-made geographical boundaries. The incom-
prehensibility to the customs officers of the "receipts new chemists / wave
at the border" suggests that the new chemicals that are continually arriving
are substances about which little is known. Invention outpacing knowledge
is a formative condition for the modern risk society, the kind of society
sketched here. The dangers of some better-known manufactured chemicals are suggested elsewhere in these lines: "compromised eggs" evoke the
thinning eggshells (and consequent reduced reproduction of some bird species) associated with DDT. This follows after allusions to ring-billed gulls, a
species susceptible to poisoning from organochlorine pesticides, including
DDT, as well as PCBs (polychlorinated biphenols) released from, among
other synthetic products, plastics. Acid rain's ability to cross borders makes
it "mess up" the relations between Canada and the United States, as well
as relations between states in the United States, since pollution produced
by burning fossil fuels on one side of a border commonly drifts across to
affect the wildlife, forests, water, and air quality on the other side; as Beck
has noted, the hazards characterizing a risk society are supranational and do
not respect national borders.

Mention of "epidermal composition" introduces yet another porous
boundary crucial to trans-corporeality and associated risks, the membrane
of the skin. The statement about this poem from "Materials and Methods"
provides a relevant, if characteristically oblique, gloss: "On the outside,
cream quietly soaks into the hands; on the inside, time signatures com-
pete for remote control" (*TP* 108). Many cosmetic products, including hand
creams, contain endocrine-disrupting chemicals such as the antimicrobial
parabens used as preservatives. These are absorbed through the skin and,
mimicking estrogen, quietly rewrite the instructions controlling the body's

reproductive system; results include more endometriosis, lower sperm counts, and more breast cancer. (Dickinson is interested in biosemiotics, an interdisciplinary field that investigates sign systems and communication within and between living systems.) This particular type of chemical pollution, which challenges conventional assumptions about the separateness of bodily inside and outside, comes to the fore in the later parts of the poem, where

> a man who has been drinking
> can make his way into any house
> and find his children
> reading hand sanitizers into the
> endocrine glands of dropped calls.
> Homonyms hunt in hand creams
> looking for out-of-season
> mammaries in textiled memories
> that have driven paper-coated milk cartons
> from grocery store shelves.　　(TP 50–51)

The notion of "reading" these chemicals conveys Dickinson's view that they are effectively words through which science is inadvertently rewriting the hormonal instructions that govern bodily processes. As an analog for the flow through the environment of chemicals that defy the policing of borders, the poem's difficult-to-follow, often alliterative Mad Lib–like lines suggest the ease with which words, too, can slip into places where they may not, in our minds, belong. The poem closes with a clear message: "It's pointless to protect / yourself from ricochet." Endocrine-disrupting chemicals are pervasive, mobile threats to our bodily security from which we cannot effectively protect ourselves, despite official pretense to the contrary.

In this era when trans-corporeality becomes so ominous, we need to understand human bodies in a much more expansive way—not only as depending on a vibrant microbiome but also as consisting inevitably of man-made materials. As Dickinson puts it in "Polyfederalsiloxane," his poem based on the Canadian Charter of Rights and Freedoms, "The age of polymers is a genital stage of articulated hybrids, campervans, and cyborgs. A human has the alien right to viruses in her genome, microbes in his gut, phthalates in her blood, pharmaceuticals in his brain, contacts in her eyes, and a battery in his heart" (TP 101). Dickinson's poems repeatedly stress the ordinariness as well as the pervasiveness of those no longer alien but nonetheless often dangerous substances that have become part of our cyborgian bodies. Several poems ironically emphasize that some of the deathless things that are killing us from within are household products intended to keep us clean—soaps, stain removers, sanitizers, latex gloves. In "Cups and Knives and Forks and Spoons," which considers the turn from glass vessels to accumulating Styrofoam cups and plastic bottles, Dickinson wryly observes that the twenty-first-century decision to ship alcoholic beverages in plastic bottles "relieves us of forethought / when it comes to throwing up / or throwing at, / and commits impulse to concealed / weapons of translucent declension" (TP 87). If the booze bottle is made of plastic rather than glass, one doesn't have to hesitate to heave it at someone or something; the new translucent bottles mark a decline, not only in civility of behavior, but in the health of our environment and even of our language: "Debris, in its finality, is our cutlery / and conversational / idiom" (TP 88).

Responding to the ready availability of verbal debris on the Internet, some of his poems rely on online material.[20] For instance, the Internet is a probable source for the poetic chain of Iraq War operations mentioned earlier and probably made readily available the license plate slogans.[21] More interestingly, the difficult poem "Habitat Disambiguation" responds to selected links on the Wikipedia page of that title. Habitat is, of course, a key ecological concept: habitat preservation has been a central aim of conservation movements, habitat destruction a major cause of extinction, habitat degradation a concern for environmental justice activists as well as environmental scientists, and so on. Dickinson's "Materials and Methods," however, offers for the poem of that title the following list apparently selected from the Wikipedia entry "Habitat (disambiguation)": "Habitat 67, Habitat for Humanity, Habitat Blinds and Shading, Habitat InsulFoam," all of which concern specifically human housing.[22] (Habitat 67 is a model community and housing project of elevated cement units in Montreal, designed for a future of high-density urban housing.) The poem itself—the first in section 3's sequencing of polyvinyl chloride (PVC or vinyl)—seems an oblique meditation on the turn away from care for the larger environment and the many life forms it supports as industrialized humans focus on the material structures in which humans dwell and on the manufacture of products to build and decorate them:

> and instead of hugging the shoreline, inroads drive inland and camp
> near refineries, and the temperature pressures the outcome, and

the thread is so repetitive all our clothes look the same, and stepwise
fashions form higher species throughout the monomer matrix,
and successive cross-links vulcanize a call for more thermal security.
(TP 47)

"Inroads" should mean progress, but here it seems to mean only the movement toward more extraction and carbon consumption, more cultural
homogenization and conformity. "Thermal security" of selected human
housing, achieved through plastic products like Habitat InsulFoam, comes
at the cost of global thermal security in the form of climate stability. That's
what it means to live in a world risk society.

The handful of poems I have discussed that feature plastic in more or
less central roles occupy only a small proportion of this volume that runs
to 111 pages. Although *The Polymers* is conceptually organized around plastic
resins, those plastics are not so much its direct subject as the prompt for its
pataphysical experiments. In an interview, Dickinson explains:

> In *The Polymers* I am interested in the sorts of ethical and epistemological
> questions that get reframed by the unexpected juxtaposition of culture and
> chemistry. What if we were to think of plastic (its proliferation as waste,
> its relationship to the oil industry) as not simply the expression of certain
> questionable cultural priorities, but also as something intrinsic to culture
> itself? In other words, what if we exposed the ways in which culture is
> polymeric; what would the identification of cultural polymers tell us about
> our complicated relationship to plastic and plasticity? Ultimately, my in-
> tention in the book is to apply the structure of polymers (their repetitions,
> chain-like dynamics, their chemical behaviour) to what I see as analogous
> phenomena in culture.[23]

Many of the poems that track or mimic cultural polymers have a far less direct connection to plastics and the environmental problems they pose than
the poems in Reilly's *Styrofoam*, which differently explore "our complicated
relationship to plastic and plasticity" and to which I will turn momentarily. Yet regardless of how directly concerned with synthetic polymers they
may be, Dickinson's intriguing experiments with an ecopoetically focused
conceptualism valuably demonstrate an alternative to conventional realism
and its deference to mimetic scientific renderings of ecological processes.
The Polymers exemplifies an exploratory adaptation of poetic forms and
language designed to keep in readers' minds the interconnection of nature
and culture and the fluidity of boundaries between natural and artificial or

inside and outside. It reveals how deeply rooted in our cultural practices, our desires, and our behavioral patterns this particular set of environmental problems may be. Implicit is the poet's hope that imaginatively rendering these patterns visible may make those that are harmful more amenable to change.

NETS OF INTERCONNECTION IN EVELYN REILLY'S *STYROFOAM*

My introductory chapter's discussion of Reilly's "Wing/Span/Screw/Cluster (Aves)" provided insight into her collage poetics—a formal contrast to the syntactic glue Dickinson favors in representing polymers—in which disjunct verbal fragments may connect in multiple directions to other words or images on the page, making of the poem and, on a larger scale, the volume a mobile branching form readily associated with the connectivity of the Internet as well as with Timothy Morton's notion of the ecological mesh.[24] Brian Reed has observed that "montage, collage, and juxtaposition were the aesthetic puzzles of the twentieth century. For the twenty-first . . . the problem is managing the information flood."[25] Reilly, however, uses the capaciousness of collage as a way to flow over and through that twenty-first-century deluge, keeping her reader's head above water, if sometimes just barely. Formally and semantically, her writing in *Styrofoam*'s nine extended, interrelated poems encourages thinking in terms of a vast net of interconnections and interactions. "Ecopoetics," she observes, "requires the abandonment of the idea of center for a position in an infinitely extensive net of relations." My introduction's discussion also introduced the environmentalist reasoning behind Reilly's resistance to poetry's traditional association with what she calls "the mesmerizing spell of the transcendent."[26] In what follows, I will explore more fully her volume's representations of the environmental toxicity of plastic along with *Styrofoam*'s explorations of the complicated relations of plastic to art and creativity, of past art to current environmental problems, and of art to science. I begin by returning to the opening poem, titled "Hence Mystical Cosmetic Over Sunset Landfill," from which I quoted above, to consider the relation between Reilly's poetry and the Internet and to examine her volume's ambivalent meditation on the intertwining of plastic with contemporary creativity and of contemporary environmental problems with problematic attitudes that art may render beautiful.

Both plastic and the Internet have been, in powerful ways, democratizing forces. The manufacture of plastic has made inexpensively available all sorts of objects that once only the wealthy could afford. (Freinkel's *Plastic* examines the comb as one such object.) Similarly, the Internet has been a means for ordinary people in industrialized nations to access far more information than had been available even in the best libraries and most comprehensive encyclopedias and to gain unprecedented powers of public expression through social media, websites, and blogs. Reilly's frequent use in *Styrofoam* of punctuation suggesting domain names indicates on the one hand an appreciation of the nonlinear, expansive modes of thinking and organizing information offered by the World Wide Web (an environmentally provocative moniker); such ways of thinking, fostered by her collage poetics, seem suited to genuinely ecological understanding. On the other hand, the current intertwining of art's resources with the Internet, a democratization of artistic production, also enables the cooptation of creative impulses by environmentally destructive corporate interests, as Reilly demonstrates in "Hence Mystical Cosmetic Over Sunset Landfill" via the Foodservice Plastic Packaging Group.[27]

The passage that displays this cooptation begins with definitions of foam and emphasizes the inexhaustible malleability of plastic foam, which makes it such a marvelous material for scientific and artistic creativity:

foam 1 : a mass of fine bubbles on the surface of a liquid
2 : a light cellular material resulting from the introduction
of gas during manufacture 3 : frothy saliva 4 : the SEA

(lit.)

which can be molded into almost anything

& cousin to.thingsartistic:

Kristen J
A low oven and a watchful eye turns bits
of used plastic meat trays into keychain ornaments.

Monica T
Soft and satisfying for infant teething if you first freeze.

posted 10/11/2007 at thriftyfun.com

hosted by FPPG the Foodservice Plastic Packaging Group   (*S* 10–11)[28]

FPPG is enlisting the creative energies of the public not to address environmental problems (though that might be a pretense, reuse being comparable to recycling), but to participate in them more intimately. Ingenious citizens—amateur artists and scientists of sorts—are encouraged to share their discoveries about how to use leftover Styrofoam trays. FPPG imposes no ethical restraints; there's no acknowledging, for instance, the dangers of using polystyrene *"for infant teething,"* although infants and children are particularly susceptible to endocrine-disrupting toxins. Science has clearly established these dangers; an article from *Environmental Health Perspectives,* for instance, asserts that almost all commercially available plastic products, including those advertised as being BPA-free, leach chemicals with reliably detectable estrogenic activity.[29] While the environmental ubiquity of chemicals like BPA reduces the usefulness of the idea of point sources, and while systematic legislative efforts at mitigation (rather than individual attempts to avoid contact and consumption) will be needed to meaningfully address this pervasive problem, precautions against avoidable exposure are nonetheless worth taking. FPPG allows the public to imagine that it's fine for babies to teethe on cooled Styrofoam, and that is profoundly irresponsible. Moreover, as the example of Kristen J demonstrates, if plastic foam products are at least "cousin to.thingsartistic," art and artistic creativity now are imbricated in contemporary capitalism's unethical marketing of unsustainable consumption and of products hazardous to the health of human and nonhuman animals.

Reilly's next lines, "All this.formation / anddeformation," might suggest not only the transformations of bodies, cultures, and landscapes to which the multitude of plastics are contributing, but also the potential within plasticity for possibly productive new forms to emerge in biological, social, and artistic life. Yet the creative potential of the malleable man-made materials proliferating in our world does not mitigate their environmental damage. As the poem goes on to point out, while some species manage to thrive amid Anthropocene habitat transformation, many more are disappearing from this world where plastic waste has become ubiquitous:

> *beyond the dense congregation of species successful in environments*
> *where the diversity of plants and animals has been radically diminished*
>
> *(for all averred, we had killed the bird*   [enter albatross
>   stand-in of choice

hence this mood of moods

this.fucked.flux.lux.crux

(broken piece of lamp garbage)

sunset	*400 lux*	
LCD computer screen	*300 lux*	
full moon	*.25 lux*	
starlight	*.0005 lux*	*(S 11)*

In this passage, allusions to earlier artworks introduce another aspect of art's plasticity: its ability to speak to multiple generations in different time periods. Here, as is often the case in *Styrofoam*, Reilly's allusions point to art's problematic ability to sustain trans-historical connections to earlier intellectual frameworks and ideologies that helped produce and still contribute to current environmental problems. By juxtaposing references to Coleridge's "Rime of the Ancient Mariner" and the chapter of Melville's *Moby-Dick* called "The Whiteness of the Whale" with references to current environmental degradation, Reilly suggests how some elements of Romantic thought represented by authors on both sides of the Atlantic helped foster the environmental mess we're in. Reilly's deployment of these allusions to art produced at the dawning of the Anthropocene as industrialism took hold draws on an understanding like Raymond Williams's that it was during the early industrial era that Nature came to be regarded as something apart from human settlement and culture, when Man and Nature formed a dichotomy, as discussed in my introduction.[30] Many environmental scholars regard such a conceptualization as having allowed for the degradation of the places industrialized humans mine and inhabit. That these artworks are widely known today speaks to the trans-historical adaptability not just of art but of the ideologies artworks embody.

Where Coleridge's ancient mariner suffered the guilt of killing a single bird ("For all averred, I had killed the bird"), "we" who are transforming habitats around the globe are collectively responsible for vastly more deaths.[31] How the mariner's murderous act and the current extinction of innumerable "albatross stand-in[s]" reflect in Reilly's view a shared Romantic orientation toward nature is suggested through allusions to Melville's meditations on the horror of whiteness—white being the predominant color of Styrofoam, as Reilly's cover image of Styrofoam packing material emphasizes. Her line "antarctic fowl.cherabim" invokes Melville's footnoted description of first sighting an albatross: "I saw a regal, feathery thing of unspotted whiteness, with a hooked, Roman bill sublime. At intervals, it arched forth its vast archangel wings, as if to embrace some holy ark . . . it uttered cries, as if some king's ghost in supernatural distress. Through its inexpressible, strange eyes, methought I peeped to secrets which took hold of God."[32] At the end of that passage Melville's narrator, Ishmael, envisions the "Antarctic fowl"—a phrase Reilly repeats—which had been caught with a "treacherous hook and line," ultimately flying "to join the wing-folding, the invoking, and adoring cherubim!" In such an idealizing perspective, the white bird's death points human thought toward heavenly rewards; that death is not ultimately anything to mourn. However—as in "Wing/Span/Screw/Cluster (Aves)," discussed in my introduction—Reilly resists such a transcendental impulse and its focus on otherworldly glory. In contrast to a Romantic vision of God-infused, sublime nature positioned apart from human civilization, she keeps her readers' attention on this world, filled with plastic detritus such as broken lamps; she presents a list similar to the one in the Wikipedia entry for "lux" (a unit of illuminance "measuring luminous flux per unit area") that registers the thorough imbrication of the synthetic and the natural by placing an LCD computer screen's illuminance alongside those of sunset and moonlight.[33]

Even the poem's title, "Hence Mystical Cosmetic Over Sunset Landfill," through its allusions, calls attention to received—and seductive—attitudes toward nature in order to show their inadequacy. Here, however, because Romanticism is neither monolithic nor simple, Reilly works partly in collusion with Melville's art, thereby highlighting positive dimensions to art's trans-historical adaptability: Romantic artworks may sometimes support environmentally savvy cultural analysis. The words "mystical cosmetic" and "sunset" derive from a later passage in "The Whiteness of the Whale" in which Melville speculates about why white acts on us as it does, "stab[bing] us from behind with the thought of annihilation." Considering white as the absence of color, his narrator ponders the theory that what we perceive as the "earthly hues" that color our environment, including "the sweet tinges of sunset skies," are in fact "subtle deceits" "only laid on from without" so that "all deified Nature absolutely paints like the harlot, whose allurements cover nothing but the charnel-house within." From this perspective, what

Melville calls "deified Nature," often celebrated in the writing of British Romantics and their American transcendentalist counterparts, is revealed as a horrifying whited sepulcher. The passage concludes:

> and when we proceed further, and consider that the mystical cosmetic which produces every one of her hues, the great principle of light, for ever remains white or colorless in itself, and if operating without medium upon matter, would touch all objects, even tulips and roses, with its own blank tinge—pondering all this, the palsied universe lies before us as a leper; and like wilful travellers in Lapland, who refuse to wear colored and coloring glasses upon their eyes, so the wretched infidel gazes himself blind at the monumental white shroud that wraps all the prospect around him.[34]

Melville, often a dark thinker among the Romantics, here steps away from the dominant philosophical model of his era that views nature as "deified" and enters the perspective of the "infidel." That's the perspective Reilly would have her readers adopt, one without colored glasses (as worn by the complacent speaker who announces late in the poem, *"Gee, this.stationaryparticulatecloud actually improves the sunset"*) and without the inherited consolations of a sacralized Nature.

In Melville's time, the sea was a realm of seemingly inexhaustible abundance. Today, after the introduction of more and more thermoplastics, "What the sea brought [is]: poly.flotsam.faux.foam / &Floam®" (*S* 12). Unlike Melville's sailors, people in the twenty-first century are "barely able to see sea," presumably because of the soup of plastic trash that achieves its greatest density in massive garbage patches in the North Pacific and Atlantic oceans. The pollution levels of today's oceans would have been unimaginable to Melville and his contemporaries; yet the whaling industry's ruthless profiteering, of which Melville was clearly cognizant, anticipated attitudes typical of today's multinational corporations, to which so much of that pollution and other environmental destruction can be traced. Reilly's frequent allusions to *Moby-Dick* suggest that the understanding prevalent in Melville's time of Nature as the realm not only for human spiritual and physical quest but also as resource to be exploited for market profit undergirds the despoiling evident in the sea's current "poly.flotsam.faux.foam."

After emphasizing the environmental damage caused by the accumulation of plastic in the oceans and suggesting the connections between that damage and specific strands of our intellectual inheritance that artworks often help sustain but sometimes critique, the poem in its closing lines returns to contemporary art's entanglement in industry irresponsibility and deception:

What the sea brought: poly.flotsam.faux.foam

&Floam®

> *a kind of slime with polystyrene beads in it*
> *that can be used to transform almost any object*
> *into a unique work of art*   (S 12)

The context undercuts the advertiser's claim that what Floam does is to radically expand the production of unique works of art, when its real transformative effect seems to be environmental degradation. Recognizing plastic foam as "cousin to.thingsartistic," Reilly's collage poetry indicates that art in the contemporary mesh is thoroughly interwoven with the marketing and consumption of products that threaten environmental health.

Reilly further explores plastic's relation to contemporary art through several of the volume's visual images that depict artworks made with Styrofoam. One displays a work by environmentally concerned New Zealand artist Andrea Gardner that, like Kristen J's key chain ornaments, takes as its material Styrofoam meat trays. Titled *Garden,* and made from prefabricated roses as well as dozens of meat trays painted black, this geometrical piece presents what looks like a row of seven stylized and identical vertical plants, perhaps analogous in their regulated homogeneity to a row of Monsanto corn. The work seems intended as commentary on what is happening to gardens and our biosphere more generally, on how proliferating products like Styrofoam create what another poem calls "the inverse.garden," the antithesis of Eden. By including this artwork along with that of Kristen J, however, Reilly also raises cautionary questions about the existence of clear distinctions between art and kitsch, between beauty and ugliness, between environmentally conscious reuse of excess or waste (attempted, presumably, by her own poetry in this collection where much of the text is online detritus) and use that is environmentally and politically suspect. That is, she suggests their interconnection.

With more complexity, Styrofoam art appears in a reproduction of Rudolf Stingel's *Untitled, 2000,* made from four thick Styrofoam panels on which Stingel apparently walked in boots dipped in lacquer thinner, which

Untitled, 2000. Styrofoam, 4 panels. Rudolf Stingel

Figure 1. Boot prints in Styrofoam. Rudolf Stingel, *Untitled, 2000*. Styrofoam, 4 panels; in Evelyn Reilly, *Styrofoam*, 18. (Courtesy of James Sherry and Roof Books)

melts Styrofoam (fig. 1). Reilly has credited the series from which this piece comes, which she saw in a Stingel retrospective exhibit at the Whitney Museum, with prompting the book's project. Striking her as "incredibly beautiful and joyous," their combination of "problematic materials" and "beauty" caught her imagination.[35] On the facing page she places a grainy photo taken from the Internet of a line of bear paw prints on a crust of snow, which she has playfully titled *Ursus Anonymous, 2008* (fig. 2). This pair of images immediately precedes a poem punningly titled "Bear.mea(e)t. polystyrene." Reilly's positioning of the images accompanied by the title insists that readers consider these two "interlaced // figures"—the wild animal and the man-made substance whose production is contributing to the melting of that animal's habitat—in the fullness of their complicated interrelations, their "meeting" in our world. The poem conveys the imag-

Ursus Anonymous, 2008

Figure 2. A polar bear's tracks. *Ursus Anonymous, 2008,* in Evelyn
Reilly, *Styrofoam,* 19. (Courtesy of James Sherry and Roof Books)

ined joy of Stingel's act of creation and the ecstasy that humans and bears
alike may feel in their brief lives, while it also calls attention to the enduring
toxic pollution generated by human scientific and artistic creativity.

The poem's opening page emphasizes the pleasure of sensory contact
with the material world, particularly the exhilaration of "impact on material" made, as the paired images establish, by both humans and bears. Yet, by
referencing plastic products, the passage also hints of humankind's larger,
problematic impact on the planet:

Standing

                                        in the foreshortened

space of
impact on material

amid immortality of plastic (the ex-
of exhilaration (the ex-
of anonymity
ex(of nihil exhil

dawn . foam . dusk

bear . moon . musk touch

the ankle bracelets of the birds
(a pvc resin cut from extruded sheets)
the multiplicity of foam and foam's conditions
(a lightweight closed-cell polystyrene)

the ecstasy

of being
containers   temporary or   not   (*S* 20)

In *Styrofoam*'s poetics of interconnection, the play with multiple meanings
of "ex" connects to "Wing/Span/Screw/Cluster (Aves)" and its critique of
Saint Teresa's transcendent ecstasy. That contrasts here with the ecstasy
simply "of being," which also entails "being / containers" for whatever substances our trans-corporeal selves take in from our surroundings.

Problems associated with human making come into sharper focus
shortly thereafter:

[enter: pseudo-kindness   *good night bear*

[enter: faux para-snowfoam   *goodnight styrene*

[enter: *keeps food warm for the elderly*
as per www.americanchemistry.com   (*S* 21)

We treat, or make a show of treating, our manufactured stuffed bears (as
in *Goodnight Moon*) with more care than live ones;[36] we blanket the planet
in toxic materials, imitating and substituting for natural ones; and we tell
ourselves or allow industry to tell us that those toxic materials are not dangerous. (The American Chemistry Council is an industry trade association
for American chemical companies.) The inventions of artists (Bernini as

well as Stingel) and scientists ("Ester among corn / Ethyl among ethylene")
become "fuel // for the way things happen"; that "way" currently produces
trash and terrible environmental toxicity:

> the smell of fumes
>
>
>   & a yellow strip
>
>
>   of smoked.brilliance
>   orange pylons discarded
>   nickel cadmium batteries
>
>   and.sleet
>
>   like small rounded plastic
>   units that frost
>
>
>   the.terrain
>
>
>   of polished visitation.ecstasy   (S 22–23)

After displaying the harmful environmental impact of human creativity
(and of transcendental aspiration—"visitation.ecstasy"), the poem closes,
more than a page later, in elegiac tones. Reilly suggests there a grievous
historical arc, perhaps a deterministic sequence, traced as "thoughts caught"
in artistic representation. It moves from Bernini's Saint Teresa, whose focus
on the next world Reilly sees as fostering the degradation of this one, to
Stingel, working from a degraded environment full of potentially beautiful
but deadly manufactured materials, to Reilly herself, writing a kind of a
requiem mass necessitated by global warming and associated mass extinctions consequent partly on products like styrene (an endocrine-disrupting
petroleum byproduct that mimics estrogen, found in, among other plastic
products, Styrofoam):

> the caught
> thoughts

of.transport . then styrene . then ex-inner sanctum

then

requiem eternal

Imposing Solitary Quadruped!

ex ex   (*S* 24)

The penultimate line is another allusion to Melville's meditation on whiteness and connects in the netting of this volume to the image that precedes
the final poem, "The Whiteness of the Foam," where a solitary polar bear
swims in open ocean ominously free of icebergs. Reilly's "Bear.Mea(e)t"
poem implies no negative judgment of Stingel, who makes genuinely
"unique works of art" from the manufactured materials filling the space in
which he's "standing." But she uses the existence of his Styrofoam creations
to register the impact of our energy consumption and toxic manufacture on
another realm of whiteness, the dwindling habitat of polar bears.

I understand "ex-inner sanctum" as a reference to the loss of separation
between inside and outside made evident, for instance, by the absorption of
endocrine-disrupting chemicals from our surroundings; the phrase acknowledges trans-corporeality, a recurrent preoccupation in this volume, prompting Reilly's critical examination of modern science. (At one point, she says
it directly: *"no important distinction between inside and outside"* [*S* 35].) While
valuing scientific knowledge and respecting the often elegant order evident
in scientific understanding, she underscores the failure of science in our risk
society to live up to its ethical obligations that follow from science's own rev-
elations of our interconnection with what surrounds us. The second poem
in this richly woven volume is titled "Permeable Mutual Diagram"; both
permeability and mutuality as ecological realities seem too little integrated
into modern science including medical science, which Reilly represents as
aligned with economic rather than humanitarian interests. These powerful
entities cover over the "polysmell / of the inverse.garden" we inhabit:

O doctors, brokers   *& other parfumists of*

current operating procedures

offering several different formulae
of eau de brutal and normal

as convulsions throughout   *(petit mal . grand mal)*   *(S* 14)

Ordinary people, finding themselves in an increasingly hazardous world
where their health is more and more threatened, are left searching the Internet, unsuccessfully, for "a place to go next." At this point Reilly introduces a multivalent term: "enter: the ether." In addition to being a class
of chemical compounds and a term that functions variously in different
Nintendo games, ether is something that Newtonian scientists posited as
the space-filling medium for the transmission of light and heat through
space. Having asked about "whose vehicles" might bring "a place to go
next," Reilly introduces through this term a cautionary reminder of science
having offered a subsequently discredited vehicle. Yet she also indicates the
positive potential in science as she then presents a drawing representing two
molecules of the solvent diisopropyl ether. By commenting on the appealing symmetry of this molecular model, she suggests that scientists' creation
of new compounds is partly an artistic act, responding to or revealing

> *the symmetries*

of our anesthetic aesthetic inter aether-ial

net   net of nodes   noded net of netted nodes
as per some sutra or is it the reflection
of Indra's jewels that forms the setting   *(S* 15)

Indra's net, a metaphor for the endless interconnection of all phenomena
taken from Hindu and Buddhist teachings, has attracted interest as an image
for ecological interconnection. This net is a wondrous structure that extends
infinitely in all directions. In each juncture of the net hangs a single glittering
jewel, and since the net itself is infinite in dimension, the jewels are infinite
in number. The polished surface of any one of these jewels reflects all the
other jewels in the net, so an infinite reflecting process is occurring as well.
As I argued in the introduction, Reilly's radically disjunctive poetic forms
cohere precisely because of the multiple underlying connections among
their parts, making the figure of such a net particularly apt for her poetics.
In this passage, she suggests the closeness of scientific experiment or inquiry

to her own artistic explorations. What she seeks is "some kind of permeable mutual // diagram in which the edge of one center / becomes the center of the next.edgeof," and in which nature and culture or manufacture are thoroughly entwined: "this intimate.multitude mixed with authentic.faux. art.products" (*S* 16).

How far scientific procedures have fallen short of respecting such interconnection and its ethical implications is registered in the volume's most polemical poem, "Plastic Plenitude Supernatant," which brings together science's failure to protect people from food-contact polystyrene and its failure to respect personal rights in taking cells from the cancerous cervix of an African American woman for research use without authorization or payment. (The line of cells stolen from Henrietta Lacks, who died of cervical cancer at age thirty-one in 1951, has been used along with prepubertal female rats to test the effects of polystyrene packaging on the female reproductive system. The two are further linked in the poem by a kind of immortality: the lasting of plastic and its effects, and the ability of Henrietta Lacks' cervical cells—HeLa cells—to keep reproducing endlessly in the laboratory.) These violations by scientists of respect and sensible precaution bring to mind Dickinson's sense of our living in a huge unprincipled experiment, which in turn recalls the unintended consequences of industrial innovation fundamental to Beck's notion of a risk society, depicted by Reilly as follows:

The modern world being filled with untold substances

(in our infinite plasticity prosperity plenitude

that serve to make life better

(x-s to ex ex, Henrietta

as long as we carry out HI, "Hazard Identification"

(s-o-s, Henrietta   (*S* 42–43; for "x-s" read excess)

The poem's opening treats the use of polystyrene packages for instant noodles as itself an experiment perpetrated on unaware girls around the age of puberty, enabled by an ideology that subordinates other concerns to technological progress (what supposedly "make[s] life better") and that idealizes the supposed objectivity of science conveyed by its impersonal language:

r e : *Identification of unknown ingredient in food contact polystyrene*

e g : noodle eating by pre, post, and presently pubescent

i e : sorry about that girls (er er, as per

Central Research Institute Nissin Food Products Co.

Ohyama having reported effects of certain oligomers
in E-screen tests of estrogen receptors

examining subjects as described in Materials and Methods

& performing immature rat uterus assays

as well as standard protocols using transfected HeLa cells

(the mother of us all, Henrietta

constructing expression plasmids (ethereal replicant, Henrietta

and reporter plasmids (unearthly circlet, Henrietta   (*S* 42)

The poem's italicized language has been adapted from an article published in 2003 in the journal *Food and Chemical Toxicology* in which Japanese researchers within Nissin Food Products Company countered some earlier studies by ascertaining that styrene oligomers have no endocrine-disrupting effects. (When a little estrogenic activity occurs with high concentrations of the test compounds, these instances are deemed "false positives.") By drawing from this article the language she implicitly critiques, Reilly calls into question the objectivity of science now, when studies like this one are carried out by the very corporation that sells the product under investigation. The speaker whose non-italicized lines are juxtaposed against but also interwoven, in a formal enactment of painful interconnection, with those of the scientific authorities speaks with tender sympathy of the rats who (with allusion to Dylan Thomas's "Do Not Go Gentle into That Good Night") "go gentle in the crook of the arm." Her companion calls attention to the anaphylactic shock experienced by these experimental subjects (who are ultimately killed so that their uteruses can be measured after a series of chemical injections) and either that person or the speaker expresses regret as she pictures herself "at the gates of heaven . . . unconscious rat in sorry hand." She would seem to be at least complicit in the animal's death. At the same time, she is aligned with other victimized females in the poem—

Henrietta, whose life in a "segregated community" as well as the medical abuse to which she was subject speaks to racial oppression, the Japanese girls whose possible reproductive problems are breezily dismissed with a "sorry about that," and the sacrificed rats; all are victims of the patriarchal order in which a reductive version of scientific truth is valued far more than imaginative truth like that of Indra's net.

"A Key to the Families of Thermoplastics," which translates abbreviations used in science and industry for readers of poetry, explores the fascination both art and science share with plastic materials, while also suggesting a critique of science's unethical pursuit of infinite plasticity in the material rather than the spiritual realm. Reilly's deployment of visual elements in this poem exemplifies her use of images in *Styrofoam* to emphasize the materiality and plentitude of the human-fabricated world in ways that expose often problematic commonalities among scientific discovery, technological invention, and artistic creativity. All are products of the human drive to manipulate and remake the world. By taking her images from the Internet and reproducing them in black and white she also renders varied and incommensurate things visually commensurate in the same way that the astonishingly diverse uses of thermoplastics ultimately homogenize the planetary environment they poison, litter, and degrade.

About a fifth of the pages in *Styrofoam* are occupied solely by single graphic images, three of them being scientific graphs or molecular drawings. In addition, four poems contain smaller images integral to Reilly's collage text. Heterogeneous in content and tone, aesthetics, and relation to the verbal text, almost all if not all of them derive from the Internet. Because scientific graphs and molecular models are treated in the same fashion as both high and low art, Reilly's visuals construct a complexly ironic cornucopia. As we'll see, its evocation of plenitude (or excess) acknowledges the appeal not just of abundance but particularly of plasticity. At the same time, the visual elements of her collage reinforce how all three ultimately interconnected enterprises, which consume resources and produce so much stuff, currently threaten human survival and the planet's environmental health. Reilly's ironic cornucopia of images might even be understood as giving visual form to the slow violence of plastic's accumulation, when slow violence, including "the cellular dramas of mutation," often goes unrecognized because its lack of spectacle makes it hard to see.[37]

The (anti-)environmentalist meaning of *cornucopia*—the view that environmental "dangers are illusory or exaggerated," that we have plenty of environmental resources, and that whatever environmental problems arise will be amenable to techno-fixes—is often the perspective disseminated by industry, including powerful plastic-producing corporations like DuPont or Dow Chemical.[38] "A Key to the Families of Thermoplastics," the poem in *Styrofoam* with the largest number of visual images, repeatedly invokes the term, implying a sharp and sometimes anguished critique of such a view. The concept of cornucopia is introduced via facing-page images that immediately precede the poem. The first depicts an ancient stone relief that Reilly captions descriptively, "King holding a cornucopia, symbol of abundance and 'inexhaustible store.'" Opposite that is a black-and-white version of the Periodic Table of Thermoplastics. (On the Web, this table appears in a dozen colors; amusingly, Reilly has reproduced the "Reduced version—For people who don't want to know about the properties!") Juxtaposed, the images suggest that what we now have in great abundance is not grains or fruits, but thermoplastics. As a caption for the right-hand image, Reilly quotes Hegel (the opening of section C of his Jena Lectures, "Art, Religion, and Science"), *"The absolutely free spirit, having taken its determinations back into itself, now generates another world."* With the godlike powers available through the "free" play of our wonderfully plastic brains, humans have invented enough types of new thermoplastic molecules to fill a table comparable to the periodic table of naturally occurring elements. The poem's title, while it alludes to works by Roger Williams and Rosmarie Waldrop, derives more immediately from the line at the bottom of the Tangram Technology table headed "Key to Major Polymeric Families" schematizing this particular new world.[39]

The allusion to Roger Williams's *A Key into the Language of America* (1643)—the first English dictionary to translate a Native American language—remains significant, however, since it positions Reilly as a translator who makes the language of science available to the larger population. Williams studied the language and culture of the Narragansett Indians when most of his compatriots were either vilifying or attempting to ignore them. Reilly, however playful much of the poem may be, invites her readers to learn about and acknowledge their connection to plastics, as Williams's "key" invited his readers to learn about the Indians whose territory they occupied. Such education in scientific information is one role that poetry may valuably assume in the self-conscious Anthropocene.

Most of the poem's text catalogs major types of thermoplastics and some of the products made from them, thereby suggesting how thoroughly this generated world has transformed the given one. Tongue in cheek, its opening provides an aggrandizing, mythologizing lineage for what are in fact recently developed materials, invented and named by modern science and produced by modern technology:

Polyethylene, Most Ancient of the Crystalline Polymers

gasoline tanks, water bottles, the plastic bag

Polypropylene, also called Mother of Abundance

carpet squares, garden furniture, automobile interiors

PVC, the Prince of Commodity Plastics

blister packaging, pipes and fittings, magnetic stripe cards

The Acrylics and their Most Adaptable Cousins

Ethyl, Methyl, Butyl, Stearl and Laurel   (S 48)

Later, as if the glamour has worn off, the listing uses only abbreviations and more matter-of-fact description:

PE-LD and PE-LLD, flexible, durable, with a waxy feel
(ENWRAP)

irrigation tubing, pallet sheets

PE-HD, semi-rigid and very tough (ENCLOSE)

shopping bag handles, cereal box liners, chemical drums

PET, with exceptional clarity, but "notch sensitive"

carbonated drink bottles MATERIAL FLOOD
throw-away condiment tubs MATERIAL STORM

POM, translucent, with good processing qualities   (S 51)

From a cornucopian perspective, the poem's catalog would substantiate how human lives have been improved by advances in technology—and, undeniably, some of the plastic products that have come to dominate our material culture have saved human lives and, in substituting for natural materials, saved plants and animals as well. Certainly, many of the products listed have come to seem essential to modern life. Simply the variety and number of images in the book taken from the seemingly inexhaustible resources of the World Wide Web would for a cornucopian only be further grounds for celebration of what Reilly elsewhere dubs "our infinite plasticity prosperity plenitude" (S 43). But the cornucopian perspective reflects a delusion: the store of oil and natural gas from which most plastics are made and that largely powers the Internet is by no means "inexhaustible"—a key word in the definition of cornucopia Reilly presents. Moreover, although plastic may be, in a phrase from the poem, "capable of being deformed continuously without rupture," living beings lack "infinite plasticity." Our brief survival is contingent on suitable environmental conditions, which are jeopardized by the "MATERIAL FLOOD" or "MATERIAL STORM" of plastics and their energy-consuming manufacture.

The abundance of plastics displayed through the Tangram table and Reilly's catalog is undoubtedly impressive, both in itself and as evidence of the power of human scientific invention; moreover, as the quotations like Hegel's "INFINITE PLASTICITY IS THE ESSENCE OF THE SPIRIT" make clear, the traits of plastic—its "immortality," its amazing malleability, adaptability, and variety—resonate with ancient, even fundamental, human aspirations. At the same time, this product of science and technology is monstrous and terrifying, as the poem's turn at its close to horror films involving insatiable plastic forms such as "The Blob" and "The Thing" emphasizes. Images like those Reilly uses to demonstrate LIVING HINGES (a product listed under PP, polypropelene) also suggest something monstrous about the invention of plastic, as if its very creation were a Frankensteinian transgression of the boundary between the living and the dead. For though not alive, plastic, as Reilly has emphasized from the volume's opening line ("Answer: Styrofoam deathlessness") is also something that refuses to die. One of these pictures of living hinges looks like a plastic coffin (though actually a Tic Tac box, from the Wikipedia page for living hinges), and the other, a figure whose right bent elbow and wrist are more literally living hinges, looks like a bloodied zombie. Though perhaps amusing in their revelation of plastic as at once unliving and undead, these images call into question the ethics of our so unrestrainedly transforming the carbon atoms that are the metamorphic remains of the abundant plant life of the Carboniferous era into a material "STUCK BETWEEN THE DEAD / AND THE LIVING (PURGATORY CORNUCOPIA)" (*S* 57).

On the facing page, three visually echoing images depicting different versions of being "changed in form" add to the poem's visual discourse on material recomposition, now bringing in forms from nature and high art. The left-hand image in this triptych is a beautiful, almost bejeweled amoeba, an organism that readily changes its shape. The center image is Correggio's depiction of Io being ravished by metamorphic Jupiter in the form of a thundercloud; her backward tilting body, upward gaze, and ecstatic expression recall Bernini's statue of Saint Teresa that figured in several of the volume's earlier poems. On the right is a cartoon female ninja, a figure of surreptitious transformation and deadly violence. Combined, the images suggest that metamorphosis is a tremendous power—one essential to many life forms, wielded by the classical gods, and cultivated by those seeking political or military dominance. Although potentially dangerous, metamorphosis here seems no more inherently bad or good than Dickinson's polymeric forms are, while its potential aesthetic appeal is clear from two of the three images. But Reilly's move from this trio to a quote from Dante about pursued desire leading to eternal grief, and then to description of "The Thing" as "an abhorrent force of plasticity [that] imitates / and destroys almost any form of life it encounters" (*S* 57) suggests that we humans have gotten ourselves in deep trouble by letting so much of this metamorphic material, plastic, loose upon the world. Importantly, the desire that led us to do so seems as based in aesthetic sensibility or social and economic ambition as in scientific curiosity. Just as her poetics insists on the interconnection of all living beings, of what is artificial with what is found in nature, and of the corporeal inside with the outside, it demonstrates the interconnectedness of the cultural forces, including both art and science, that have produced the currently airing drama: "MATERIAL CHANGE THE PILOT / UNCONTROLLED GROWTH THE SERIES" (*S* 58).

Styrofoam's final poem, "The Whiteness of the Foam," is a meditation on white bodies and materials that connects our blanketing the planet with (white) thermoplastics to global warming and the melting of the arctic habitat of polar bears. (Borrowing from the playbook of environmental organizations like the World Wildlife Fund, Reilly deploys anthropogenic threats to charismatic megafauna—polar bears' "white ears above the flood. melt" or a humpback whale killed by a cruise ship—to give readers an emotional focus for the consequences of environmental degradation.) Reilly puns on carbon footprint to merge the current self-destructive situation of the human species warming its own planet with the image of Rudolf Stingel dissolving the Styrofoam panels he walks on: "to ride on the heat of y/our own melting . . . to melt on the foam of y/our own molding" (*S* 61). Evidently, the artist cannot hold him or herself apart. Drawing from Melville's chapter on whiteness, Reilly paints a stark portrait of our deadly situation as Styrofoam waste takes the place of snow cover and vegetation (the italicized words are Melville's):

here *in* [un]*eternal* [de]*frosted desolateness*

where the solvent properties
of our insolvent imprints

admit not (even) *the cheerful greenness of complete decay*   (*S* 64)

Yet she won't completely give up on the blue marble ("Yet still driving.for-thin.blue.carbon / beneath this white blanket debris.galaxypicture") or on the human love for it that she juxtaposes against plasticization:

having been pieces   *ofcosmos   once*

        polymerization of the reaction *beloved*
        catalyst for the reaction *cherished*
        product of the reaction *tenderest*
        aftermath of the reaction *dearest*   (*S* 64–65)

Moreover, the poem contains what I take to be an example of a better use of human creativity and scientific ingenuity than the invention of additional plastic polymers. That is the development of nanolight technology derived from cloning florescent proteins in marine organisms—a technology that medical science can use in place of toxic radioisotopes or radioactive agents. I don't want to push too far in claiming that this new science is positively represented here; it is clearly part of a capitalist economy (Reilly includes a list of prices for differently sized vials), and it depends on humans presuming rights over other creatures and their genomes. (A distinctive resource of art is its ability to present a multifaceted vision, easily displaying multiple and even conflicting truths.) But these vials present a heartening alternative to the enwrapped vial (think Saran Wrap) held by the muse of plastic at the volume's opening. The bioluminescent materials being developed from luciferin remain within the cycles of decay that govern the biosphere, and they can substitute for toxic manufactured materials that have potentially devastating effects on trans-corporeal planetary life.

In that final poem in *Styrofoam*, Reilly offers a three-line characterization of the book—"this apoplexy apocalypse incantation / this devastation deflection invocation / this reflex context perplex" (*S* 63)—which leads her back to plastics through the rhyming Perspex®, an acrylic more widely known as Plexiglass. The last two formulations in her trio seem to me most apt: the volume enacts a hope to deflect devastation by cultivating an ecologically embedded sense of plastic's threats to environmental and human health and by highlighting our trans-corporeal interconnection. And it muses, sometimes with an ambivalence that bespeaks perplexity, on the contexts for our situation and the seemingly automatic behaviors that drive it. Even her visual images, which convey various forms of human creativity and aspiration expressed in Western culture over the centuries, function as material emblems of values and attitudes that provide contexts for our contemporary addiction to plastic. Dickinson's pataphysical project in *The Polymers*, too, can be read as an attempt at rethinking and reenvisioning that aims to deflect disaster, while many of his cultural polymers point to contexts for producing the manufactured ones.

What about "this apoplexy apocalypse incantation"? Reilly's visions of humans "holding hands for the briefest moment of shared materiality / among longtermheritage styrene" (*S* 12) and of "white ears above the flood.melt" (*S* 62) signaling "the possibility(optionshift) // mammalless" (*S* 35) invoke looming catastrophe, and perhaps her cataloging of plastics in her "Key" should be heard as a catastrophic incantation. For more extended, direct engagement with "apocalypse incantation," I turn in the next chapter to Reilly's subsequent volume, along with other recent poetry that responds to the self-conscious Anthropocene through the discourse of environmental apocalypse.

CHAPTER 3

"Under These Apo-calypso Rays"

Crisis, Pleasure, and Eco-Apocalyptic Poetry

Apocalyptic discourse is, in the eyes of some environmentalists and eco-critics, a key resource for inciting environmental concern and activism; others see it as counterproductively generating pastoral nostalgia, distrust of scientific data, or emotional exhaustion. But for better or worse, apocalyptic thinking is so much a part of the Judeo-Christian inheritance that apocalyptic rhetoric attracts even writers who are skeptical of its power or keenly aware of its limitations. That is the case with the two poets whose work I will examine here: Jorie Graham and Evelyn Reilly. In their respective volumes *Sea Change* (2008) and *Apocalypso* (2012), these poets are engaged in eco-apocalyptic writing, adapting it to the particular pressures posed by the increasing sense of crisis experienced in the self-conscious Anthropocene, even as they critique the mode or attempt self-consciously to avoid its pitfalls.

This chapter, then, will explore two different approaches to apocalyptic writing that together suggest how the pressures of the self-conscious Anthropocene are molding apocalyptic discourse employed in relation to environmental threats. Using not Beck's concept of risk society that figured in chapter 2 but Frederick Buell's related notion of dwelling in crisis, I will demonstrate that the prominent function of environmental apocalyptic writing to date—as a warning that conveys to readers the gravity of current circumstances so as to avoid disaster—is being destabilized as human impact on the planet increases and the sense of ongoing crisis intensifies.[1] While holding onto the hope that apocalyptic writing might help avert planetary environmental catastrophe, these two poets seem unable to maintain a steady faith in that possibility. The result is a rhetoric that, while highlighting the complex temporality of apocalyptic vision, mixes avertive warning and despairing prediction. Both poets also counterbalance the grief and despair of apocalyptic awareness through deliberate cultivation of pleasures grounded in immediate physical experience and perception. Without some counterforce, such grief and despair can prove paralyzing, both artistically and politically; Reilly has observed in her essay, "The Grief of Ecopoetics,"

> if you combine grief over our limited role as citizen-artists with environmental grief, the place from which you are writing can get almost paralyzingly grim. Jonathan Skinner has talked about the power of silence, meaning, I believe, that sometimes we shouldn't look to poetry for the kinds of power that might better come from direct action. But if you also think, as I do (and I feel pretty certain that Jonathan does as well), that there is a kind of power that comes through art, then even in the grip of overwhelming grief, the key may be to find a way to still work out of the joy and aesthetic pleasure that are essential to that kind of power.[2]

Graham in the earnestly apocalyptic poems of *Sea Change* and Reilly in the mockingly metapoetic and self-consciously ambivalent exploration of apocalyptic discourse in *Apocalypso* employ differing poetics as well as contrasting tones, yet both offer distinct modes of pleasure that serve as counterpoint to the potentially overwhelming darkness of apocalyptic thinking.

Those pleasures are connected to a shared awareness of embodied embeddedness in threatened ecosystems. In Graham's poetry, such embeddedness puts into sharp relief the aesthetic pleasures of the pastoral, which has long provided a literary foil to apocalyptic destruction. In Reilly's apocalyptic writing, embeddedness is registered most through human connections to nonhuman animal species and their destinies, while paying attention to oncoming disaster in the context of ongoing crisis requires most especially the pleasures of humor—even if, as in the blues, laughter may be mixed with pain. As in Graham's work, the double burden of ongoing crisis and looming catastrophe encourages renewed appreciation of presently available sensory delight, suggested by her title's reference to a spirited music developed in resistance to oppression, calypso. The poets' inclusion of compensatory pleasure focused in the physical world does not make apocalypse welcome as the promise of the New Jerusalem's earthly paradise does in the Christian narrative. It does, however, make anticipation of catastrophe momentarily more bearable, while it may support a reinvestment in environmental well-being. Although neither artist's poetry says so explicitly, this approach to apocalyptic discourse that includes reminders of worldly pleasures may renew—and may well be intended to renew—readers' personal commitments to do what they can to mitigate and minimize ongoing environmental damage and reduce the threat of utter devastation.

ENVIRONMENTAL APOCALYPTICISM AND DWELLING IN CRISIS

The previous chapter's discussion of poetry concerned with the toxicity of plastics was framed partly through risk theory as formulated by Ulrich Beck. Beck examines relatively new types of ecological and high-tech risks that have a "new quality": "In the afflictions they produce they are no longer tied to their place of origin. . . . By their nature they endanger *all* forms of life on this planet." Consequently, "in the risk society the unknown and unintended consequences come to be a dominant force in history and society."[3] If all forms of life on this planet are now inadvertently threatened because of multiple types of industrial or military production and energy generation, it is not surprising that current awareness of risk is often linked to the anticipation of catastrophe. It's equally unsurprising that Rachel Carson's *Silent Spring* (1962), which Lawrence Buell identifies as the "effective beginning" for contemporary environmentalism's toxic discourse, is also considered, due especially to the prefatory fable, its inaugural example of apocalyptic discourse.[4] Carson, in Buell's words, "invented doomsday by environmental genocide."[5] The shift from the last chapter's exploration of ecopoetic engagement with one contemporary form of toxicity—one set of the "toxic things" that "will far outlast current social and biological forms" dubbed "hyperobjects" by Timothy Morton[6]—to this chapter's concern with poetry that envisions environmental apocalypse and engages apocalyptic discourse seems almost inevitable.

Ursula Heise has even suggested that the "vision of a terminally polluted planet" typical of toxic discourse is a "subgenre of apocalyptic narrative."[7] Heise's views are worth elaborating because, although characteristically insightful, they seem to me not entirely accurate in relation to twenty-first-century ecopoetics. In addition to subsuming toxic discourse within apocalyptic discourse, Heise claims that the secular version of apocalypticism found in environmental writing of the 1960s and 1970s "can appropriately be understood as a form of risk perception." But she goes on, "Yet to the extent that such narrative, even in its secular version, articulates quite clear-cut distinctions between good and evil, desirable and undesirable futures, it indeed relies on a different mode of projecting the future than theories of risk, which tend to emphasize persistent uncertainties, unintended consequences, and necessary trade-offs."[8] In Frederick Buell's diagnosis of "the demise of environmental apocalypticism," which I will soon examine more extensively, Heise finds valuable the suggestion "that apocalyptic scenarios differ from risk scenarios in the way they construe the relation between present, future, and crisis. In the apocalyptic perspective, utter destruction lies ahead but can be averted and replaced by an alternative future society; in the risk perspective, crises are already underway all around, and while their consequences can be mitigated, a future without their impact has become impossible to envision." She goes on to state that this is not a dichotomy, but nonetheless maintains that the important difference between the two "lies in the way that many (though not all) environmental apocalypses continue to hold up, implicitly or explicitly, ideals of naturally self-regenerating ecosystems and holistic communities in harmony with their surroundings as a counter model to the visions of exploitation and devastation they describe, while perspectives grounded in risk analysis tend to outline more or less desirable consequences and futures of certain courses of action, but by definition none that are completely exempt from risk."[9] Although we will see ways in which Graham does hold up a countermodel to devastation, it is a profoundly damaged or doomed rather than a self-regenerating ecosystem. Reilly's and Graham's approaches to apocalyptic rhetoric—approaches that combine what Frederick Buell calls "dwelling in crisis" with visions of planetary catastrophe—render the distinction between apocalyptic rhetoric and the language of risk less clear than Heise's argument suggests, even given how she qualifies her claims. Similarly, their work, as we will see, challenges Frederick Buell's presentation of apocalyptic vision as an alternative to the acknowledgment of living in crisis. Both visions coexist, however uneasily, for these twenty-first-century poets.

The usefulness of apocalyptic rhetoric for advancing environmentalist awareness and reining in environmentally destructive behaviors is contested, both in popular journalism and in ecocriticism. There's a widespread sense that too much doom talk tends to produce a kind of deafness in those addressed. The telling phrase "apocalypse fatigue" appeared in the headline of a November 2009 article in the *Guardian* by environmental strategists Ted Nordhaus and Michael Shellenberger, where they assert that apocalyptic rhetoric has only polarized the politics surrounding climate change and undermined public faith in climate science. Yet in May of 2013 the *Guardian* ran a monitory article headlined "Apocalypse? No. But Unless We Change Tack, the Planet Is Running Out of Time." Similarly, in May of 2012 *Scientific American* ran an article focusing on the forecasts of the MIT computer model World 3, titled "Apocalypse Soon: Has Civilization Passed the Environmental Point of No Return?" Also playing on the 1979 Vietnam War movie title *Apocalypse Now*, in August of 2015 *Rolling Stone* ran "Apocalypse Soon: 9 Terrifying Signs of Environmental Doom." In 2011 the *Wall Street Journal* even published a *Guide to Investing in the Apocalypse*.[10] Such journalistic venues seem to believe that talk of apocalypse at least attracts rather than deters readers, and perhaps they hope it will produce environmentally beneficial social or political changes in the process.

Lawrence Buell has argued that "apocalypse is the single most powerful master metaphor that the contemporary environmental imagination has at its disposal." He continues, "Of no other dimension of contemporary environmentalism, furthermore, can it be so unequivocally said that the role of the imagination is central to the project; for the rhetoric of apocalypticism implies that the fate of the world hinges on the arousal of the imagination to a sense of crisis. It presupposes that 'the most dangerous threat to our global environment may not be the strategic threats themselves but rather our perception of them, for most people do not yet accept the fact that this crisis is extremely grave.'"[11] As Buell sees it, such writing, in which "the imagination is being used to anticipate and, if possible, forestall actual apocalypse," may be justified by the hope of practical efficacy: "Even the slimmest of possibilities is enough to justify the nightmare." Robin Globus Veldman has drawn on sociological studies to argue for an association between environmental apocalyptic thinking and environmental activism. Some, such as Lisa Garforth, have made a case for apocalyptic scenarios claiming they can, by prompting recognition of the need for radical action, "effect, metaphorically, a fresh start in terms of the imagination of future social possibilities."[12]

Yet the potential pitfalls are many. The most often cited risk is of seeming to cry wolf; the public learns to dismiss claims of impending catastrophe as earlier dire predictions fail to prove true—even when the predicted scenarios may not have come true because people recognized and averted the danger. After all, as James Berger among others has emphasized, despite the long history of apocalyptic writing, the end of the world has not come about; the paradox of apocalyptic texts is that "the end is never the end" (and according to Berger, what remains after the end is the true object of the apocalyptic writer's concern). Other acknowledged problems with apocalyptic environmental literature include its extreme moral dualism and, as Heise notes, the genre's implicit or explicit "rel[iance] on pastoral as the template for alternative scenarios." At its most culpable, Lawrence Buell observes, the turn to the pastoral enacts a "willful retreat from social and political responsibility" (though he cautions that this gesture may be strategic and that "the job of setting a pastoral moment in an appropriate ideological frame is trickier than it might seem"). When explaining "The Trouble with Apocalypse," Greg Garrard notes that the rhetoric of catastrophe tends to *produce* the crisis it purportedly describes, that it generates polarized responses, and that it tends to simplify scientific findings and compromise scientific caution because of millennial panic.[13]

Whatever its limitations, however, eco-apocalyptic writing seems unlikely to diminish in the near future, both because of the intensifying stream of environmental bad news and, importantly, because of the centrality of apocalypse to Christian thought and hence to Western cultures. Except when employed by evangelical Christians, eco-apocalyptic discourse generally differs from the pattern established in the Book of Revelation in envisioning a "blank apocalypse" without a welcome paradise, without the city of God here on earth to follow the destruction.[14] The vast majority of environmentalists who foresee doom for current planetary life or for the human species find nothing redeeming about it and want desperately to avoid the catastrophe that looms. The framework of their eco-apocalyptic thinking is predominantly secular. Nonetheless, as will be evident in Graham's and Reilly's poetry, both the narrative structure and the imagistic particulars of the biblical story in Revelation and in the Old Testament books thought to anticipate its story, as well as the temporal complexity of apocalyptic prediction, provide compelling resources for environmentally concerned writers. In both poets' work, an array of allusions to this tradition signals their apocalyptic perspective.

However deep its roots in an influential tradition, eco-apocalypticism in the twenty-first century is having to adapt to new pressures. Earlier consensus held that the function of apocalypticism—"a strategy of persuasion or coercion that interrupts routine and acquiescence with a call of alarm"—is to persuade the audience to change courses, to modify or abandon reigning ideologies.[15] Environmental apocalyptic writings, as Jamie Killingsworth and Jacqueline Palmer noted in the mid-1990s, "are not to be taken literally. Their aim is not to predict the future but to change it." Killingsworth and Palmer argue that "millennial ecology" is a radical attempt at social change, aiming to "replace the ideology of progress and to dislodge from power its primary perpetuators and beneficiaries." Observing that apocalyptic narrative appears at moments when the environmental movement is seeking to appeal to new segments of the public, they assert that "the hyperbole with which the impending doom is presented—the image of total ruin and destruction—implies the need for an ideological shift. If the 'predicted' devastation is extreme in the apocalyptic narrative, then the change in consciousness or political agenda recommended by the narrator is correspondingly extreme or radical." This is interesting rhetorical history, but what happens when the "predictions" of apocalyptic discourse can't so easily be put within quotation marks and the doom depicted appears less evidently hyperbolic? A similar question emerges in relation to Lawrence Buell's characterization of environmental apocalyptic literature, also from the mid-1990s, as embracing "the challenge of imagining the remote consequences of the transformation of environment that seem to follow from the unprecedented instability widely perceived to mark . . . the actual state of physical nature, as human power over it increases." In the self-conscious Anthropocene the consequences of that instability may no longer seem "remote." Observing that "technology is advancing at an ever more rapid pace even as our world appears to accelerate toward a plunge into chaos more profound than any pre-technological civilization would be able to take," Benjamin Kunkel notes that this lends a "grim plausibility" to both dystopian and apocalyptic scenarios.[16]

One possible response is exemplified by Ed Roberson's "To See the Earth Before the End of the World," which figured in the first chapter's discussion of dissonant scales. His apocalyptic poem locates contemporary humankind in the midst of the "world's death"—the demise of the planet as humans have known it—with the current population witnessing the final, lethal stages of ongoing disasters, in particular the rapid acceleration of what the poem presents as anthropogenic global warming that will cause human extinction. The poem's perspective is deterministic; the coming end is inevitable, human destruction having been assured ever since we first became hunters and assumed dominion over the natural world more than 2 million years ago. In stressing the inevitability of the end it foresees, "To See the Earth Before the End of the World" fits the "tragic" framework in the tragic/comic schema of apocalyptic writing that Garrard adopts for ecocriticism from rhetorician Stephen O'Leary.[17] Roberson, however, does not present the radically dualistic battle of good vs. evil associated with tragic apocalypticism. Good and evil are also not the terms on which either Graham or Reilly structures apocalyptic writing. All three seem closer to the comic frame in that they depict "human agency [as] real but flawed," so that fallibility rather than evil is at issue.[18]

But how can poets who do not share, or at least resist, Roberson's fatalistic view respond to current apparently dire circumstances? The eco-apocalyptic writing of both Graham and Reilly seems more fully aligned than Roberson's with "comic" apocalypticism, in which, because "the End may or may not be nigh, believers must live in the light of its possibility whilst refraining from relinquishing their worldly duties."[19] This less deterministic frame lends itself to warnings designed to change behavior or keep people on the path of virtue—or, in this case, on the path of protection and care for the environment; it suits what Veldman calls "avertive" apocalypticism. Yet Garrard rightly cautions that a clear distinction between prophesy and exhortation cannot be sustained either by the history of apocalypticism or by rhetorical theory, and I regard the two modes as becoming only less extricable now, as the rhetoric of risk becomes entangled with that of apocalypse. Both Reilly and Graham seem to want to embrace hope that humans might have the will and the ability to change course with sufficient speed; Graham writes of the "obligatory / hope" that the artist must take up despite inner resistance in order to continue to create: "hope forced upon oneself by one's self" "before the next catastrophe."[20] Once assumed, however, that hopeful perspective proves difficult to maintain as the consequentiality of environmental changes humans have made or precipitated becomes ever more evident. What rhetoric will serve to acknowledge current environmental realities without relinquishing the hope of fostering a positive impact on the future?

And in this context of the self-conscious Anthropocene, how will readers respond to apocalyptic discourse? Beyond the emotional and cognitive exhaustion that Nordhaus and Shellenberger noted, the onslaught of dire news concerning an endless stream of sometimes irreversible anthropogenic environmental changes can produce an emotional and intellectual shutdown that discourages acts or activism that might help avert catastrophe. The predictions of doom can feel too convincing, while the awareness of environmental transformation on scales vast enough to warrant the epochal designation Anthropocene only reinforces feelings of hopeless disempowerment. Politically consequential, those emotions may weaken the will toward collective action. What I'm describing may be the inverse of Garrard's assertion that "only if we imagine that the planet *has* a future, after all, are we likely to take responsibility for it."[21]

Some of the ways in which eco-apocalyptic poets like Reilly and Graham are navigating this morass are usefully illuminated by the thinking of Frederick Buell (Lawrence's brother) in his study *From Apocalypse to Way of Life* (2004). His central claim is that "environmental crisis seems increasingly a feature of present normality, not an imminent, radical rupture of it."[22] In response, he proposes that wise voices "will abandon apocalypse for a sadder realism that looks closely at social and environmental changes in process and recognizes crisis as a place where people dwell, both in their commonalities and in their differences from each other. Seen thus, problems will have both gone beyond and become too intimate to suggest authoritarian solutions or escape—for dwelling in crisis means facing the fact that one dwells in a body and in ecosystems, both of which are already subject to considerable degradation, modification, and pressure. No credible refuge from damage to these is at hand." He advocates an initially individual act of "coming to one's senses in a damaged world." A "persistent awareness of 'embodiment' and 'embeddedness' in ecosystems," he argues, can teach one to "[dwell] actively within rather than accommodating oneself to environmental crisis." Such awareness "makes people experience in their senses the full impact of dwelling in environmental and ecosocial deterioration and rising risk," which in turn, he optimistically claims, prompts more focus on ecological and social health and more caring behavior toward the environment.[23] Happily for environmental poets with similar views, among poetry's long-celebrated powers is its ability to help us come to our senses in literal as well as figurative ways. Moreover, although this is my emphasis not Buell's, "coming to one's senses" while embodied within ecosystems can bring joy as well as knowledge of damage or vulnerability; "sadder realism" therefore proves an inadequate term for the ecologically grounded vision of these poets.

While Frederick Buell urges abandonment of apocalyptic discourse in favor of writing that emphasizes an ongoing crisis in which humans are ecologically entangled sufferers, actively "dwelling in crisis" does not, from what I can see, preclude the anticipation of dramatic catastrophe on top of the already occurring creeping degradations one inhabits. Although Buell regards such active dwelling as generating a commitment to environmental care that will "help reverse society's environmentally destructive momentum," nonetheless, that mode of thinking and behaving does not necessarily increase one's empowerment or ensure social change so much that the sense of impending doom disappears. This may well be more evident now than it was when his book was published more than a decade ago. Poets like Reilly and Graham, and Roberson as well, write with an awareness of inhabiting a world already in crisis even as they *also* anticipate or prophesy much more devastating changes to come. While observing that combination in the readings that follow, I will expose the differing ways in which Graham and Reilly convey awareness of embodiment and embeddedness in (damaged) ecosystems. In so doing, they counterbalance cataclysmic vision with kinds of perception that make it more bearable and less emotionally exhausting. Desired consequences include freeing politically and existentially useful energy and inspiring its devotion to (re)opening the search for meaningful courses of environmental action.

LOOKING BACK ON THE PASTORAL PRESENT: JORIE GRAHAM'S *SEA CHANGE*

The temporality of apocalyptic writing is complex, since, as Berger observes, "the narrative logic of apocalyptic writing insists that post-apocalypse precede the apocalypse"; additionally, "the writer and reader must be both places at once, imagining the post-apocalyptic world and then paradoxically 'remembering' the world as it was, as it is."[24] This is a part of the discursive apocalyptic tradition that we will see Graham adapts in *Sea Change*, one that richly complicates her representation of the present. On the one hand, she calls attention to ongoing and worsening crisis in the form of present environmental disturbance; although (as she represents it) only beginning to be registered in damage to humans, its cascading force is evident in damage to ecosystems whose intricate and fragile interrelations she details. On the other hand, rather like Roberson turning his attention to the beautiful piece of melting glacier before him, she focuses intently on the beauties of her present surroundings. She often does so from the prospective-retrospective perspective of an apocalyptic or postapocalyptic future, so as both to heighten her readers' sensory pleasure in embeddedness in a wondrous world and also to awaken readers to the awfulness of ongoing and catastrophically impending losses. Her intensification of present appreciation alleviates the darkness of apocalyptic vision, even if it sharpens grief as well.

The poem that begins Graham's eleventh volume, *Sea Change*, its title poem, emerges from a perspective of conscious dwelling within crisis that is also apocalyptic. "Sea Change" opens onto an extreme weather event perceived as part of an ongoing "unnegotiable drama" of environmental dissolution:

One day: stronger wind than anyone expected. Stronger than
                              ever before in the recording
                              of such. Un-
natural says the news. Also the body says it. Which part of the body—I look
                              down, can
                              feel it, yes, don't know
where. Also submerging us,
                              making of the fields, the trees, a cast of
                                  characters in an
                              unnegotiable
drama, ordained, iron-gloom of low light, everything at once undoing
                              itself.[25]

The line break between "Un" and "natural" conveys at once the wrenching, hitherto abnormal changes taking place and their production of a new normal that we now must face as "natural." Capturing the near inconceivability of this "sea change," Graham oxymoronically observes, "The permanent is ebbing"—neatly conveying the sense of living in dire, almost unimaginable crisis that Frederick Buell points to as the contemporary condition. The notion that permanence itself is disappearing highlights the speaker's expectation of continuing transformation as crises inexorably unfold. Then, in a single sentence whose unspooling over two pages itself suggests the cascading consequences of current changes in our ecosystems, Graham records some of the ways global warming is affecting our ecologically interdependent biosphere. For instance,

                              at the very bottom of
                          the food
                          chain, sprung
from undercurrents, warming by 1 degree, the in-
                              dispensable
plankton is forced north now, & yet farther north,
                              spawning too late for the cod larvae hatch,
                              such

that the hatch will not survive, nor the
                                    species in the end, in the right-now forever
                                    un-
                                    interruptible slowing of the
                                    gulf
stream   (*SC* 4–5)

Here again, the line breaks separating "in" from "dispensable" and "un" from "interruptible"—more breakages that suggest mind-boggling reversal—convey how what had seemed impossible is now not just possible but inescapably taking place. Feeling in this context the uselessness of the poems she has written, Graham moves from speaking "in this wind today, out loud in it, to no one" to speaking for the wind. This wind, which urges "consider your affliction . . . do not plead ignorance," recalls the destructive winds mentioned in Job or Jeremiah, two touchstones of apocalyptic writing:

                                                                    & quicken
                              me further says this new wind, &
                              according to thy
                              judgment, &
I am inclining my heart towards the end,
                              I cannot fail, this Saturday, early pm, hurling
                                    myself,
wiry furies riding my many backs, against your foundations and your
                              best young
tree, which you have come outside to stake again, & the loose stones in the
    sill.   (*SC* 5)

That the civilization or the species may well be doomed is suggested by the word "foundations," which denotes not just the substructure of the speaker's home but the things fundamental to her or her society's life, while the line break temporarily isolating "best young" speaks to the precarious position of the younger generation, whose future is in jeopardy. Using biblical phrasing that suggests its work enacts divine judgment, the voice—at once the poet's and the wind's—becomes the voice of an apocalyptic prophet.[26]

   In several of the volume's poems where the speaker's immediate experience is shadowed by her consciousness both of present degradation and risk and also of a devastating future, Graham addresses or assumes the perspective of someone living in that future when lifestyles we in the developed world now consider ordinary will appear almost unimaginably luxurious.

"Loan," whose title indicates that we don't own the environmental gifts we have, however we may take their loan for granted, is an example. The speaker, who has been tracing the rivulets of water after a rain, wanting "to know where everything's / going, runnelling, & what's / really dead here and what's only changing," suddenly shifts to address someone living in the future she foresees, someone who looks back on our present time:

> do you remember it, the faucet flared like a glare of
> open speech, a cry, you could say what you
> pleased, you could turn it
> off, then on again—at will—and how it fell, teeming, too much, all over your
> hands, much as you please—from where
> you are now
> try to
> feel it—what
> was it, this thick / thin blurry coil
> flowing into the sink   (*SC* 25)

Later Graham's speaker similarly comments on how we can presently "jump in the shower—just like that," so that her readers will recognize how wondrously fortunate, and perhaps how lavishly irresponsible, we are, given that

> the day which comes when there are to be no more harvests from now on,
> irrigation returns only as history, a thing made
> of text,
> & yet, listen,
> there was
> rain   (*SC* 25–6)

In the volume's final poem, "No Long Way Round" (that is, no way to avoid what lies in the route ahead), the horror associated with this future perspective, from a time when the fundamental orders of civilization will have disappeared along with the familiar patterns of the natural environment, is even clearer. At the same time, the human imagination capable of giving insight into the future consequent upon present human conduct is revealed to be already in mortal danger:

> You will not believe it
> when the time
> comes. Also how we mourned our dead—had

ample earth, took time, opened it, closed
it—"our earth, our
dead" we called
them, & lived
bereavement, & had strict understandings of defeat and victory. . . . Evening,
what are the betrayals that are left,
and whose? I ask now
as the sensation of what is coming places its shoulders on the whole horizon,
I see it
though it is headless, intent
fuzzy, possible outcomes
unimaginable. You have your imagination, says the evening. It is all you have
left, but its neck is open, the throat is
cut, you have not forgotten how to sing, or to want
to sing.   (*SC* 55, ellipsis in original)

Circumstances are desperate; the poet must sing while she still can.

In a 2008 interview Graham explains her manipulation of temporal perspectives as a strategy she hopes might avert precisely the postapocalyptic perspective she sees us approaching:

What is the imagination supposed to do with its capacity to "imagine" the end? Is the imagination of the unimaginable possible, and, perhaps, as I have come to believe, might it be one of the most central roles the human gift of imagination is being called upon to enact? Perhaps if we use it to summon the imagination of where we are headed—what that will feel like—what it will feel like to look back at this juncture—maybe we will wake up in time? I have written [*Sea Change*] in order to make myself not only understand—we all seem to "understand"—but to actually "feel" (and thus physically believe) what we have and what we are losing—and furthermore what devastatingly much more of creation we are going to be losing.[27]

Graham's emphasis here on "actually" feeling is evident throughout *Sea Change*, beginning with the very opening of "Sea Change," where the speaker's body conveys to her the unnaturalness of the record-setting winds. Graham's belief that physical registration of "what we have and what we are losing" might prompt action and motivate sacrifices in what we regard as our standard of living so as to slow global warming aligns with Frederick Buell's call for "living in one's senses while one dwells in environmental crisis."[28]

Sea Change enacts on multiple scales a tension between an impulse to focus on the terrible future and a desire to give the fullest possible sensory attention to the present and its wonders, the latter helping us feel the value not only of our immediate lives but also of what we might work to preserve. For Graham, this duality emerges even in the formal character of the verse, its combination of long and short lines with often jolting mid-phrase or mid-word enjambments, for which one of her explanations is

> [by] letting the sentences move along this grid of very long and very short lines . . . I also was able to enact a sense of a "tipping point"—the feeling of falling forward, or "down" in the hyper-short lines at the same time as one feels suspended, as long as possible, in the "here and now" of the long line—so that the pull of the "future" is constrained by the desire to stay in the "now," which is itself broken again, as a spell is, by the presence of the oncoming future. This also involves a tipping back and forth between hope and the brink of its opposite.[29]

In relation to present time, fullness of feeling appears to be among the poet's primary aims. Central to her version of embodied embeddedness in ecosystems, such feeling is enacted both in the volume's acute attention to deeply pleasurable moments of seasonal suspension and, more generally, in its emphasis on sensory experience, especially sight. "This" for instance, details the sensory character of a moonlit winter night through the observed action of "wind in trees blocking and / revealing moon" (*SC* 8). The tips of the trees are described as literally "scratch[ing] at" the "idea of the universal," underscoring the material particularity of the moment. In this moonlight, the speaker's senses awaken to the outer world—"All the light there is / playing these limbs like strings until / you can / hear the / icy offering of winter" (*SC* 8)—and to her inner being—"things one feels instantly / ashamed about." Here, as elsewhere in *Sea Change*, language itself is described in sensuous embodied terms: "the feeling of the mother tongue in the mouth" (*SC* 9).

The two poems that open the volume's second section, "Later in Life," and "Just Before," extend Graham's exploration of the present moment, now focusing on times when awareness of the future seems held at bay. "Later in Life" opens on the first early morning of summer heat during a moment when two workers call to each other and their cries make a round with bird cries, a musical phenomenon richly registered via rhyme and alliteration as "a round from which sound is sturdied-up without dissipation or dilation." In this suspended and extended present, "summer arrives, has arrived, is arriving" (*SC* 19). Immersed in this moment, the speaker declares, "The / future is a superfluity I do not / taste" and asserts "we have it all, now, & all / there ever was is / us, now" (*SC* 20). The poem almost fiercely asserts "your right to be so entertained" and savor this moment of bless-edness ("there is no angel to / wrestle"), although its ending implies the ephemerality of such experience: "these words, praise be, they can for now be / said" (*SC* 21). For now.

In "Just Before" Graham elaborates on such a moment of temporal di-lation—"a pool. Of / stillness"—as an experience of embeddedness in the earth, in planetary history and planetary life. The experience of this stilled temporal motion was, she states, "full / of earth," while kenning-like word combinations such as "undersoil," "earthwide," "wood-rings," and "fish-mouth" reinforce the asserted materiality in such stillness:

> of copper mines and thick under-leaf-vein sucking in of
>   light, and isinglass, and dusty heat—wood-
>   rings
>   bloating their tree-cells with more
> life—and grass and weed and tree intermingling in the
>   undersoil—& the
>   earth's whole body round
>   filled with
>   uninterrupted continents of
>   burrowing—& earthwide miles of
>   tunnelling by the
> mole, bark beetle, snail, spider, worm—& ants making their cross-
>   nationstate cloths of
>   soil, & planetwide the
>   chewing of insect upon leaf—fish-mouth
>   on krill,
>   the spinning of
> coral, sponge, cocoon—this is what entered the pool of stopped thought—
>   (*SC* 22–23)

This moment of individual opening into an expansive present is also a moment of planetary awareness and awareness of multispecies interdepen-dence. The passage may be among those Graham had in mind when she remarked in an interview about *Sea Change* that she was trying to awaken in herself and others "earlier, more ancient, human feelings of belonging in creation."[30] Certainly, her depiction of the moment enacts what Buell calls embeddedness in ecosystems.

Although Graham registers the changes associated with global warming through her senses (as well as through her knowledge of what is happening to other species—the plankton, for instance, or the cod), in contrast to Reilly and Dickinson in chapter 2, Graham in *Sea Change* does not exhibit much sense that environmental changes are a threat to her own body or to the bodies of other humans. She's well aware that, however terrible the changes taking place, she "cannot / go somewhere / else than this body" (*SC* 6), and she attends to what her "body says." Yet the poems reflect not so much Frederick Buell's awareness of human bodily vulnerability within compromised ecosystems as an intense appreciation of the sensory experience of still relatively normal surroundings, along with a desire to record for the future the precious traits of what is currently taken for granted as "normal." If, as Wallace Stevens wrote, "death is the mother of beauty," then, going beyond awareness of her own mortality to anticipate the extinction of vast numbers of nonhuman species and perhaps of humankind as well further intensifies Graham's appreciation of the wonders of her surroundings.[31] In often synesthetic terms, she details and savors the experience of an environment that still has a progression of seasons, impressive biodiversity, and air one can inhale with pleasure. At the close of "Loan"—the poem in which she asks future readers whether they can remember when clean water was abundant—her warning about a dry, harvestless future gives way to a loving detailing of the sounds, sights, and tactile sensations of our easily taken-for-granted yet wondrous present world:

> & yet, listen,
> there was
> rain, then the swift interval before evaporation, & the stillness
> of brimming, & the
> wet rainbowing where oil from exhaust picks up light, sheds glow, then
> echoes in the drains where
> deep inside the
> drops fall individually, plink
> & the places where birds

interject, & the coming-on of heat, & the girl looking sideways carrying the
large
                    bouquet of blue hydrangeas, shaking the
                    water off, &
the wondering if this is it, or are we in for another round, a glance up, a quick
step
                    over the puddle
                    carrying speedy clouds,
birdcall now confident again, heat drying, suddenly no evidence of its having
been wet—but no, you
                    didn't even notice it—it rained.
                    (*SC* 26)

The particularization of this appreciative catalog encourages readers to use
their own ears and eyes, to take notice.

The pleasures of sensory experience on which Graham focuses generally fall within the realm of the literary pastoral. I say that despite details
like "rainbowing" on "oil from exhaust" not just because such references
to beauty that stress an industrialized context are rare in these poems, but
more importantly because the perhaps suburban world in which Graham's
speakers take pleasure functions as the "green world" of the pastoral mode
traditionally has: as a precious oasis that offers an escape from a diminished
or corrupted world and that is the focus of nostalgic longing. That last assertion may seem curious in that the speaker inhabits the described world—
and it's one whose environmental health is evidently diminished. But because Graham keeps in her readers' view the backward-looking perspective
from a drastically degraded future in which our current world will look
paradisal, her speaker's present time becomes also an already nostalgically
viewed past. And while the current environment Graham describes is not
necessarily rural, its nesting ring-necked doves, falcons, fields in which "new
shoots glow" (*SC* 37), creeks with minnows, and blossoming trees—even if
those trees are blossoming at the wrong times and the doves are buffeted
by high winds—make it seem a bucolic *locus amoenus* in comparison to the
harvestless desert lacking in songbirds and other familiar animals that constitutes the environment of her prophesied future.

Invoking a pastoral realm as a foil to the horrors of apocalypse is a
common move in apocalyptic writing.[32] Lawrence Buell has observed, "the

pastoral logic that undergirds environmental apocalypse . . . rests on the appeal to the moral superiority of an antecedent state of existence when humankind was not at war with nature in the way that prevails now." In *Sea Change*, that antecedent state seems precariously preserved in the backyard pastoralism of the speaker's domestic life, a real-world version of Rachel Carson's pastoral: "The mythical American small community, the desecration of whose integral leafy exurban bliss is portrayed in her introductory 'Fable for Tomorrow.'" Apocalyptic texts like Carson's—and, I would add, Graham's—that invoke the pastoral are, Buell notes, examples of the "doubleness of American pastoral ideology": "activist appeals to nostalgia, accomplishing their interventions by invocations of actual green worlds about to be lost." He adds that one shouldn't assume the authors "believe that their portrayals of these about-to-be-lost worlds say all there is to be a said about them" but rather that they intend "to create moral antitheses that would force readers to confront the possibility that history has reached a turning point" for the environment.[33] Even so, the pastoral tends to produce wariness in current ecocritics, including Heise and some-times Buell himself, because of its association with a dichotomous vision of nature in opposition to culture as well as with outdated understandings of ecology, and also because it can serve as a retreat and a turn away from environmental problems.

Examining two apocalyptic poems from *Sea Change,* I will demonstrate how Graham, in whose writing the pastoral impulse is strong and tied to her tendency toward aestheticization, navigates the risks it poses—in one poem, by offering a reflexive critique of her own pastoral impulse and in another poem more typical of the collection, by making the pastoral clearly only a temporary refuge. The speaker in "Futures" explores from a critical perspec-tive how attention to the visible world can become a form of ownership. (The title evokes the futures market as well as temporal futures.) Through the language of capitalism, Graham critiques what the poem calls the poet's "action of beauty," an aestheticization connected to pastoral's simplifying vision of a green world. The poem begins, "Midwinter. Dead of. I own you says my mind. Own what, own / whom. I look up. Own the looking at us / say the cuttlefish branchings [of bare deciduous trees], lichen-black, moist." The sense of personal ownership associated with seeing is presented as essential to the act; it cannot be "scoured from inside the / glance." What prevents this "thrilling" "push of owning" the natural scene from bringing happiness to the observer is awareness of ongoing (present and future) environmental destruction, only some of which is or will be visible: "the crop destroyed, / water everywhere not / drinkable, & radioactive waste in it, & human bodily / waste" (*SC* 14). In the poem's closing passages, Graham presents a vignette, introduced with the past tense but ambiguously set in the future, in which the speaker finds herself turning a painfully degraded pastoral scene into one in which she can feel pleasure in ownership. This emotional shift from pain to the pleasure registered in her smile takes place through an act of enumeration that is also an aestheticization:

> one day a swan appeared out of nowhere on the drying river,
>
> $\qquad\qquad\qquad\qquad\qquad$ it
>
> was sick, but it floated, and the eye felt the pain of rising to take it in—I own you
>
> $\qquad\qquad\qquad\qquad\qquad$ said the old feeling, I want
>
> $\qquad\qquad\qquad\qquad\qquad$ to begin counting
>
> again, I will count what is mine, it is moving quickly now, I will begin this
>
> $\qquad\qquad\qquad\qquad\qquad$ message "I"—I feel the
>
> smile, put my hand up to be sure, yes on my lips—the yes—I touch it again, I
>
> $\qquad\qquad\qquad\qquad\qquad$ begin counting, I say *one* to the swan, *one*,
>
> do not be angry with me o my god, I have begun the action of beauty again, on
>
> $\qquad\qquad\qquad\qquad\qquad$ the burning river I have started the catalogue,
>
> $\qquad\qquad\qquad\qquad\qquad$ your world, $\qquad$ (*SC* 15–16)

The burning river is an apocalyptic image, recalling the many destructive fires in Revelation, including 8:10–11, in which a burning star called Wormwood "fell upon the third part of the rivers, and upon the fountains of waters" rendering the waters poisonous and causing the deaths of many men.[34] To begin the action of beauty in analogous circumstances seems gruesomely inappropriate. The speaker's apostrophe to her god conveys her sense of transgression in this act of beautification and enumeration. The lines immediately following further taint that action by linking it to the attraction of money—which, ironically, smells like the natural realm of pastoral beauty that the poem makes clear exists only in the imagination, not in the external environment. It can be imagined and remembered, but, with "water everywhere not / drinkable," its physical sustenance is no longer available in unpolluted form:

> I your speck tremble remembering money, its dry touch, sweet strange
>
> $\qquad\qquad\qquad\qquad\qquad$ smell, it's a long time, the smell of it like lily
>
> $\qquad\qquad\qquad\qquad\qquad$ of the valley

sometimes, and pondwater, and how
                              one could bend down close to it
and drink.   (*SC* 16)

"Futures" conveys Graham's unease with her own tendency to aestheticize her surroundings. The artist risks becoming more taken up with the potentially endless imaginative act of beautifully naming entities in (or once in) nature than with acts of stewardship or attempts at ecopolitical change. And the same goes for the reader. Lawrence Buell astutely observes that "in pastoral, beauty never functions *only* as critique. At some level there is always the chance that the text will tempt the reader to see all sugar and no pill and that even hard thrusts will get deflected into quaint excursions."[35] If this is a risk in Graham's *Sea Change*, "Futures" might be read as a combination of confession and warning to readers to resist such deflection.

"Positive Feedback Loop" exposes the escapist potential in the pastoral that some ecocritics have noted. ("Positive feedback loop" is a phrase often used in connection with global climate change, since many consequences of the earth's warming themselves amplify it.) The speaker at the poem's opening is intensely conscious of a present impinged upon by the future, what Graham calls the "silence that precedes." This is a suspension more ominously weighted than, say, the summer morning experienced as ongoing arrival in "Later in Life." What this silence both holds and heralds is catastrophic environmental transformation:

                    complete collapse, in the North Atlantic
                       Drift, in the
                    thermohaline circulation, this
                    will happen,
fish are starving to death in the Great Barrier Reef, the new Age of
    Extinctions is

                       now   (*SC* 42)

As the speaker's consciousness moves in and out of meditation on imminent danger, the poem looks also to the past, noting that for ages cultures have feared and tried to ward off disaster, usually through religious ritual. At the close the speaker ends her divagating meditation by relocating herself first "in the Great Dying again"—that is, dwelling in the crisis of extinctions— but then almost immediately thereafter in the anticipation of "a / lovely evening" when, after "a bit of food a bit of drink" we

shall walk
out onto the porch and the evening shall come on around us, unconcealed,
blinking, abundant, as if catching sight of us,
everything in and out under the eaves, even the grass seeming to push up into
this our
world as if out of
homesickness for it,
gleaming.   (*SC* 44)

This moment, the poem's ending, is one of pastoral pleasure; "we" inhabit a simpler green world, a realm of abundance where swallows or bats fly near the eaves, the stars become visible, the grass gleams. Readers may find disturbing the incongruity of such a moment in juxtaposition to The Great Dying, particularly since the experience reflects social privilege of a kind that has been seen as dulling awareness of environmental injustice. If this turn to the pastoral is redeemed, it is so through its implicitly acknowledged brevity. This lovely moment is tied to the coming on of evanescent evening, sure to be followed by night's darkness. The imagined homesickness of the grass projects the speaker's own longing for a world she precariously inhabits and treasures but also feels she is both losing and has already lost.

While some of Graham's catalogs record the anthropogenic ills of the ecosystems in which we are embedded, she is repeatedly drawn back to naming what is wondrous in what is still, precariously, the "normal." This iterative reminder that we are not yet at the end of the world, so that it remains possible to sustain momentary appreciation of our blessings, seems to me Graham's way of making both living in crisis and her own apocalyptic perspective bearable. This interpretation fits with conventional understandings of the restorative function of pastoral as a *temporary* reprieve; Leo Marx calls attention to this brevity when describing the idyllic episodes characteristic of American pastoral, clearly relevant to *Sea Change,* in which "the protagonist enjoys a sense of ecstatic fulfillment, a feeling of calm selfhood and integration with his or her surroundings." Such moments "are linked to the old pastoral by a setting that often resembles the *locus amoenus* or pleasance: the lovely, peaceful shaded natural site that has figured prominently in the Arcadian mode since Virgil's first eclogue." Marx goes on, "As might be expected, however, this experience of transcendence is fleeting; it proves, in [Robert] Frost's fine phrase, to be only 'a momentary stay against confusion.'"[36] The blinking lights at the close of "Positive Feedback Loop" and the evanescence of evening itself signal the temporariness of this respite in Graham's work and serve both to criticize and to limit the escapism associated with the pastoral.

However much she wishes to sustain the pleasure-filled moments of presence that feel suspended out of time, Graham's speaker is always pulled back into history. As a momentary stay, however, the pastoral in all its beauty has great value in her work as a mode for registering the sensory pleasure produced in endangered and even damaged environments. The pastoral helps Graham hold out to readers the hope implicit in comic or avertive apocalypse, that all is not yet lost. Capturing nature's beauties, the world's sensory pleasures may bring into focus something worth fighting to preserve while implying a strong critique of all that threatens it.

The volume's closing poem "Long Way Round," which I discussed in connection with Graham's compulsion to tell a future audience "what / normal was" (SC 56), records, as the opening poem does, a moment of seemingly unnatural weather—"High winds again"—when, with symbolic significance, evening is coming on. Two successive sentences in this poem aptly record the tension that animates Sea Change and much serious eco-apocalyptic writing of the self-conscious Anthropocene: "One has to believe / furthermore in the voyage of others. The dark / gathers" (SC 54). On the one hand, the writer remains invested in ongoing life, and in changing the present to make a future possible; this is the stance underlying comic apocalypse. At the same time, that future possibility seems to be disappearing. Unable to either resolve this tension or simply sustain it, in the book's closing lines Graham moves toward the consolation of a deep ecological perspective: "there are sounds the planet will always make, even / if there is no one to hear them" (SC 56). The volume's combination of dire scientific information about global warming and personal meditations on the beauty of life embedded in damaged ecosystems seems to enact the kind of wake-up call we expect of eco-apocalyptic writing. But the pressures of living in crisis make this particularly difficult to sustain. When Graham in closing looks with a kind of Zen acceptance to a world without humans or sentient life forms (an acceptance not unlike Roberson's as he contemplates the vanishing figurative ice sculpture in the deep time context of "our small human extinction"), she nearly abandons much of what has made apocalyptic writing a motivator for change. Nearly, but not quite completely: she still says "if," not "when."

ANTI-PASTORAL HUMOR AND MULTISPECIES
EMBEDDEDNESS IN EVELYN REILLY'S *APOCALYPSO*

Evelyn Reilly's *Apocalypso* offers few if any pastoral pleasures. The immediate pleasures with which she lightens the gloom of apocalyptic awareness are, as we will see, less tainted by nostalgia, while her foregrounding of apocalyptic rhetoric as an ancient practice—one she mocks even as she seriously deploys it—makes her volume seem more removed from declensionist perspectives. Instead of representing beautiful nature, the poems of *Apocalypso* emphasize the dominance of technology in contemporary living—especially digital technology, which Reilly, with an ambivalence like Graham's toward the pastoral, both enjoys and critiques—and the too often overlooked interdependence of human and nonhuman animals.[37]

Reilly's eschewing of the pastoral is evident, for instance, in a passage from "Chilled Harold," a poem that combines aspects of Byron's *Childe Harold's Pilgrimage* with the narrative methods of the children's book, *Harold and the Purple Crayon*, in which the protagonist's story emerges as he draws it.[38] The passage begins "where a forest / was supposed to be," a place that might have promised a green world, but where Harold instead finds "one remaining tree, / with fruit needing protection." The poem continues:

So he drew some fierce protection
and got so caught up

in the violence of his depiction,
he scared even himself.

Shaking, he drew the ripples
of a sea by accident,

then quickly got in over his head.
Eventually, he climbed onto some sand,

where a sign said, "Reserved for American
Picnic" before an astonishing spread.

He ate a huge amount of appalling pie
and then shared the rest with a moose[39]

The manner of this fast-moving narrative is jocular, enhanced by puns (apple / appall) and the literalization of banal figuration ("in over his head"), and although the pastoral landscape seems to have been destroyed there's no evident nostalgia, only a sharp critique of America's disproportionate consumption of the world's so-called natural resources. When characterizing her sense of ecopoetics, Reilly explicitly rejects the pastoral as she seeks "a poetry that is not one of retreat and meditation, but of engagement and innovation—one that is not rural, regional, or pastoral, but is of a world in a continuum of crisis and ecological in scope, a community of communities." She believes "ecopoetics must be a matter of finding formal strategies that effect a larger paradigm shift and that actually participate in the task of abolishing the aesthetic use of nature as mirror for human narcissism."[40] Presumably, the pastoral is one version of such narcissism, its rural haven having been constructed as a counterpoint to the corruptions of court, urban, or industrialized life. The Romantic traditions of nature description and first-person lyricism to which Graham retains ties also fit that perspective Reilly would like to see abolished.

Reilly's approach to apocalyptic discourse in *Apocalypso* reflects her curiosity when composing the volume "as to whether our moment was uniquely marked by a kind of catastrophic end-time imagination or if this was just an amping up of something always in the human psyche—the fight-or-flight mechanism compulsively monitoring, on a micro-to-macro scale, the potential for various kinds of impending disaster."[41] She seems to have landed on the "amping up" side of things, which might align with Frederick Buell's sense of dwelling in crisis. Her reliance in the volume's title poem on the Book of Revelation as well as her references to works like Pieter Breugel the Elder's *Fall of the Rebel Angels* underscore that apocalyptic thinking is nothing new. However, the dystopian poems, which set the stage for "Apocalypso: A Comedy," emphasize that our current technologies promise a very different version of postapocalyptic conditions than any imaginable in previous eras.

The first section of the opening sequence, "Dreamquest Malware," for instance, presents a series of epistles sent from variously numbered "build sites" at various time stamps (e.g., ZMT 96927) reporting on the circumstances and difficulties an engineer encounters in a future world where technology is used to try to replace and mimic what nature once provided. (Reilly may be playing on the epistles concerning the future that are directed to different cities early in Revelation.) In an unusual moment of celebrating successful technological improvements, the speaker reports:

Brighter dimmers replaced the blighted meters
and the blinded windows
were given decorative grills

Even the situation drive restarted
which had exhausted us for weeks

So today the sun is ambulatory! the planet ambulatory!

The surplus bark in spite of snow
peels in permeable tentacles of façade plu! (*A* 16)

That the speaker is ecstatically grateful for a functioning mechanical "situation drive" that gives the illusion of the sun's normal movement across the sky makes clear the desperate deprivations of this engineer's future circumstances. "Plu" suggests not only the French for rain and past participle of being pleased but also the current Internet slang abbreviation for "people like us." It seems that at least two of the three meanings—pleasure and community—have to be artificially generated in "this sober landscape // littered with so much / dreamware wreckage" (*A* 18) where the speaker is "so lonely / [s/he's] been talking to [his/her] software / for three years" (*A* 14).

The darkness of this dystopian series arises in part from the way in which technical vocabularies are interposed on emotional ones, conveying half-successful attempts to repress emotion, particularly a nearly disabling grief. Here, for instance, is a report sent from one of the original build sites:

The signal is so sticky with procedure dreck
we grow desperate
for dislocation lubricant

Yet today we completed
2 fulfillment interstices
and 6 perfusion upsinks

after which it took hours to adjust
the nose cone of rampant grief

We have now pried countless tender chordate features
from the slab encasement

105 translation blockages
79 embedded snares

kneeling

yrs   (*A* 11)

Talk of "dislocation lubricant" and "fulfillment interstices" may suggest
technological management of dislocation and unfulfillment, but ultimately
neither the jargon nor the inventions it denotes can keep the speaker from
assuming a position of supplication or defeat.

"Chordate" refers to the phylum *chordata,* which encompasses a range
of animals possessing a notochord, a flexible rodlike cord of cells that provides longitudinal structure; the phylum includes all vertebrates (as well as
tunicates and cephalochordates), so it contains everything from humans to
blue whales to peregrine falcons, with about half the living species being
bony fish. The collective term may function in the poem as a euphemism,
enabling the speaker to avoid naming the species whose remains she or he
has been handling. Whatever the species involved, confronting the horror of
mass die-off seems part of what brings the speaker to his or her knees. This
mention of "chordate features" is one of many references in *Apocalypso* to
nonhuman species, which often are referred to via scientific taxonomies of
phylum, genus, and species, for animals and animality figure importantly in
Reilly's thinking about ecopoetics. She positions her ecopoetic work within
"the far larger project—which transcends all genres—of radically reforming
language as part of coming to understand ourselves as animals, and as such,
revisiting the notion of the human subject within a trans-species context.
In many ways, this is a search for language that 'coheres' with evolution,
in other words with our destiny as animals among other animals and living
things."[42] Using the term *chordate,* which lumps the human together with
ostensibly dissimilar creatures, points toward that sense of *Homo sapiens* as
an animal among other animals and also toward Frederick Buell's recommended awareness of ecological embeddedness. Both Buell and Reilly seek
recognition that the fate of humankind is inseparable from that of other life
forms, with clear implications for our planetary stewardship.

That Reilly values thinking in terms of embodiedness as Buell does is evident in the essay from which I just quoted, "The Grief of Ecopoetics," as she elaborates on the language she seeks: "Another aspect of this project is the exploration of a language that is deeply imbedded in materiality, not just in the sense of being an artistic or plastic medium, but as an action of our material being. . . . I see ecopoetics as search for a poetry that is firmly attached to earthly being."[43] While Graham conveys the preciousness of sensuous earthly being through catalogs and descriptions of what we can still enjoy, Reilly frequently communicates the preciousness of embodied experience through its deeply disturbing erasure. Key to the horror of the dystopic realm of "Dreamquest Malware" is its reliance on virtual and false versions of material phenomena in the context of the ruins of the material world familiar to us; what remains after some kind of apocalyptic transformation includes dust composed of "so many kinds of pulverized materials," "*blown fragments*" of animal bodies, and itemized things of dubious materiality such as "dreamware wreckage," "ceaseless moral deficiency showers," "veiled impediment confluences," "blog storage device[s]," "vision replacement apparition[s]," "large containers rigid with organic grief," and finally, to close the work, "fields // of unintended / result flowers."

Yet, like Graham, Reilly counters her grim future vision with present pleasures that the reader can savor, including bodily pleasures that remain available now even if largely vanished from the imagined future and, notably, the pleasures of humor. Here is Reilly's description, from "The Grief of Ecopoetics," of how she found a way to relieve her gloom while working on this volume or its title poem. The Western notion of apocalypse, she notes, is

linked to revelation—the vision of an escape from history into ahistorical bliss, prefaced however by an era of extreme violence and devastation. And it's the descriptions of devastation that tend to dominate the literature of apocalypse. . . . Thus, the more I worked on this project, the more I began to be subsumed by despair.

I was struggling with this for quite a while and getting gloomier and gloomier until one day I changed my working title from Apocalypse to Apocalypso, on one level just a tinkering with language, but on another level thinking of [Wallace] Stevens' "It must give pleasure," and needing to dig myself out of an emotional and creative hole. And then I started reading about calypso, . . . the Afro-Caribbean music with roots in both underground communication systems used by slaves and French troubadour poetry. . . . Putting these two ideas together—apocalypse and calypso—began to solve something for me about the role of poetry and the joy of the aesthetic impulse, about how to bring that back into our notion of ourselves as animals, and perhaps how to love ourselves again as animals, and maybe find a base of action and of language in that love.[44]

As will be evident shortly, "Apocalypso" focuses on loving animals while it also exposes cultural deterrents to doing so. Much of the joy to be found not just in that poem but in all five sequences in *Apocalypso*, each of which reflects an apocalyptic or dystopic vision of the future, comes from Reilly's engagement in some form of play or humorous wit that counters gloom. Such play seems crucial to her sense of the aesthetic impulse. Think, for instance, of the wordplay already observed in "Chilled Harold." As another example, the "time stamps" for "Dreamquest Malware" make an allusive joke since ZMP, with which they all begin, is a drug for migraines. Drawing sometimes upon the linguistic inventiveness of the French architect François Blanciak, who in his book *Siteless* has drawn 1,001 imagined site-less "building forms" to which he gives names (*A* 111), Reilly produces some grimly hilarious documents.[45] Here's the beginning of one, from "Dreamquest Malware," addressed to a Ms. T, where the speaker's righteous tone in the context of the faux-techno vocabulary produces a comic effect:

> It was a shock that you would send
> this ignition system
>
> instead of the slogan-infestation compress
> we had so explicitly requested
>
>
> *What exactly was your intent?*   (*A* 10)

The irritated entitlement communicated in the manner of a formal business letter collides amusingly with the speaker's degraded circumstances and with the absurd idea of a bandage that would alleviate an infestation of slogans. The circumstances remain bleak, but the reader enjoys a chuckle nonetheless.

Having shown how Reilly's representation of embodied embeddedness involves environments severely damaged by industrial and digital technology where human and nonhuman species remain nonetheless interdependent, and having identified the pleasures that enable her apocalyptic rhetoric to produce responses other than paralysis and despair, I turn now to the volume's longest sequence to see these traits in action within a work that self-consciously scrutinizes the apocalyptic imagination as both an historical and a present phenomenon. "Apocalypso: A Comedy" enacts what Lawrence Buell notes Douglas Robinson has identified as "one of the hallmarks of American literary apocalypticism": metanarrative irony. Buell adds, "In the era of *Cat's Cradle, Doctor Strangelove,* and *Star Wars* it is hard for apocalypticism to keep a straight face." In line with that tradition's "self-reflexivity about the possible fanaticism of one's discourse," Reilly's "Apocalypso" offers a critical and partly mocking, reflexive treatment of the apocalyptic writing of Revelation, even while she employs the devices of apocalyptic rhetoric to warn of oncoming doom.[46]

The disjunctive poem "Apocalypso: A Comedy" is a quest journey through the Book of Revelation, filled with quotations from the "revised standard / sedition edition" of that text, as the speaker, equipped with a glue gun and accompanied by the one animal humans claim unabashedly to love, her dog, measures the apocalyptic vision of John of Patmos against what is happening in her own apparently doomed world and critiques his underlying values. *"Come,"* the work begins, calling attention to the tortuous temporality of apocalyptic discourse that we saw Graham engaging, *"and I'll show you what once / shall have taken place after this"* (A 75). Far from being awed by John, the spunky speaker is angry and defiant; John's having *"abandoned the love / he had at first"* (in Rev. 2:4; A 77)—which the speaker seems to understand to be love for life forms other than humans—has *"unleashed the dog / of* [her] *darkest humor / to devour the chapters / that verseth"* (A 77). Here, while playing with puns on *leashes,* Reilly announces her most fundamental critique of Christian apocalyptic traditions (and perhaps of Christianity itself): their anthropocentrism.[47] At every opportunity, Reilly's speaker, who is in several senses "down with the animals," gestures lovingly toward them. She lists in her "sting-ray version / of the beatitudes" (A 90) species often disparaged in Western cultures: sea slugs, bottom dwellers, predators, and "those who stridulate" (crickets and grasshoppers) (A 102)—expanding her appreciation well beyond the charismatic megafauna championed by conservation organizations and implicitly highlighting the different functions enacted by different species within ecosystems. Playing on the anagrammatic presence of the word "rats" within "stars," she declares, "and I mean to vindicate the innocent / and address vermin love

words // to the seven rats of the seven stars" (*A* 81). The biotic egalitar-
ianism that Lawrence Buell has identified as one of the central traits of
environmental apocalyptic writing is clearly central to Reilly's version of
that discourse.[48]

Ironically, however, Reilly's speaker is at the same time complicit in her
culture's pervasive disparaging of animals. She admits, in connection with
rats, to having hired an exterminator. Calling attention to our language's
conventionalized denigration of animals and animality, she apologizes to *ca-
nis familiaris* for that phrase about the dog of her darkest humor. At another
point, she takes back a derogatory usage of the word "cockroach," using
the opportunity to educate her readers about the diversity of cockroaches
through scientific terminology free of negative connotations:

> But delete this derogation
> of Phylum Arthropod
> Order Blattaria
>
> with so many genera
> including the oriental roach
> (*Blatta orientalis*) and the American
> (*Periplaneta americana*)
>
> and some, especially in the genus Ectobius,
>
> which are "small temperate species that live outdoors"   (*A* 84)

The speaker's amusingly presented inconsistency of caring about nonhuman animals yet also insulting them highlights "how much our notion of
our 'species position' is embedded in our language."[49] The unfortunate durability in our culture of both the human/animal dichotomy and the ideology of animal inferiority is suggested in the passage where the speaker's
invitation to her beloved companion animal echoes the children's game in
which those on one team shout a challenge to their opponents, "red rover,
red rover, let [a named member of the other team] come over," and that
person tries to break through the callers' line. "Come over lover rover,"
Reilly pleads, conveying devotion but also an edge of enmity. The invitation,
poignantly, is to participate jointly in magical environmental restoration:
"help spread some phoenix ashes / in this bit of ravaged woods" (*A* 78).
These lines suggest a hope that awareness of our interdependence with

other species, while hard to achieve fully, might yield better environmental stewardship and even some forms of environmental recovery.

In addition to criticizing the focus of traditional apocalyptic discourse on exclusively human salvation—an ethical and ecological error—Reilly also challenges what she conveys as the irresponsibility of its absurd temporality. By definition, the future apocalypse can, presently, only be imagined, even though apocalyptic writing depicts what is believed to be already determined, and even though the apocalyptic chain of events will, if realized, have proved unstoppable. As one of the poem's epigraphs puts it, "strange verb tenses must be enacted: these are those things that *will have had to have been,* that *will have had to yet occur*" (A 71). This produces lines like the following in Reilly's poem, "For we have stepped into the sacred areas / and wept over our waste procedures // which is will have been being our transcendence" (A 82). Here we tumble from present perfect, designating an action that has happened, to the present tense "is," to the future perfect, used for an action that will have been completed in the future, and back to the continuousness of the present participle, "being," entwined in the future perfect as "will have been being." The lines' landing on "transcendence" points to the aspect of apocalyptic temporality that is most problematic for Reilly: its "escape from history into ahistorical bliss," which she fears allows people to look beyond this world and detach themselves from the challenges of problem solving within the conditions of historical time—here, the environmental problems caused by humans' waste.[50] Reilly's speaker directly challenges John the Revelator on this score in a passage that humorously rewrites Robert Creeley's "I Know a Man"—a minimalistic masterpiece capturing first the tendency to stew anxiously and self-consciously in a crisis situation, and then an emphatic rejoinder that urges taking immediate preventive action when disaster threatens:

As I sd to my
friend, because I am
always talking,—John, I

sd, which was not his
name, the darkness sur-
rounds us, what

can we do against
it, or else, shall we &

why not, buy a goddamn big car,

drive, he sd, for
christ's sake, look
out where yr going.[51]

Here's Reilly's speaker, who addresses John of Patmos, "as we are just about
to cross / the George Washington Bridge":

Excuse me,
a question while we are driving
I sd., John, I sd
what do you have anyway
against historical time?   (A 83)

Even as the lack of apparent urgency in her question with its stalling "anyway" resonates comically against Creeley's hard-hitting conclusion, the
question nonetheless carries considerable force. For while Reilly invites
an awareness of human insignificance in geological time, historical time is
what matters immediately to her—and, she implies, should be what matters
to us all. If historical time is only something to be transcended en route to a
blessed eternity where all is made new, then we've little reason to look out
where we're going.[52]

   For all its light-hearted mockery of its ethically inconsistent protagonist
and its playful invocations of the absurd temporality of apocalyptic writing, "Apocalypso: A Comedy" keeps readers aware of the grim realities of
the present. Where we're going—indeed, where we already are in Reilly's
representation—matches all too closely John's prophesies in the Book of
Revelation, in which seas fill with blood, multitudes of creatures die, and
waters become lethally bitter. These connections are evident through Reilly's extensive quotation (or, misquotation—hers is the sedition edition, after
all) and paraphrase of the Bible, which make clear that she is serious about
the possibility of looming apocalypse, however apocalyptic traditions may
be ironized in her text. Dwelling in crisis, the speaker is aware of constantly
increasing environmental degradation—"Every morning reveals another
crevice / of this denatured nature canvas" (A 90)—and she uses language
that echoes the Book of Revelation to convey this accumulating damage.
Where Graham focused primarily on global warming, Reilly introduces
a variety of issues. For instance, evoking Rev. 6:14, "every mountain and
island were moved out of their places," she points to mountaintop removal

mining: "the mountains were removed from their places" (*A* 99); where John of Patmos was shown the pure river of the water of life flowing from the throne of God, she is shown "the river / of the waste water of life" (*A* 106), with its suggestions of deadly pollution. She combines, compresses, and modifies biblical images in ways that make the envisioned cataclysmic future difficult to distinguish from the present, as she refers to "tainted soil" (*A* 98), "the sea thick with apo-oceanic scum" (*A* 100), or "the flowers / of the apocalypse—// stalky ashen broken caked / with coral reef skeletal remnants / and the dust of lichen," which are particularly vulnerable to air pollution (*A* 103).

Not all her mentions of current environmental problems are directly tied to biblical references. For instance, she observes that her canine partner is suffering "dermatological troubles / probably resulting from long-term exposure / to environmental chemicals" (*A* 95), and the only tie to apoca-lyptic discourse in the passage is that these are designated "tense issues," a reminder of the strange verb tenses inherent to apocalyptic writing. Yet with or without evident allusions, analogies and modifications to the trib-ulations prophesied in the Bible are everywhere. Mention of clock hands in the poem suggests the Atomic Energy Commission's Doomsday Clock, here adapted from its initial function of registering nuclear threat to sig-nal multiple forms of environmental disaster, like those often cataloged in Revelation. In Revelation these disturbances of nature serve to eliminate the wicked; Reilly instead notes that they are inequitably suffered most by the impoverished and disempowered:

> But we are getting rather out of order
> still holding the bomb in our clock hands
> I mean the tsunami I mean the flood
> I mean the hurricane that pummels
> the poor and the weak   (*A* 97)

Where Revelation prophesies the destruction of the "merchants of the earth" who were made rich from jewels, precious woods, marble, agricul-tural products, and other materials gleaned from the earth, Reilly gestures toward current political, legal, and financial corruption. Her spirited speaker is one who (alluding to Johnny Cash's "The Man Comes Around") is "kick-ing against the pricks / of wholesale legislative / abandonment" (*A* 85), and she sometimes sketches examples of that abandonment. For instance, that passage about the disasters pummeling the poor and the weak continues:

                              as a voice
in the midst of chapter six verse
eight is speaking building codes
deficient regulatory powers international
aid diversions and the darkest rider
(in both legal and equestrian senses)
flails its financial instrument vehicle
with fiscal irresponsibility reins

And a third of the waters
became wormwood
and many died
because they were made bitter   (A 97)

(Rev. 6:8, to which the passage refers, speaks of the pale horse ridden by
Death and followed by Hades and proclaims the destructive power given
them over a fourth part of the earth.) The italicized biblical passage that
Reilly includes, a nearly exact quotation from Revelation 8:11, seems not so
much a threat of supernatural punishment that will come to those who fail
to impose protective regulations or who divert aid from where it is needed
as a description of what people through their economic and governmental
institutions are tragically doing to themselves.

    As was the case in Graham's work, Reilly's sense of present degrada-
tion and ongoing crisis does not preclude her also experiencing apocalyptic
threat in "these cataclysmic lyrics" any more than her awareness of the
sometimes ridiculous qualities of apocalyptic rhetoric and its failure to date
to predict an actual end of the world precludes her from employing it. Near
the work's close Reilly confesses,

    This is how
    what would will have been
    being a diversion

    merged instead
    into a vision
    of preliminary descent

    while sleeping on your carbon cushion
    Flight 267
    New York from Kiev   (A 110)

Presenting the poem's contents as a dream vision experienced in a traveler's fitful sleep, she admits not only to an all-too-comfortable recourse to airplane travel despite its terrible carbon footprint, but also to feeling increasingly pessimistic about the future; "preliminary descent" is the early stage of a downward course soon to become more precipitous.

If people for millennia have found in visions of postapocalyptic transcendence or of pastoral retreat inherited conceptual structures that can mitigate—for better or worse, in terms of worldly reform—the fearful aspects of threatening catastrophe, Reilly's "Apocalypso" exposes the digital realm as currently proffering another equally ambivalent alternative to focusing on the threatened biosphere. As "Dreamquest Malware" demonstrates, the substitutions for destroyed nature enabled by digital technology are in Reilly's view thoroughly inadequate, and her work suggests that the digital environment that so many Americans regularly inhabit can be as much an escape as the sublime wilderness or the pastoral garden has ever been. Indeed, the digital is probably more dangerously seductive now than the pastoral precisely because digital reality is not disappearing, and because while we hide there, we can avoid seeing all that *is* being lost.

Reilly depicts people, including her speaker/persona, as too much shut into the digital realm, in the "usual enclosures [of] (Word, Facebook, Linked-in, Google,)" (*A* 93). Yet, recognizing humans as technology-using animals, Reilly doesn't condemn digital technology, and this helps her avoid pastoral's temptation to focus nostalgically on the past. The poems in her preceding volume, *Styrofoam*, discussed in both the introduction and chapter 2, are unapologetically full of information lifted from the Internet. She probably means it when she exclaims "(how I love my Apple)" after speaking of "passing through security / carrying as much fruit of the tree / of knowledge as possible" (*A* 87). (The page containing those lines plays more extensively with Rev. 2:7: "To him that overcometh will I give to eat of the tree of life.") But she offers no visions of techno-engineering as a means of salvation from environmental disaster. Rather, recognizing that the not-here of the digital realm offers its own version of escape, and that it, like the pastoral, is more readily available to those with social and economic privilege, she admits to being "Disturbed just a bit today / by my own privilege screen / comfort mechanisms" (*A* 84). Wanting to make a change, she determines to find her "home page"—figuratively, her fundamental orientation—in a perspective that connects her to even the most disparaged of animal species such as cockroaches. It's a perspective, moreover, that draws on the pleasures of embodiment—that is, on coming to one's senses—and on what she calls "the joy of the aesthetic impulse."[53] That section of the poem ends, compellingly:

> singing loving my vermin
> singing sunniest day
>
> dancing my aptest app-dance
> under these apo-calypso rays   (A 84)

The passage brings together much that "Apocalypso" values in this moment of environmental crisis and incipient apocalypse: concern for the well-being of nonhuman life; embrace of technology as an aid, though not a sole solution; recognition of the needs of the weak and oppressed, in recalling the Afro-Caribbeans who invented calypso; and appreciation of the very real pleasures of inhabiting a body on this planet—of singing and dancing and enjoying the sunshine.

At one point in her apocalyptic comedy, Reilly contemplates the section of Bruegel's *Fall of the Rebel Angels* that appears on her book's cover and remarks, "So many pretty revels / in these devastation pictures" (A 76). There's a critique of aestheticization there—and a reflexive acknowledgment that artists like herself may be tempted to play with apocalypse just because it offers such an amazing array of powerful images: "A big artistic impetus this endtime vision" (A 95). Reilly is wary of the "prettiness" that is Graham's forte, just as her sharp irony contrasts with the earnest self-examination Graham offers. By staying with the Book of Revelation throughout "Apocalypso: A Comedy," Reilly remains more consistently focused on apocalyptic discourse than Graham does in any of the poems of *Sea Change.* Yet Reilly's poetry also acknowledges, as Graham's demonstrates, the psychological difficulties of dwelling unrelentingly in pre-apocalyptic crisis. Their poetics differ significantly, yet both poets' work highlights the precarious dynamics and unsteady purposes of apocalyptic writing in the context of ongoing environmental crisis, particularly given the instability of their own relations to a sense like Roberson's that it's already after the end of the world.

All three poets combine an awareness of living in crisis like that theorized by Frederick Buell, with a belief that we are either poised on the cusp of environmental apocalypse or already tipped into it. Rather than following Buell's advice to leave aside apocalyptic prediction, then, they have brought such warning together with an ecologically grounded vision that recognizes dwelling in crisis. Their poetry concurs with Buell's sense that acknowledging "one dwells in a body and in ecosystems" initiates the most environmentally and socially responsible stance available. But in order to bear their double awareness of crisis and apocalypse, the poets, unlike Buell, have brought into focus the pleasures available within that awareness. All three poets regard narratives of unmitigated sadness or unmitigated doom as unproductive. Roberson turns to the rewards of attention to one's surroundings, knowing that what we have to attend to is in part unfolding doom. Reilly and Graham, who have not entirely abandoned the hope that apocalyptic warning might produce meaningful action as well as attention, seem to believe that eco-apocalyptic art must offer some kind of revelry or pleasure if it is to help people immersed in ongoing crisis muster the will to avert devastation.

CHAPTER 4

Understanding Nonhumans

Interspecies Communication in Poetry

Evelyn Reilly is far from being the only contemporary North American poet who is "down with the animals" and whose writing reflects a desire to establish more ethically and environmentally responsible relations with earth others. Chapter 3's discussion of her critique of Judeo-Christian anthropocentrism in *Apocalypso* lays groundwork for this chapter's examination of animal-focused work by Angela Rawlings, a Canadian poet and performance artist who publishes as a.rawlings; Jody Gladding, an American translator, poet, and installation artist; and Jonathan Skinner, a U.S. poet, birder, and editor of the field-altering journal *ecopoetics*. Representing one strand of environmentally invested contemporary poetry concerned with animals, these three experiment with formal strategies for representing other-than-human animals in ways that respect both their difference from humans and the richness of their lifeworlds, a richness registered as comparable to that enjoyed by humans. Even as these poets attempt in some ways to translate nonhuman languages into a human tongue, they at the same time use animal signs to modify the English language, pushing its syntax and sounds away from the human / nonhuman divide on which human exceptionalism depends and toward greater recognition of animal agency and of varied forms of communication in the biosphere.[1] Seeking better understanding of nonhuman species as well as more respectful relations with them, in their scientifically informed representations of animals or animal messages they approach as best they can the elusive anti-anthropocentric ideal that Joan Retallack calls "reciprocal alterity."[2] Employing what I will present as varied grammars of animacy, their visually and aurally inventive work encourages appreciation of nonhuman species and their modes of communication; in so doing, it fosters compassionate attention to the plight of nonhuman animals in the self-conscious Anthropocene.

THE CONTESTED POSSIBILITY OF INTERSUBJECTIVITY
BETWEEN HUMANS AND NONHUMANS

In his widely cited lecture "The Animal That Therefore I Am (More to Follow)," delivered in 1997 and published in English in 2002, Jacques Derrida points to an alarming acceleration during the past two centuries in the anthropogenic transformation of the experience of those beings we call animals:

> traditional forms of treatment of the animal have been turned upside down by the joint developments of zoological, ethological, biological and genetic *forms of knowledge* and the always inseparable *techniques* of intervention with respect to their object, the transformation of the actual object, its milieu, its world, namely the living animal. This has occurred by means of farming and regimentalization at a demographic level unknown in the past, by means of genetic experimentation, the industrialization of what can be called the production for consumption of animal meat, artificial insemination on a massive scale, more and more audacious manipulations of the genome, the reduction of the animal not only to production and overactive reproduction (hormones, genetic crossbreeding, cloning, and so on) of meat for consumption but also of all sorts of other end products, and all of that in the service of a certain being and the so-called human well-being of man.[3]

To this impassioned list of deliberate manipulations of other-than-human beings we might add the less intentional destruction of habitats that has accompanied the explosion in the world's human population and its increasing industrialization, including the poisoning of land and rivers by herbicides, "pesticides," and other pollutants; the degradation of marine environments resulting from ocean acidification, heavy fishing, oceanic noise pollution; the threats to various animal populations posed by global warming; along with such inadvertent developments as the deadly transmission of animal pathogens through globalized trade and travel. In addition to noting "the *unprecedented* proportions of this subjection of the animal" that's being practiced for the purported protection of humans, Derrida observes that we are now living through a turning point.[4] That sense of a turning point for the planet's animals has only intensified in the self-conscious Anthropocene with the growing recognition that we have entered a period of mass extinction on a scale unmatched since the last mass extinction 65 million years ago, the Cretaceous-Paleogene extinction of an estimated 75 percent of the earth's species, including all the non-avian dinosaurs. The currently unfolding biotic crisis is referred to as the Sixth Great Extinction or the Holocene Extinction.[5]

Donna Haraway, whose earlier championing of the cyborg has developed into advocacy of an ethical otherness-in-relation involving a capaciously understood "companion species," is among those who have acknowledged the importance of Derrida's essay. Haraway commends Derrida—who devotes much of the essay to contemplating his cat looking at him naked—for recognizing that his cat is someone (not some thing) able to look back at him and for "not fall[ing] into the trap of making the subaltern speak." Nonetheless, she points critically to the philosopher's failure to "become curious about what the cat might actually be doing, feeling, thinking, or perhaps making available to him in looking back at him that morning." By being insufficiently curious, Derrida stopped short of full respect for the animal. Pondering the contrasting example of noted scientists who have not "refused the risk of an intersecting gaze" and who thereby seem to be gaining "positive knowledge of and with animals," Haraway asks: "Why did Derrida leave unexamined the practices of communication outside the writing technologies he did know how to talk about?"[6] In answer, she proposes that the philosophical tradition in which he writes did not provide the tools to practice the sort of curiosity she advocates and which is for her the basis of an ethical "alertness to otherness-in-relation."[7]

In line with this aspect of Haraway's thought, the poets whose work I will examine in this chapter are immensely curious about both inter- and intraspecies communication by animals. They experiment boldly with poetry—with the materiality of its language and with its visual and aural resources along with extra-poetic visual and aural material to supplement those resources—to gain knowledge *"from, about, and with"* other-than-human animals.[8] Determined to attend to both animal expression and the limitations of their human language and human sensory apparatus, they imaginatively transcribe, translate, and transmute verbal and nonverbal signs made by animals. While such efforts could be dismissed as presumptuous, appropriative, or just silly, I see their explorations as serious and respectful efforts to expand human listening and attending to earth others.

The motivation for their curiosity is partly but not exclusively environmentalist. Here's Jonathan Skinner, contemplating "slow listening," which in his practice involves literally slowing down recordings of birdsong as well as producing spectrograms in order to make available to human ears and eyes more of that song's intricacy. Metaphorically, however, the phrase points more generally to deliberately focused modes of attention to animal sign systems:

> Our limited overlap with the way our other-than-human neighbors see and hear the world, which includes our ability to take in what they might be telling us, constrains our appreciation of their brilliance and impacts our understanding of their needs. As the noisiest, neediest (and nosiest) residents on the block, it may be our job to stop and listen. . . . Just as translation makes opportunities of the constraints our language encounters in another's hearing, slow listening can turn our lumbering ears into instruments for unwinding the musical microcosm inside a sparrow's ear. We at least begin to hear what we aren't hearing. Our algorithmic manipulations of space and time [as in the slowed recordings] might offer a probe into the seismic channel of perceptual distance between us and those we share the planet with. Finding ways to see what we hear [as with the spectrograms] offers a purchase into translations that become ways of performing other than human being. We will listen differently after a journey into the sparrow's ear and we might act differently if we can become sparrows, speaking or singing into what we hear, even briefly.⁹

This passage illuminates the intertwining of environmental with aesthetic aims—wanting to appreciate both the needs and the brilliance of the other in what Haraway calls "significant otherness-in-connection"¹⁰—while it implicitly acknowledges that the poetry derived from such listening may reveal as much about the humbling limitations of our own senses and sign systems as about other animals.

The notion of becoming the other, "even briefly," is fraught; the degree to which humans can empathize with or enter into the experience or perspective of other animals has been a crucial debate in critical animal studies. Because all three poets discussed here produce some kind of translation of nonhuman experience or signals into human language, it's worth laying out these debates more fully and positioning the poets' work within them. Matthew Calarco's useful three-part schematization of recent theoretical approaches to human–animal relations, each with its strengths and limitations, can frame this discussion. The first is an identity-based approach whose advocates "seek to establish a relevantly similar moral identity

between human beings and animals." Such thinkers have effectively challenged a simplistic binary between human and animal, but their position
has been criticized for its logocentrism and persistent anthropocentrism;
quintessentially human traits provide rational grounds for extending (or
not extending) moral status to particular nonhuman species. The second
is a difference-based approach, represented by Derrida, that involves not
the old, humanist dichotomy between animals and humans, but an "exploration of the nonanthropocentric dimensions of post- or antihumanism."
This approach avoids both logocentrism and anthropocentrism, but tends to
present Human and Animal as monolithic categories so that "complicated
lines of mutual affect and relation" are obscured. Moreover, its reinforcement of difference between human and animal, Calarco argues, plays into
the powerful received binary. The third approach, which Calarco believes
warrants more development and attention, he labels indistinction: these
thinkers are trying to identify "new modes of thought and practice beyond
the human/animal distinction" that would "enable alternative modes of
living, relating, and being with others of all sorts (human and nonhuman)."
Haraway's work exemplifies this approach that reflects a "desire to inhabit
the world from perspectives other than those of the classically human subject and to explore the passions and potentials that are found in such spaces
of encounter."[11]

The identity-based perspective is well represented by J. M. Coetzee's
character Elizabeth Costello, who asserts "there is no limit to the extent
to which we can think ourselves into the being of another. There are no
bounds to the sympathetic imagination." A novelist like her creator, this
character claims she can think her way "into the existence of a bat or a
chimpanzee or an oyster, any being with whom I share the substrate of life";
she asserts that Ted Hughes does that in some of his animal poems, which
she says don't inhabit another mind but rather another body.[12]

Her mention of a bat is part of her attempt to refute the difference-based
view of Thomas Nagel in his widely known philosophical essay "What Is
It Like to Be a Bat?" There, Nagel observes that because our experience as
humans provides the basis for our imagination, its range is limited. I can
imagine "only what it would be like for *me* to behave as a bat behaves"
but not what it is like for a *bat* to be a bat, Nagel argues. He reasons that
the experience of any species has "a specific subjective character, which it
is beyond our ability to conceive." "If extrapolation from our own case is
involved in the idea of what it is like to be a bat, the extrapolation must be

incompletable." However, he acknowledges in a footnote the possibility that the imagination might extend such extrapolation: "It may be easier than I suppose to transcend inter-species barriers with the aid of the imagination. For example, blind people are able to detect objects near them by a form of sonar, using vocal clicks or taps of a cane. Perhaps if one knew what that was like, one could by extension imagine roughly what it was like to possess the much more refined sonar of a bat. The distance between oneself and other persons and other species can fall anywhere on a continuum."[13] In a more recent work than Nagel's, which urges respect for difference, Kate Soper cautions that it is anthropocentric "to assume that our desires and capacities offer direct access to knowledge of their 'analogues' in the worlds and life-styles of other species." She presents a forceful critique of the current romance with "'transgressive border crossing,'" challenging the logic and the political ramifications of the popular "refusal to treat the differences between humans and other animals as anything but matters of degree within an essential ontological continuity."[14] Soper denies that a fluid sense of the divide between the human and the animal necessarily will yield more ecofriendly policies or less tolerance for mistreatment of animals, pointing instead to its possible dystopian consequences.

Yet Haraway, who focuses on the co-constitutive relationships between animals and humans, places far more hope in cultivating awareness of what Calarco calls indistinction. Comments from several of the poets suggest that they, too, are exploring this territory of indistinction, though in ways that avoid anthropocentrism or making the subaltern speak and that maintain a respect for interspecies differences. None of these poets claims really to perceive, or speak, from another species' point of view à la Costello. For instance, while noting the benefits of listening in a way that expands both "the boundaries of what we allow to be language" and the "realm of 'linguistic beings,'" Gladding expresses the hope that the poems that result from her own listening to the language of bark beetles will be "closer . . . to translation than to imposition, to play than to betrayal," but she acknowledges "there's always the danger of making things up."[15] Her stated aim is to skirt that danger and remain in a collaborative relation with the beings she works with. Yet even as Gladding engages in imaginative translation—"trying to stretch beyond my own frame of reference as a human in the world and to think of other beings as linguistic"—she isn't making truth claims about that thinking; "I'm not making the argument that they are," she adds.[16] She implies that what's of value is the stretch, the attempt to expand beyond human beings' usual perceptions, and in so doing possibly to gain some knowledge or wisdom about and from the nonhuman other. We'll see that the work of the poets under consideration here suggests a faith that what Nagel reminds us are necessarily partial imaginings may nonetheless help us see the world differently.

Importantly, Skinner, Gladding, and a.rawlings approach the nonhumans represented in their poetry as real beings who occupy particular ecological webs and have distinctive habitats, behaviors, and life cycles. In an environmental context, it's significant that the species these poets write about are not particularly threatened; the poems are not composed to wrench heartstrings in service of any "Save the Whales"–style campaign. Indeed, at least some species of the bark beetles whose material language Gladding translates tend to be seen as the enemy by conservationists, among others: thanks to drought and climate change, native mountain pine beetles are killing off millions of acres of especially lodgepole and Ponderosa pines in the western United States and Canada (and affecting birds, bears, and other species in the process). Producing vast dead forests and thereby reducing carbon sequestration, the beetles are part of a feedback loop that intensifies global warming. But that does not diminish Gladding's interest in this family of beetles (*Scolytinae*) or her admiration for the beauty of the engravings their larvae produce in the bark of the trees they inhabit.

The conspicuous differences between a beetle or a beetle larva and an adult female human—or between moths or songbirds and humans—ensure readers' awareness of the divergences between the species' experiences of the phenomenal world we all, though with very different sensory equipment, occupy. As I ponder the images of tunneled bark that Gladding includes in her *Translations from Bark Beetle,* it's clear to me that she is indeed "making things up." But this is not necessarily problematic. For as she translates the larval tracks into a grammar that relies on a pronoun that does not distinguish between first and second person or singular and plural, in which prepositional phrases are particularly important and verbs are in either "the cyclical or the radiant" tense, her inventions reflect an ethically disciplined imagination of otherness.[17] Her "translations" evidently emerge from careful sympathetic attention to the shapes and trajectories of the channels beetle larvae carve, mindful of the creatures' life cycles, of what is known about their communication systems and their particular ecological needs.

By focusing their curiosity on nonmammalian animals, these three poets reduce the likelihood of their poetry enacting the romanticized and "sentimental glorification of humans' proximity with animals" that Rosi Braidotti observes is "especially problematic in contemporary culture."[18] Because they do not write about creatures who can easily be made to seem like humans, they avoid the problematic tendency evident in identity-based philosophical discourse to "allocate moral consideration to non-human beings entirely on the basis of their similarity to the human." Instead, they encourage recognition of these independent beings as having "potential needs, excellences and claims to flourish of their own."[19]

Additionally, animals do not function in these poems simply or primarily as figures for exploring the "animal within" the human, although in the sensual fabric of a.rawlings's *Wide Slumber for Lepidopterists* human animality does come to the fore. Exploring the animal within humans is potentially an environmentalist project as it attempts an opening of human senses that, in David Abram's words, "own[s] up to being . . . a creature of earth."[20] Such projects are most curious about the human rather than the other, however, while the works examined here seek greater understanding of nonhuman species. In different degrees and forms these three poets do suggest the possibility of temporarily merging the other's experience with their own or approximating another's language with human voicing. While they approach that expansion of perception and expression through focused attention on the other, they also recognize their translation or transmutation of other-than-human expression as, in Skinner's terms, a performance.

In their exploration of nonlinguistic communication by earth others, then, these poets are engaged in something far less presumptuous and less extreme than the "conceptual meltdown," the abandonment of ontological discrimination that Soper sees in the trendy dissolution of boundaries.[21] The figure Skinner employs of performing karaoke, for instance, captures an amused self-consciousness about the limitations of his own attempts to "translate" bird vocalization. After all, karaoke—Japanese for "empty orchestra"—is a form of entertainment in which the real star is absent and the aspiring amateur singing in his or her place is almost always a poor substitute. Skinner describes his "performance genre" of Birdsong Karaoke as follows: "I play back birdsong at half or quarter speed and read or sing along lyrics composed to fit the bird's tune. The bird is the composer and I am just trying to sing along with my poor human vocal cords. I often fail, but where there is a match, it's as though I get to be the bird, for a brief instant, and the audience gets to hear birdsong in human language. If all that comes of the experiment is heightened attention to the specifics of these avian performances, then I am happy." He adds in the next paragraph: "The text, or language, exists wholly within the world of the human" and goes on to explain the sources for his poem, "Countersong: Rising and Falling," which re-scripts the duet of two hermit thrushes, in movies he had recently seen or was half-watching while typing, as well as in the topography over which his airplane was flying as he wrote.[22] The experiment enacts an openness to varied aspects of the poet's environment, including but not limited to his repeated listenings to the recorded birdsong. His is a form of translation that aims to expose the wondrous intricacy of bird communication, and to re-code, without presuming to de-code, its content.

Of the three poets treated here, a.rawlings would seem most to partici- pate in the contemporary ethos of species blurring that Soper deplores. As will shortly become clear, I think it one of the remarkable achievements of a.rawlings's *Wide Slumber for Lepidopterists* that it manages through varied devices frequently to blur the otherwise obviously divergent embodied ex- periences of moths and humans. I would argue that producing moments of porosity between species, as she does, need not constitute an eradication of distinctions between those species or an appropriative speaking for the other. To imagine sensorily vivid shared experiences is not to claim unob- structed channels of empathy running between species. It can, however, foster more ready sympathy, compassion, appreciation, and respectful con- cern on the part of the planet's now dominant animal.

The work of ecofeminist philosopher Val Plumwood, which, like Har- away's, represents Calarco's indistinction approach, illuminates the poetry under consideration here. Plumwood agrees with Soper and many other environmental thinkers that anthropocentrism is deeply problematic: "To the extent that anthropocentric frameworks prevent us from experiencing the others of nature in their fullness, we not only help to imperil ourselves through loss of sensitivity but also deprive ourselves of the unique kinds of richness and joy the encounter with the more-than-human presences of nature can provide." But Plumwood distinguishes anthropocentrism, which she contends is as avoidable as ethnocentrism or androcentrism, from an inescapable "epistemic locatedness" (what we saw Nagel exploring); the latter does not preclude empathy or the broadening of ethical concern beyond the self. She proposes that we "need a reconception of the human self in more mutualistic terms as a self-in-relationship with nature, formed not in the drive for mastery and control of the other but in a balance of mutual transformation and negotiation." Such a reconception seems to her possible. It requires being open to and aware of the potential agency and communicative powers of earth others—potentialities "that are closed off to us in the reductive model that strips intentional qualities from out of nature and hands them back to us as 'our projections'":

> To treat the other as a potentially intentional and communicative being and narrative subject is part of moving from monological modes of encounter (such as those of anthropocentrism) to dialogical modes of encounter. Communicative models of relationships with nature and animals can improve our receptivity and responsiveness, which clearly need much improvement. They seem likely to offer us a better chance of survival in the difficult times ahead than dominant mechanistic models which promote insensitivity to the others' agency and denial of our dependency on them. This clash of models is critical for our times.[23]

Sharing Plumwood's sense of potential agency and intentionality in earth others, a.rawlings, Gladding, and Skinner work to generate just such communicative models. Their interest in the specifics of particular species' life cycles, sensory capabilities, and ecological needs perhaps suggests a degree of sympathy with those who think in terms of difference, while their attempt to render animal communication in English might be seen as participating in the logocentrism of the identity camp. But most fundamentally they are aligned with the indistinction thinkers like Plumwood, who "aim to have us notice and attend to the fact that what our culture takes to be 'mere' animals are capable of entering into modes of relation and ways of life that can never be fully anticipated."[24]

Calarco's phrase "our culture" is a reminder that not all cultures have the reductive perspective on animals evident in the modern West. To complete my framing of the poets' thinking about their linguistic representations of animal others, I turn to observations the ethnobotanist Robin Wall Kimmerer offers about the cultural perspective of her Potawatomi ancestors. I do so because her insights highlight the key role that language plays in people's ways of thinking about earth others. Her meditations on one Native American "grammar of animacy" underscore the potential importance of experimental poetics for transforming the relations that English speakers perceive and enact with earth others.

In her essay "Learning the Grammar of Animacy," Kimmerer, a member of the Potawatomi tribe (one of the Ojibwe or Anishinaabe peoples of North America), recounts her experiences trying to learn the Potawatomi language—a tremendously difficult challenge because Potawatomi differs so profoundly from English, both in its grammatical structures and in the worldview they convey. Where English is noun-based, Potawatomi is 70 percent verbs. Moreover, in Potawatomi, both nouns and verbs are classified as either "animate" or "inanimate": "Pronouns, articles, plurals, demonstratives, verbs . . . are all aligned in Potawatomi to provide different ways to speak of the living world and the lifeless one. Different verb forms, different plurals, different everything apply depending on whether what you are speaking of is alive." Kimmerer recounts being stunned when she learned of the word *Puhpowee,* meaning "'the force which causes mushrooms to push up from the earth overnight,'" for "the makers of this word understood a world of being, full of unseen energies that animate everything."[25]

The difficulties of learning Potawatomi were so great that Kimmerer was on the verge of giving up the struggle, until a revelatory moment when she encountered the verb *wiikwegamaa,* which means "to be a bay." She recalls:

> In that moment I could smell the water of the bay, watch it rock against the shore and hear it sift onto the sand. A bay is a noun only if water is *dead.* When *bay* is a noun, it is defined by humans, trapped between its shores and contained by the word. But the verb *wiikegamaa*—to *be* a bay—releases the water from bondage and lets it live. "To be a bay" holds the wonder that, for this moment, the living water has decided to shelter itself between these shores, conversing with cedar roots and a flock of baby mergansers.

This language, she recognizes, is "a mirror for seeing the animacy of the world, the life that pulses through all things." Potawatomi extends the grammar of animacy not only to humans, nonhuman animals, and plants, but also to rocks and "mountains and water and fire and places." In every sentence, its speakers are reminded of their kinship with all that the language establishes as the animate world. Consequently, in teaching her ecology students, Kimmerer takes a bilingual approach, using both "the lexicon of science and the grammar of animacy."[26] She explains: "Although they still have to learn [the plants'] scientific roles and Latin names, I hope I am also teaching them to know the world as a neighborhood of nonhuman residents, to know that, as ecotheologian Thomas Berry has written, 'we must say of the universe that it is a communion of subjects, not a collection of objects.'" Kimmerer makes clear she's not advocating that we all learn Native American languages, but she does urge a transformation in conception and attitude that would allow us all to speak the grammar of animacy from our hearts. Internalizing that grammar, she suggests, "could well be a restraint on our mindless exploitation of land." By enabling us to walk "through a richly inhabited world of Birch people, Bear people, Rock people, beings we think of and therefore speak of as persons worthy of our respect, of inclusion in a peopled world," it would give us access to other perspectives and sources of wisdom.[27]

Western languages such as English do attribute animacy to animals, but not in the fulsome way that Potawatomi's grammar of animacy does; inherent in that grammar is a fundamental equality and respect granted to all the parts of the natural world that possess linguistic animacy, and this nonhierarchical orientation is key to what I wish to convey when I use Kimmerer's phrase "grammar of animacy." The idea implicit in Kimmerer's essay that because language shapes perception and thought, changes in language might generate as well as reflect changes in perception is congenial to many contemporary North American poets with experimentalist leanings; they have derived from constructivism and poststructuralist theory a belief that disruption of linguistic conventions might open the way for fundamental ideological change. Those with environmental concerns seem very like Kimmerer in using the powers of language to initiate what Forrest Gander calls "a reorientation from objectivity to intersubjectivity."[28] It is in this sense that they are engaged in what I am calling—adapting Kimmerer's usage—a grammar of animacy. Joan Retallack, for instance, in "What Is Experimental Poetry & Why Do We Need It?" positions the experimental poet as "radical epistemologist" and language as an "instrument of investigative engagement" that "takes part in the recomposing of contemporary consciousness, contemporary sensibilities." She observes that "the human imagination has always done a brilliant job of occupying the 'empty spaces' of alterity" and proposes that, having inherited "a monodirectional dynamic of voluble us and silent them," poets need to find "a reciprocal alterity" by engaging in the "hard work of acquiring accurate [scientific] knowledge" and combining that with an experimental stance that may free us from our anthropocentric preconceptions. "The very word ecopoetics," Retallack suggests, "may be seen as an experimental instrument that creates a new order of attention to the possibility of a poetics of precise observations and conversational interspecies relations with all contributing to the nature of the form."[29] We might question whether such conversational reciprocity can be achieved, but approaches to language that foster the kind of attitudes Kimmerer locates in a "grammar of animacy" may expand our listening skills and bring us closer to the respectful nonhierarchical connection Retallack (along with such explorers of "indistinction" as Plumwood and Haraway) envisions.

A.RAWLINGS'S *WIDE SLUMBER FOR LEPIDOPTERISTS*

Angela Rawlings is one of those seeking, in Retallack's words, "correctives to 'nature' narratives of segregation, dominance and nostalgia" that fail "to acknowledge 'them' as inextricably intertwined with 'us.'" Her 2006 volume *Wide Slumber for Lepidopterists* enhances its readers' sense of kinship and interdependence with other life forms through, in particular, extraordinary attention to and representations of embodied sensation. There is a relevant passage in Coetzee's *Elizabeth Costello* in which the title character, objecting to the implication in Descartes's assertion "Cogito, ergo sum" that "a living being that does not do what we call thinking is somehow second-class," announces: "To thinking, cogitation, I oppose fullness, embodiedness, the sensation of being—not a consciousness of yourself as a kind of ghostly reasoning machine thinking thoughts, but on the contrary the sensation—a heavily affective sensation—of being a body with limbs that have extension in space, of being alive to the world."[30] *Wide Slumber for Lepidopterists* works to create just that kind of sensation for a body that may be human and/or may be lepidopteral, as the lines between these species often blur. A.rawlings's text approaches a biocentric perspective not just through what it suggests about common somatic experiences shared by humans and nonhumans but in what it does to language itself: by highlighting the physicality of both sounding and reading words, and by making language evidently participate in the processes of the biosphere—processes of predation and consumption, of metamorphosis and decay, of reproduction, development, and evolution. The respectful and reciprocal engagement with other life forms based in, or taking place through, our bodily senses that Costello proposes—and which harmonizes with Kimmerer's, Plumwood's, and Retallack's senses of how we may move forward in addressing the current ecological crisis—is central to a.rawlings's exploration of interspecies identifications.

As I will demonstrate, in *Wide Slumber for Lepidopterists*, a.rawlings does generate species blurrings and "mutual transformations" between *Homo sapiens sapiens* and Lepidoptera, yet she also maintains her readers' respect for the differences between butterflies or moths and humans. As suggested earlier, respect for difference is made easier by her not having chosen to

"think with" one of the charismatic megafauna,[31] by not choosing a species that is large-brained, readily imagined as neotenic, frequently linked
to a particular human trait (as with the "sly fox," say), or even associated
with aspects of animality recognized—and often deplored—in the human.
With the exception of the monarch butterfly, the order Lepidoptera hasn't
much caught the popular environmental imagination, and this, along with
the marked differences between insect and mammalian anatomy, makes
the creatures' alterity easier to respect than might otherwise have been the
case. Conversely, generating a sense of kinship may be correspondingly
difficult, yet through an intense collaging that prevents clear separation of
human from lepidopteral experience, a.rawlings manages it. By revealing
correspondences and overlaps between human experience and admittedly
imagined butterfly experience, a.rawlings challenges some of the ways
in which we Western humans set ourselves apart from other animal life.
Through its densely disjunctive, highly sensory techniques, her work fosters
the appreciation of connectedness and commonalities among life forms that
a grammar of animacy conveys.

   Wide Slumber for Lepidopterists is a dazzlingly metamorphic volume that
manipulates visual images and text to explore embodiment and various
forms of eroticism; the life cycle of Lepidoptera; the practices of lepidopterists (particularly the collection and mounting of specimens); the stages
of sleep; the study of sleep and sleep disorders; and the analysis of literary
texts. According to an interview, it was prompted by a.rawlings wondering:
"If a poet writes poems during sleep, how might a lepidopterist work while
she sleeps? What effect does intimate examination of insects have on long-
term information processing and subconscious behaviour?"[32] It originated,
then, from speculations on human consciousness, but more specifically on
the human as it may be affected by intimacy with the nonhuman.

   A readily visible textual instability is key to this book's challenging version of animacy; this strategy, which asks us to see and experience both
human language and butterflies and moths in unfamiliar ways, is fundamental to the poem's attempt to reposition humans and human epistemology
in relation to the beings humans have categorized as Lepidoptera. Reliance
on visual forms of communication contributes importantly to the book's
foregrounding of sensory experience, an emphasis that suggests how much
human consciousness, at least in sleep, is a somatic phenomenon.[33] Visual
elements are one means by which the work calls upon not just cogitation
but, in Elizabeth Costello's phrase, the sensation of being.

On the cover appears what I have identified as a northern pearly-eye butterfly (*Enodia anthedon*) whose body aligns with the spine of the book so that one set of wings folds over each cover. This is the first of more than a dozen images by Matt Ceolin that appear in the book. Many of these images represent butterflies or moths either dead or in various life stages, inviting attention to lepidopteral bodies. Additionally, there are three images of jars and bottles that would be part of the lepidopterist's equipment, including a stoppered bottle containing a butterfly specimen; one of a book opened to a schematized image of a butterfly with labeled parts; and another that presents a similar schematized drawing without representing a book. These constitute visual reminders that Western humans have typically sought knowledge of Lepidoptera by killing them so that they can be collected, categorized, and either dissected or preserved.

More experimentally, the text is placed in remarkably varied eye-catching visual arrangements. Sometimes these provide a scoring of the breath in the projectivist tradition; sometimes spatial arrangement coupled with variation in font highlights the juxtaposition of different kinds of discourse. But much of this visual variety turns pages into objects of visual art whose meaning—beyond a refusal of standard arrangement—is difficult to discern. Some page designs suggest concrete poetry, as when facing pages resemble open butterfly wings. Thus, on four pages associated with "bruxism," "a parasomnia where the sleeper grinds or clenches her teeth,"[34] near mirrorings of text create a winglike design made of boldface words, and of clusters of letters with isolated consonants scattered at the edges (fig. 3). It's appropriate to "bruxism" that these are mostly the "dental" consonants t, d, n, l, made with the tongue against the teeth. The words on the left-hand pages are fragments of English, mostly nouns and adjectives; on the right are disjunct parts of Latin names for species of moths or butterflies.

These winglike textual designs might be considered a crude example of a.rawlings using language as bioform, making pages into butterflies—though we might equally well read this as highlighting the textually mediated character of our knowledge of butterflies, the distance between representation and the living animal. In a more compelling instance of displaying language as part of the biosphere, a tightly curled caterpillar of text gradually uncurls and moves to the right over a few pages (figs. 4 and 5). In the process its letters modulate from reading "count by slumber" to "faint bystander" to "pant by number" to "cunt by umber" (that last term evoking the umber moths) to—when the text is flat—"ti ur tor foknur" (where

Figure 3. Text in butterfly pattern from a.rawlings, *Wide Slumber for Lepidopterists*, 68–69. (By Angela Rawlings; courtesy of Angela Rawlings and Coach House Books)

Hold specimen by thorax, and force insect pin
through middle of body between wings.
Pin specimen to mounting board.

Figure 4. Curled text from a.rawlings, *Wide Slumber for Lepidopterists,* 25. (By Angela Rawlings; courtesy of Angela Rawlings and Coach House Books)

Pin wings near large veins to avoid tears.
Place paper over wings to prevent curling while drying.

Figure 5. Text uncurling from a.rawlings, *Wide Slumber for Lepidopterists,* 27. (By Angela Rawlings; courtesy of Angela Rawlings and Coach House Books)

"tor" as anagrammatic "rot" seems potentially significant) so that this textual creature doesn't just crawl, it *develops* in the process of its own motion through space and time. Elsewhere, letters progressively vanish from the text, as if eaten out, leaving tattered remnants of words, again giving material language a kind of organic life as it participates in processual change. Retallack in her essay adapts John Cage's thinking to propose "adopting nature's manner of operations" as one experimental ecopoetic strategy, and the practices I have just described can be understood as linguistic versions of doing just that.[35] Even when analogs to biological processes are less clear, as when recognizable words are replaced by illegible clusters of letters that may or may not be anagrammatically decipherable, language in this book tends to be an unstable, rapidly evolving material—and the visual qualities of this text contribute crucially to that animation.

Like the visual elements, sounds also enrich the sensory quality of *Wide Slumber for Lepidopterists.* For instance, in sounding those dental consonants just mentioned, the reader is forced to be more aware of tongue and teeth than in usual reading experiences. A.rawlings often employs conventional techniques like alliteration and assonance in ways that heighten readers' consciousness of their own embodiment. In her hands, even such traditional poetic devices serve to defamiliarize human somatic experience and to blur it with that of the moth or butterfly. A brief example of such aural density appears in the largely monosyllabic lines: "wood nymphs spin and hang

crude cocoons // we hold our slow high flight" (WS 15). Here's a more
extended example, the lower half of an unbroken page:

<pre>
        our wings   our breath
      heavy as   wails, our   wet
    soul, sail, th   gall of th 'th,' th 'of' of th 'of' or th 'th,' th
      ways lips hug proboscis   th vulva, yes, th vulva
  water is fire   protrusion   velour
                      penetration   vellum
                chrysalistalization dark valium
                   row of fine-lipped, of
              up   tubular, a
              thin   (WS 65)
</pre>

Clearly, the echoing and modulating sounds—for instance, of proboscis,
protrusion, and penetration (which could be read downward in immediate
succession), or of vulva, velour, vellum, and valium—give these lines a sensual richness on the tongue. But beyond that, partly through the progression
and dissolution of sound patterns as well as through its visual design, the
passage enacts a shift from what seems a clear distinction between species—
"our wings" (which belong to butterflies and not humans) on the left-hand
side of the page, "our breath" (produced by humans and not butterflies) on
the right-hand side—to a confusion of bodies. Either breath or wings could
be heavy and wet, and both have associations with the soul (as the soul
passes, or flies, from the mortal body with its last breath)—although a term
like "wails" designates sounds not, to our knowledge, made by insects. The
line of "of"s and "th"s could sound like either panting breath or the movement of air with a fluttering of wings. The insect's alliteratively stressed
protruding proboscis penetrates flowers, but the human vulva might also
be the entryway of penetration, while the lips here seem human as well,
whether associated with the mouth or with female genitalia. Perhaps these
lines suggest an analogy between the butterfly's pleasure in feeding and the
human male's pleasure in sexual penetration. Perhaps they point to commonalities between the objectified position of the female in a patriarchal
order and that of the butterfly in an anthropocentric one. Going further
in their imagining, perhaps these lines attempt to bring alive for us the experience of an insect feeding, sticking that thin proboscis up the velvety
softness of a tubular flower.[36] A.rawlings creates a first-person plural that is

not appropriative but inclusive, to borrow Retallack's useful distinction; this "we" acknowledges a commonality of embodiment, hunger, and desire but within a context of also recognizing mutual alterity. Flying remains fundamentally different from breathing, and vice versa.

The important role sound plays in this poem's blurring of the bodies and bodily experiences of butterflies or moths and humans is evident from the book's opening pages. The first four pages of verbal text (that is, the pages that follow immediately after the dedication "To Northern Ontario," a page of translucent vellum, and one with a small drawing of a northern pearly-eye), contain only the phrase "a hoosh a ha," which is repeated different numbers of times and arranged differently on each page to map varying rhythms and increasing speeds with which the phrase is articulated. Calling those syllables a "phrase" is misleading, since they seem closer to a sounded breath or breaths, inhalations and exhalations. A.rawlings's 2007 performance of those pages (designated "Prologue") on the PennSound website is eerily ambiguous in its combination of human and inhuman elements.[37] While her voice dominates, one hears multiple voices, male as well as female, and the sounds, including some squeaks, don't register as necessarily human.[38] "A hoosh a ha" might well mimic the sounds butterfly or moth wings make as they move through the air, as perceived by hearing organs finely tuned enough to register their being raised and lowered. (As hearing organs, Lepidoptera have tympanal membranes on their wings or abdomens. They are sensitive to sounds produced by predators—birds in the case of butterflies, which are active in the day, and bats in the case of moths, which tend to be nocturnal. They are also sensitive to vibrations in the plant substrate and may communicate with one another or with other species through such vibrations.) In a.rawlings's recorded reading, those pages assume an eroticized character, as if the being "hoosh"ing were approaching and then reaching orgasm before subsiding into stillness. Perhaps, though, one could imagine the sounds to register the gathering of more and more butterflies, who, once assembled, then come to rest. The northern pearly-eye does gather in large groups, particularly in the cooler, northwestern-most portion of its range.

We have seen that the visual and aural elements of *Wide Slumber for Lepidopterists* require a degree of sensual and somatic involvement unusual even in poetry, the literary genre in which the material qualities of language are usually thought to play the largest part. This emphasis on embodied experience draws readers toward aspects of our being we most evidently share with nonhuman animals (or sometimes plants, suggested, for instance, by reference to the scent of honeysuckles as "honeysuckle sweat") and away from the rational cognitive functions traditionally thought to distinguish the human. We have seen, too, that the insistently metamorphic character a.rawlings gives to both sounded words or letters and their visual arrangement contributes to her unsettling of conventional distinctions between human and nonhuman species and perhaps even—in giving an unusual life to letters—between the biotic and nonbiotic realms.

Metamorphosis, particularly multistaged metamorphosis, also provides the basis for the book's structure, and exploring this structurally embedded thematic further will allow me to more fully develop my argument about the poem's creation of a grammar of animacy. The book has six sections, in each of which a lepidopteral life stage is explicitly linked with a stage of human sleep or a category of sleep disturbance—for instance, the first section is "EGG - INSOMNIA," the next "EGG, LARVA - DYSSOMNIA," the third "LARVA - NREM," and so forth. Each page announcing a new stage also has on it a large-font typographic symbol or combination of symbols (e.g., {#} or ~ or ~}); one effect of these is to foster more inclusive thinking about languages by signaling that communicative systems need not involve words. Four of the poem's sections contain pages where the name of a sleep stage or disorder—"sleep spindles," say, or "somnambulism"—appears in a small capitalized font on the lower outside corner by the page number. According to the description on the book's back cover, "sleep is read here through the life cycle of a moth." However, that does not accord with my readerly experience: the book does not seem to me to be more about sleep than it is about moth life. The two are thoroughly intertwined so that the book is about both, and also about their construction in language and their examination by science. After I shared with Angela Rawlings an earlier reading that made these claims, she responded, "Yes, I approved the back-cover copy. However, I thought I'd mention that I am in agreement with your experience of the book. My experience writing it was that there was no intended hierarchy of one subject over another. Indeed, it could be said that sleep is read through the moth's life cycle, but the inverse is equally valid—the moth's life cycle can be read through sleep."[39] Sleep seems to be where humans come closest to the kind of metamorphosis butterflies undergo: when we sleep, without our choice our brains and bodies enter distinct states with different modes of experience or consciousness. The book's structure, then, emphasizes the analogous ways in which humans

and butterflies or moths undergo change through successive bodily transformations not subject to cognitive control.

The experience of reading *Wide Slumber for Lepidopterists,* while certainly
fascinating, is unsettling and at times disturbing as well. The back cover
identifies the book as "an erotic nightmarescape." That disturbance is pro-
voked partly by the book's content—horrifying evocations of moths caught
in one's throat, for instance—which is what the anonymous blurber seems
to have in mind. But it is also produced by the unpredictable ways "words
breed" (*WS* 81) suggesting uncontrolled genetic modifications. More generally, discomfort arises because the reader's orientation is so precarious, and
any sense of cognitive mastery so ephemeral.[40] Beginning with the very first
lines after the (ah hoosh a ha) prologue, the reader has to accept or in some
way accommodate a condition like the illogic of dream narrative. Here are
those opening lines:

> We descend on a field by a lake. *a hoosh* The lupin, sleep, the fog. *a ha* Fire-
> flies, silent moths. We bury our legs in sand. Sound through the sand is
> dormant. We desire sleep to enter, virginal.
>
> We stretch our feelers toward the warm body. *a a* Slowly, hands fog-damp
> spin plants, form air-filled hollows, breath cocooned, fur soft and blurred,
> heavy even heavenly. *hoosh* Soft like quiet. *ha*
>
> Soft like we quiver.   (*WS* 14)

The first-personal plural speaker might well, at least initially, be lepidopteral,
but the perspective seems ambiguously human as well. Perhaps the writing
moves between the two species' experiences, perhaps it joins them, but certainly any impulse in the reader to separate human neatly from Lepidoptera
is thwarted. Once the reader relinquishes the quest for categorization, she
or he can appreciate that whether the legs in sand or the desire for sleep
belong to one species or both, the bodies with hands and/or feelers occupy
the same dreamily fog-filled field and possess a similar soft vulnerability.
They share not only the natural environment of this summer evening in (if
the dedication locates the work) northern Ontario but also a condition of
desire for a change of somatic state that involves both sleep and sexualized
bodily contact.

Similarly, the page that follows begins with the clearly human action and
predominantly human perspective of "Slow light touch of hand on wing,
scales brush off like butterfly kisses" (the anthropomorphizing attribution

of kissing to butterflies, which imagines the act would feel like brushing one's eye lashes against another's skin) but shortly, when "we tongue our shell, our conch," "we" seems to speak also for larvae eating the eggshells from which they emerge and then acquiring nutrition from plants with "tongue buried deep in the suckle the honey" (WS 15). The we subsequently becomes even more intensely indeterminate with the eroticized language that accompanies "the story's arousal":

> we are taut while we thrust against the inner wall. Sleep is bruised or screams or none comes but we desire, we feel the full hot flesh of our wing swipe grass, scrape sand, we push ourselves out of ourselves, into our sound our hand our sweet wet hot our path, mourn, rake, master or muster. Glisten swell come and the story's arousal, twenty eyes unblink when the sun's awake and even when it's not the brain speaks, screams, swells

> and huge battened eyes of a hundred hungry mouths, no moths, wait this will move.   (WS 16–17)

As the first-person plural pronoun gathers in the reader as well, s/he is drawn into an experience that seems both the human progress toward the "sweet hot full the electricity" of orgasm and the compound-eyed moth's effortful emergence from an earlier stage of itself, the pupa.

If we readers cannot distinguish human from butterfly desire or human from butterfly arousal here, and if we have to acknowledge that both are present, then we can no longer take up the hierarchical, anthropocentric vantage offered by a language that devalues the nonhuman. If, prompted by this dense weave of words—the text's grammar of animacy—we have imaginatively entered a state where human and lepidopteral experiences, equally vibrant and equally defamiliarized, interpenetrate without our losing awareness that significant differences exist between insects and mammals, we may be approaching Kimmerer's vision of the world as a "communion of subjects." This is a remarkable achievement and one likely to enhance readers' sense of Lepidoptera as creatures with their own intentions and desires, keenly responsive to their environments; it is also likely to stimulate curiosity about the entanglement of human and lepidopteral lives (or extinctions).

Of the three poets discussed in this chapter, a.rawlings goes the furthest in developing somatic commonalities between humans and nonhuman species. The sensory experiences she invokes often involve primal activities such as eating or sex or moving between involuntary stages of being, and they often assume a violent cast. Consequently, she may risk playing into some very old, derogatory thinking about animality. It's hardly news that humans and nonhuman animals have sexual drives in common; one could even see the work, particularly through its violence, as reinforcing traditional, problematic linkages of the animal with humans' "lower" functions. This lends special importance to the work's treatment of language—a "higher" activity that some view as distinguishing the human—particularly its rendering of language as thoroughly metamorphic and material. A.rawlings's reinforcement of how much we humans *are* our bodies even in such an "elevated" trait as our ability to invent sign systems, moreover, fosters recognition of—to recall Frederick Buell's phrase—embodied embeddedness in ecosystems. In most of this volume, a.rawlings's presentations are too mobile, too multifaceted and multiperspectival, to allow any sense of the human apart from the dense linguistic environments of animacy she creates—environments in which plant, human, and nonhuman animal bodies as well as alphabetic ones join, divide, caress, tear, devour, pin, penetrate, entangle, and transform.

In its representation of the work of lepidopterists, however, the book presents a contrasting model of using language and the intellect that substitutes familiar dualisms for the inclusive grammar of animacy. Beginning in the EGG, LARVA - DYSSOMNIA section, a.rawlings incorporates what appear to be selections from a set of instructions for those seeking the epistemological control that is expressed in tidy taxonomies. Inserted in documentary fashion are instructions for how to *"collect, kill, and mount specimen[s]"* (*WS* 23), such as:

> *Manipulate wings simultaneously to avoid twisting body.*
> *Pin wings to mounting board.*
> . . .
> *Pin wings near large veins to avoid tears.*
> *Place paper over wings to prevent curling while drying.*   (*WS* 26–27)

or

> *Keep mounted specimen in low-moisture condition to prevent mould.*
> *Avoid direct sunlight to prevent fading.*
> *Store in tightly closed box with insecticide to prevent dermestid beetle larvae and book lice from feeding on body parts.*   (*WS* 29)

These passages associate traditional methods of scientific investigation with a fixing that is counter to the processes of life and of ecology; not only do those collecting specimens kill the creatures they study, but they deliberately remove the bodies from the cycles of decay and nourishment in which they would otherwise participate. A.rawlings gives immediacy to these implied, familiar judgments of scientific "objectivity" by implicating the reader in analogous processes. Poetry critics, the text warns us, can enact a similar destruction. Parallel to those who *"Pinch thorax between thumb and forefinger. / Slide specimen into envelope; store in box with insecticide"* (WS 23) are those who wish to *"Collect, sort and frame text . . . Pinch meaning between morpheme and phoneme . . . Slide meaning into envelope; store in box with semanticide"* (WS 42). In presenting parallel critiques of literary study and the science of lepidoptery, a.rawlings puts at least certain forms of intellectual activity—forms in which the reader may have participated—at odds with the pleasure in Costello's "sensation of being."

On the facing page, which has as its sleep term in the bottom corner "restoration," a.rawlings offers a set of italicized instructions that return us to the alternative approach taken by the bulk of her poem. Notably, though perhaps not murderous, these instructions have their own violence. They involve forcefully manipulating the text so that it becomes an active medium that does things, or they involve doing things to the text that defamiliarize and reveal it more truly:

Force a pen through the body of the text.

Translate texts simultaneously to twist meaning. Pen words on bed frame.
Pen anagrams on mirror.

Pin words near vowels to avoid tears. Place paper over words to curl while drying.
Watch text uncurl dusk.

Place punctuation under lamp to increase integrity. (WS 43)

(*Tears* as in torn wings on the left-hand page may become wept *tears* on the right—an example of the text's prevalent polysemy.) It would be reductive, then, to suggest that the experimental writer's activities are positioned in simple opposition to those of the scientist—or literary critic—but the poet clearly is critical of taxonomic science's insistence on fixed and distinct categories. One way to understand the late pages that list fragmented Latin names for butterflies, or the pages that turn lists of lepidopteral pupae or

larvae into a kind of rhythmic chant—for example, "tiliae larva nd smer-
inthus ocellata larva nd hemaris fuciformis larva nd cerura vinula larva nd
notodonta dromedaries larva nd ptildontella cucullina larva" (WS 86)—is
to see a.rawlings forcing her pen through the body of lepidoperists' foun-
dational text, that of Linnaean classification according to classes, orders,
genera, and species. In a similar gesture, she performs transformative twists
on the line "Welcome to the Centre for Sleep and Dream Studies," gnawing
away at its words to reveal other possibilities they contain: "Welcome to th
// Enter. Sleep nd ream. elcm" (WS 24). Opposing herself to the dissective
activity of much science, but not denying the destructive aspects of her own
practices, a.rawlings uses scientific terms as material for productive verbal
and conceptual metamorphosis. This activity has a feminist dimension as
well: there are clear suggestions in the text that women and their bodies are
labeled, collected, violently pinned, and in several senses mounted ("does
th vahlvā speak / how does th vulvaw speak" the text asks [WS 62], evoking
Gayatri Spivak's subaltern). Women are another Other whom the book
challenges us to perceive more fully and more fluidly. The text's emphasis
remains nonetheless on tapping—through the altered states of dream, of
sexual arousal, perhaps of drugged consciousness and also through play
with several languages and bodies of knowledge—kinds of somatically
based understanding that would be available, albeit somewhat differently,
to both men and women. Wide Slumber models using that somatic knowledge to experience the animal other from an inevitably incomplete but still
radical within-ness that also gives voice to specifics of difference.

At the beginning of the "LARVA, PUPA - REM" section of Wide Slumber
is a striking pair of facing pages that combine visual images with brief text.
On the left "so we dream the same" appears above a sharp image of the
left wings of a northern pearly-eye, the other half of its body dissolving in
a watery wash; on the right an image of a specimen trapped in a stoppered
killing bottle appears above the line "do we dream the same" (WS 50–51;
fig. 6). Clearly, when human dreams are of power and domination, they
differ chillingly from those of butterflies. On a later page, a similar pattern
repeats: "do we have plans for them" appears above an image of a dead
moth on its back, and below in bold, "no we have plans for us" (WS 79;
fig. 7). The crucial replacement of "them" with "us" enacts the shift from
standard English to a grammar of animacy like that offered by Potawatomi
or by much of Wide Slumber for Lepidopterists. In recognizing interspecies
community, we have to recognize a "we" that includes both human and

so we dream the same

do we dream the same

Figure 6. Pages with digitally altered photographs of a butterfly and a butterfly in a bottle from a.rawlings, *Wide Slumber for Lepidopterists*, 50–51. (Text by Angela Rawlings, illustrations by Matt Ceolin; courtesy of Angela Rawlings, Matt Ceolin, and Coach House Books)

do we have plans for them

no we have plans for us

Figure 7. Page with digitally altered photograph of a moth from a.rawlings, *Wide Slumber for Lepidopterists*, 79. (Text by Angela Rawlings, illustration by Matt Ceolin; courtesy of Angela Rawlings, Matt Ceolin, and Coach House Books)

nonhuman others, and face that our destruction of the world around us constitutes our own destruction as well.

Imaginative and linguistic play that defamiliarizes human experience and its representation and in the process expands our thinking to include an interspecies "we" is only that—imaginative and linguistic play. Without having to make claims of authenticity for her modeling of cross-species communication, a.rawlings in *Wide Slumber* gives readers valuable practice in a kind of imaginative identification that resituates the human, opening conceptual channels that may yield less destructive plans for all kinds of species, including our own. Applying such perspectives beyond the textual and imaginative realms will demand interdisciplinary collaboration; it will depend on challenging and expanding but not shutting off rational faculties. *Wide Slumber* suggests this will require changing our scientific aims and practices, and also changing the ways of thinking embedded in our language, which grants nonhumans only a reductive, non-egalitarian animacy.

JODY GLADDING'S *TRANSLATIONS FROM BARK BEETLE*

The beetle larvae that carve channels in the soft inner bark of trees are white grublike creatures, approximately the size of a cooked grain of rice. In Western cultures, these are barely acknowledged as life forms and, whether in larval or adult beetle form, register mainly as repulsive pests. Yet Jody Gladding approaches their carvings as poems in a language worthy of translation, thereby cultivating a grammar of animacy. No doubt some readers would dismiss this translation as nothing more than a game, an over-the-top device. But any translation involves a bold venture across conceptual and perceptual gaps. There are significant impediments to translating with full accuracy between English, a Germanic language, and French, a Romance language, and greater ones in translating between Potowatomi and English or French. Much is necessarily missed, changed, or lost in translation. The project of translating from an animal language into a human one might be entered into without frivolousness as an exercise presenting the same challenges in considerably exaggerated form. Gladding earns her living as a translator from French to English; her website lists thirty books she has translated, mostly for prestigious university presses such as Columbia, Yale, Princeton, and Notre Dame (including books by such noted intellectuals as Alain Badiou and Julia Kristeva), along with some for a small press that publishes on Eastern religions and alternative health practices. While her title, *Translations from Bark Beetle: Poems,* may allude playfully to those other books she produces—and indeed, much about the book is playful—she also appears to invest herself seriously in the figure of translating a beetle language recorded in the wood that beetles inhabit.

The volume contains half a dozen of these bark beetle poems, each accompanied by a rubbing Gladding did of the beetle engraving she is working from, usually arranged as facing-page translations would be. (Numerous other poems in the volume share the material and visual emphasis of this work; originally written literally as well as figuratively "on" stones, feathers, eggs, a mobile, even on paper strips woven through the author's liver scan; photos of the originals for these appear at the back of the book as "illustrations.") The cover looks like a yellowed old leather-framed museum exhibit; in the center appears a piece of wood displaying "Larval galleries"; on the left is an adult specimen of the American elm bark beetle with its Latin name and institutional source (Ward's Natural Science Establishment, Inc. / Rochester, N.Y.) typed below its identification in English, and on the right a specimen of the European elm bark beetle, also given its Latin as well as English name and the same source. As Gladding has commented, the cover makes the book (which, like a.rawlings's, is printed in landscape orientation) look like a box of specimens one is opening, while the typeface on the cover and throughout the book imitates old typewriting, creating the impression of "provisional" field notes.[41] I take this visual information as suggesting seriousness, but not finality or certainty, about both translation and scientific understanding, while presenting the volume as an assemblage of curiosities.

The bark beetle poems demonstrate the poet's desire to be informed about and imaginatively aware of the physical conditions in which these insects leave their records in tree bark. After the adult beetles have chewed through the bark, mated, and deposited eggs within it, for a period of about six to eight weeks each larva chews its own path through the bark, producing a tunnel that usually widens as the larva grows—doing so at the same time that other larvae are carving their own tunnels. Scientists speak of these tunnel complexes as galleries, and several species of bark beetle are named engraver beetles, so Gladding's sense of these beings as artists has been anticipated by the language entomologists provided. Asked by an interviewer how bark beetle poems relate to the lives of the beetles, she replied: "My feeling is that they are love poems. Like many of our poems, they speak of longing. It takes many bark beetles, developing through many stages of their lives, to complete a bark beetle poem. Often they are working parallel to one another, making lines that never cross, though they can sense one another's vibrations through the wood."[42] Her understanding draws on scientific knowledge of vibrational communication within and between species through the substrate of the host tree, to which she adds perception of an emotional dynamic. Because these engravings are a communal product resulting from the labor of multiple beetles and larvae, it makes sense that Gladding posits a pronoun form, indicated by •, that "is used for first and second person in singular, plural, and all cases." She translates into conventional English grammar but leaves the • that invites us to hear "•' ve" as "I/we/you have," "m•" as "me/us/you." "yo•" as "you/me/us."

To demonstrate, here's the first bark beetle poem in the collection, part 1 of "Spending Most of Their Time in Galleries, Adults Come into the Open on Warm Sunny Days: Translations from Bark Beetle":

> •'ve learned through wood
> yo• can only travel in one direction
>   but turn again with m• there love
>   sap in the chamber
>   red the friable
>   taste of yo• •'ve learned
>   there are other ways in the wood's
>   growing
>   if not for m•—
>   find hollow
>   find spell   (*TBB* 6)

The opening might be read "We've learned through wood / we can only travel in one direction / but turn again with us" or "You've learned through wood / you can only travel in one direction / but turn again with us" (and so on), though Gladding has given preference to the singular speaker conventional to English-language love poems. Her translation, that is, minimizes the strangeness of the "foreign" language, as is the usual aim of translation, while her dots keep in view that the beetles' language reflects a much more fluid and capacious sense of self or speaker than ours.

In these poems, there is no attempt like a.rawlings made to merge animal and human experience, but rendering animal experience in human language itself challenges the conventional animal/human divide, particularly when emotions like love are attributed to the nonhumans. Does this result in an anthropomorphism that impedes the recognition of the otherness of this communicative being? Several of Gladding's strategies seem designed to avoid that. First, the perspective of the beetles in her poems diverges notably from a human perspective. Take, for instance, "Engraver Beetle Cycle," which contains the lines "m•y sweet m•y rolled / m•y x as in xylem / *cambrial*   *phloem*   *corridor*" (*TBB* 8). (The phloem is the layer of the bark that conducts nutrients downward from the leaves, while the xylem transports water and nutrients from the roots in the soil.) Calling another beetle or larva or a collection thereof "my/your/our x as in xylem" is analogous to a human addressing the beloved as "my H as in honey" or "my H as in home," or "my L as in love nest," since true bark beetles breed and feed in the phloem and outer xylem of the tree. But we humans would not tell others we care for that they are our xylem. The adjective "cambrial" is, as far as I can determine, a neologism: it might bring to mind the cambium tissue layer located between the xylem and the phloem; it may reference the urban slang usage of "cambria" to refer to a blonde bombshell; but its primary evocation here is of the Cambria Forest in California, a rare Monterey pine forest that has been devastated by a bark beetle infestation.[43] For humans, the adjective "cambrial" might characterize an environmental disaster, but for a bark beetle it would presumably denote a happy abundance of food and sociality; human and beetle perspectives diverge radically. This poem ends abruptly midphrase: "there are rumors of flight and fungi / (of light and lying) / the death of a tree's"; we can't determine whether that last apostrophe signals a contraction for "tree is" or a possessive. If the former, we might imagine completing the phrase, "the death of a tree's imminent"; if the latter, perhaps the speaker is anticipating the end not of a tree but of the colony of tubular ("rolled") pupal beetles who inhabit the tree and are nearing their adult flights out of the tree into sunlight and on to the next host tree. Bark beetles are often vectors for fungi that can kill trees, as is the case with Dutch elm disease, but fungi can also be threats to the beetles themselves, and perhaps that is how they function in these lines. In any case, to interpret what is going on in this poem, the human reader has to entertain decidedly unfamiliar perspectives.

The second strategy I see Gladding employing to counter a reductive anthropocentrism involves linguistic inventions, as already observed with "cambrial." Like a.rawlings, Gladding playfully highlights the animacy within language itself (an extension beyond Kimmerer's concerns), pointing to its mobility and continual evolution. But in addition, her manipulations of conventional wording also convey a difference in the language of the nonhuman other. Particularly in the series of three "Bark Beetle Fragments in Regional Dialects," which translate engravings of different beetle species—an acknowledgment of the uniqueness of the gallery pattern carved by each species—Gladding modifies familiar English phrases to mark the distinctive perspective of beetles. "Southwestern," for instance, which laments the way strip malls have ruined the beetles' quiet, begins "through think on thin," which torques the English "through thick and thin." The poem continues: "through think on thin   commercial / success going under / strip malls" (*TBB* 61); to paraphrase this simply as "through thinking on the thin commercial success of failing strip malls" seems insufficient since "through think on thin" invites contemplation of what thinness and thickness would mean within the wood-centered world of a beetle. Because bark has both inner and outer layers, the meaning of thin bark becomes potentially complex. Thicker bark would offer more resistance to the adult beetles tunneling into the tree; so thin bark means easier home-making. But thin outer bark (the rhytidome) might also mean less protection of beetles inside the bark from predators such as woodpeckers. Thin inner bark (phloem), might mean less nourishment available to beetles, though it also might mean fewer or less generative ducts producing resin that, in addition to healing the wounds beetles cause, can trap beetles. "Through think on thin" certainly supposes that beetles engage in thinking, and it may suggest a multifaceted meditation on what are for beetles beneficial and detrimen-

```
Bark Beetle Fragments in Regional Dialects

1     Southwestern


      through think on thin                      commercial
               success going under
                    strip malls                      they've ruined
                                           m•y quiet        cul-de-sac
          whole up
```

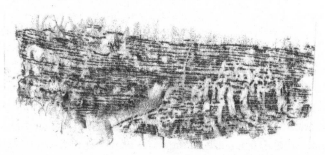

Figure 8. Bark beetle rubbing and poem from Jody Gladding, *Translations from Bark Beetle*, 61. (By Jody Gladding; courtesy of Milkweed Editions; from *Translations from Bark Beetle* [Minneapolis: Milkweed Editions, 2015]; © 2015 by Jody Gladding; milkweed.org)

tal environmental conditions. The poem's final line is "whole up," which plays on "hole up"—something beetles do for much of their life cycle—but reminds readers of the communal circumstances of beetle life in which it takes many individuals to make a whole poem or engraving. Perhaps, too, "whole up" is a command for all the engravers to turn their tunnels upward; Gladding's rubbing does reveal a series of vertical tunnels on the right side of the piece of bark (fig. 8).

Another poem demonstrating this torquing of English in ways that highlight beetle-specific perspectives is the "Red Turpentine Beetle (Northeastern)" dialect poem, based on a rubbing in which the tunnels are mostly parallel and relatively straight vertical lines:

lightivore

would have cut stars

but of

more than •

could chew

a fibrous skyful

black holes
all no through

but yes!   horizon   up against   basal
             lines   cleanly   spit
         way clear   !
             this is o•r boredom of heaven   (*TBB* 63)

This poem presents an even more speculative beetle or collectivity of beetles, one imagining an other who eats not bark but light—though the epistemically located beetle speaker naturally imagines hunks of sky as "fibrous." The poem hints at a number of puns—bit off more than you / we / I could chew, gnaw through, cleanly split—and again each variation points toward bark beetle behavior and surroundings. Most delightful is the final celebratory line about our boredom of heaven, where boredom (boredome?) seems to refer positively to the action of boring through wood, stars, or sky itself.

However much fun Gladding is having as her translations' grammar of animacy imaginatively registers a rich lifeworld for bark beetles (as well as the lively possibilities within human language), those translations always convey an ample multidimensionality in the creatures' otherness. One of the book's poems that is based not on a bark beetle engraving but on an aphorism from the poet Ralph Angel—"Art is an act of violence against the violent silence"—may capture the ethics of this project. For in important ways, Western humanity's failure to listen to earth others and to recognize the full animacy and communicative power of the nonhuman world has produced a violent silence. Gladding's lyrical elaboration of Angel's statement ends, "the most beautiful word / is / trespass" (*TBB* 45). Creating these trans-species translations is a bold and perhaps even violent trespass that contributes to the breaking of that violent silence.

JONATHAN SKINNER LISTENING IN TO BIRDSONG

The kinds of poems Jonathan Skinner has written concerning birds include straightforward descriptions of birds he observes, transcriptions of the sounds of various bird calls, and recently a delightful series of poems he calls "warblers" composed about different species in accordance with particular constraints about sound and content that Skinner established. Warblers may be written only about a bird species the poet has actually seen; each poem must translate the rhythms and pitches of that bird's song, note something about its coloring, attend to its habitat and habits, mention a distant place "since warblers link humans across hemispheres," include words from poets writing in both North and South America, and include some nonsense in acknowledgment that "warblers are restless, hard to see, and give you a crick in the neck."[44] Skinner's 2011 collection *Birds of Tifft* includes constraint-free poems that simply log the birds and other animals he has seen while walking in the Tifft Nature Preserve, or record field notes in a manner reminiscent of some of Gary Snyder's poetry. Tifft is an urban "preserve" in Buffalo, New York, part of it on the city's remediated former refuse dump, so that the environment recorded includes highway traffic, power lines, city lights, and industrial buildings; in this volume depicting one version of contemporary nature, Skinner observes native and invasive plants, beavers, rabbits, an overpopulation of deer, and black and white fishermen, along with birds of various habitats, shapes, and colors.[45] In all these works, his project is consciously an ethical one: "Poetry might help us to use, study, and deploy animal morphologies in ways that hope to better, rather than merely exploit, the human relation with such life forms, if not to improve the welfare of the species themselves."[46]

The poems I'll consider here, where my focus is on animal expression and grammars of animacy, are not-yet-collected works in which he focuses particularly on developing responses to birdsongs he has recorded. Despite the familiarity of designating extended bird vocalizations as songs, Skinner's attention to birdsong in his lyrics is a reminder that "we bring metaphors from the arts of music and poetry to complement our limited scientific understanding of the intricacies of animal communication." The poems are written with a consciousness of "ongoing biocide" and the current "human war on other species," but, like most of his other poems about birds and wildlife, rarely address either directly. Skinner's hope is that these "poetry animals" will "allow foreign organizations into the sphere of our nervous system."[47]

Although not written according to specific constraints like his "warblers," works like "Blackbird Stanzas" should also be understood as proceduralist because they are based on both audio recordings and spectrograms of birdsongs—in this case, the song of a particular type of thrush. Skinner explains his understanding of the resources provided by procedural constraints as follows: "Procedural writing can initiate a system of feedback loops between constraint and the poem-in-process, a system that might involve multiple authors, and that models an organism's relationship to environment. Just as constraints limit and challenge authorial agency, a procedure allows a site to determine the writing in ways less filtered through the subject, inviting more distributed agency."[48] Distributed agency—like Jane Bennett's related notion of distributive agency—moves toward Retallack's reciprocal alterity and an interactive sense of dynamic collective agency or authorship. Skinner is particularly interested in allowing into poems more of their sonic environments, and in the works he's calling poetry animals, he's interested particularly in the intersection between sound or prosody and "animal vocalizations."[49] This interest led him to conduct interviews with people working in the Bioacoustics Research Program and the Macaulay Library of Natural Sounds at the Cornell Lab of Ornithology, selections from which appear in his fascinating hour-long podcast, "Animal Transcriptions." In that podcast, which includes amazing animal sounds as well as commentary by professionals, one learns that slowing birdsong brings it closer to what birds hear because their (internal) ears have much better temporal resolution than human ears, while spectrograms can reveal to the human eye sounds and sound patterns that cannot be detected by human ears. By using technologically altered vocalizations as constraints, Skinner attempts with his poems to enhance our limited sensory equipment in ways that bring us closer to kinds of awareness that birds—along with other species that gather information from birdsongs and calls—possess.

Skinner has described his "Blackbird Stanzas" as "lyrics to a performance, a translation or transcript of eleven vocalizations of a European Blackbird" that he recorded; he slowed the recordings and produced spectrograms from them "to reveal the distinctive parts of each vocalization, modeling variety, density and rhythm for the five to eight lines of each stanza." He derived the words for this series from the above-mentioned interviews; many of them can be heard in context on the podcast. When he performs, he uses the recording as the sound track for his "attempt to vocalize, karaoke style, the bird's song." Ideally, he would also move visibly through the spectrogram as he "sings," but he doesn't have access to technology that would animate the spectrograms. His statement of process concludes: "If in the interviews and associated poems I listen to listening, the performance of 'Blackbird Stanzas' listens in to listening to listen."[50] That is to say, in conducting the interviews and in composing the poems derived from their text, he listens to people who spend their working hours listening to animal sounds (these include not only birdsongs but the sounds produced, for instance, by whales and elephants, along with others in the animals' acoustic habitats); in so doing, he listens to listening. When performing those words to the slowed birdsong, he adds another level of listening, which I understand to be listening to—and adjusting—the immediate interactions between his vocalization and the birdsong his words perform. He is, then, trying to enrich readers' appreciation of the elaborate construction of bird calls and songs with their multiple communicative functions and to generate an aural expression of his own—his grammar of animacy—that may stretch conventional syntax and usage to allow for more attentive response to bird vocalization. The series is an ecopoetic extension of Stevens's "Thirteen Ways of Looking at a Blackbird"—not looking at, but attempting to listen in or listen from within.[51]

The "Blackbird Stanzas" are composed in short, usually disjointed lines, but if one keeps in mind the text's derivation from discussions of animal sound and its recording (and even more helpfully, if one listens to Skinner's podcast), cohesive concerns emerge. The first of the lyrics, for instance, emphasizes the extraordinary power of these recordings and the transformative experience they offer:

> the whole woods
>> connected
>> naturally plucked
>>> roar
>> pulling us into thin air
> whether we like it or not

Sound recordings enable one to hear the acoustics of an entire habitat (audio recordings readily reveal to the experienced listener the level of biodiversity in the vicinity). The listener, both connected to that integrated ecosystem and hearing its connectivity, is inevitably transported into the airy realm of both sound waves and bird life.

As another example, the third stanza emphasizes the recovery, discovery, or analysis through sound recording of what is otherwise ineffable or lost:

> they can resolve
>> degauss   what
>> animals   cough up
> night flights
>> arriving with rain
>> recordings of ivory

Degaussing is a popular technique for destroying data on magnetic storage tapes. Degaussed data can in some circumstances be recovered; the more general implication of the first two lines is that what would otherwise be erased or simply unregistered is saved through technologies that listen to animals and the information the overheard animals divulge. "Night flights" points to one way in which sound recordings can bring us close to what we cannot record visually: they can capture bird activity in the dark. "Recordings of ivory" denotes the rare recordings of the probably extinct ivory-billed woodpecker. The Cornell Lab of Ornithology has invested in elaborate acoustic searches for living ivory-billed woodpeckers without any sure success. Recordings of these large and striking birds made in the 1930s do exist, however; while there have been recordings since that may possibly be from survivors, those old recordings may well be the only remaining aural evidence of a species destroyed by human encroachment on their habitat. Further emphasizing the loss inherent to extinction, ivory recurs in the tenth of the stanzas in reference to elephants whose survival is threatened by poachers ("rifle shots crack") who kill for their tusks: "ivory's market."[52]

My interpretive comments so far have not addressed the crucial importance of sound to the structure and effect of these poems. Both the spectrograms and the slowed audio recordings highlight the radical differences between parts of the bird's song that are captured in these disjunct lines. As Skinner notes, the spectrograms provide visual signatures for specific vocalizations: "Some parts are continuous with upsweeps and downsweeps, some jagged as a series of staccato strokes, some are smeared and some are sharp, some zigzag and some straight, some compressed and some spread across the spectra, some complex and some relatively clear." Spectrograms, he states in an instructional prompt for producing such work, can provide a "crib for translating bird song" since one can analyze the graphic image, developing one's own code to identify different kinds of vocalization present, and from that model, in concert with the slowed audio, generate a translation. The language may "be taken from almost any source, since birds and humans, let's face it, don't speak the same language." Skinner continues: "We nevertheless communicate—a vibrational communication that should be the focus of your translation, one that doesn't end with the writing."[53]

The published stanzas are accompanied by their spectrograms—as with Gladding's images of beetle engravings, the arrangement is comparable to a facing-page translation—so that a reader can break the visual image into line units and see the source of the poet's sonar interpretations. (Skinner also provides a link to three minutes and twenty seconds of sound recording.) Here, for instance, is the eleventh and final stanza with its spectrogram (fig. 9):

> value   accumulates
> inside
> a different kind of game
> loon calls
> syrinx
> boxing   our ears

The forceful syllables of "boxing" that resound as the climax of this stanza are visible in the double sharply peaked acoustic event near the end of the image strip. "Syrinx," another distinctly two-syllabled word, is suggested by the simpler paired sonic events of the preceding section. In passerine birds the bilateral formation of the syrinx (birds' vocal organ) can enable the

Figure 9. Spectrogram of birdsong from Jonathan Skinner, "Blackbird Stanzas."
(By Jonathan Skinner; courtesy of Jonathan Skinner and BlazeVOX)

production of two sounds simultaneously; that fact may have influenced the poet's selection of text for the two strokes here. The shortest event in the image yields "inside" while the longest yields the stanza's most flowing line in which the dactyl of "different" trippingly pushes the rhythm forward (the "game" of listening to birds indeed differs from the game elephants are for poachers in the preceding stanza). The section corresponding to "loon calls" has the smoothest horizontal curves, mimicked in the extended vowel of "loon" and in the gentleness of the line's predominant consonant sounds of l and n. Studying the image helps bring into focus both the stanza's and the thrush's music.

In "Poetry Animal" Skinner asserts that "poetic language structures acoustic signals before they are organized as coded meaning." Vibrational communication, then, is always crucial to poetry, but in work where the poet opens him- or herself to the vibrations of an earth other and attempts to translate that message, it assumes tremendous ethical importance. I return to Robin Wall Kimmerer: "We Americans are reluctant to learn a foreign language of our own species, let alone another species. But imagine the possibilities. Imagine the access we would have to different perspectives, the things we might see through other eyes, the wisdom that surrounds us."[54] All three of the poets discussed here have tried to imagine such access and, daringly but respectfully, to create it for their readers. All three would probably concur with the closing statement of Skinner's prompt: "The important thing is what happens when you are done with the poem." Each hopes to set in motion not just an enhanced listening to earth others but an enduring sense of closer, far less hierarchical relation to them.

CHAPTER 5

Global Rearrangements

Sense of Place in Twenty-First-Century Ecopoetics

The importance that place and a sense of place have held for environmental activism, environmental studies, and environmental literature could hardly be overstated. The very word "environment," understood as the surroundings or conditions in which a person, plant, or animal lives, implies a locale, a terrain, a habitat—that is, emplacement. Usually tied to rootedness in a rural or wild location, a sense of place has been particularly valued as a counter to the alienating effects of modern industrial life. Geographer Tim Cresswell notes, "It is commonplace in Western societies in the twenty-first century to bemoan a loss of a sense of place as the forces of globalization have eroded local cultures and produced homogenized global spaces."[1] Such lamentation is not, however, what the environmentally invested poets to be discussed in this chapter are engaged in. Juliana Spahr, Forrest Gander, and Jena Osman do not celebrate the forces of globalization, but, keenly aware of unequal distribution of both resources and environmental degradation, they also do not see the globalized world as homogeneous, or as lacking a sense of place. They take as givens highly mobile societies in the Western world, with histories behind them of colonialist circulation of cultures and species; globalized flows of trade, information, and bioforms; and fluid interdependencies across geographies. While their poetry may convey an appreciation of rootedness, it does not take rootedness as a core value or as the starting point for environmental awareness and responsibility. Place in their writings is translocal and markedly in flux so that terms like "native" and "foreign" acquire complex meanings, while consequences of various intertwined forms of invasion or miscegenation—biological, ecological, martial, (neo)colonial, economic—continually evolve. For these poets of the self-conscious Anthropocene, the meaningfulness that conventionally distinguishes place from space is derived more from mobility than stability, even as they recognize that ecosystems are not infinitely flexible and adaptable so that the rate of current environmental change is of great concern.

While geographers in the twentieth century often defined place in terms of bounded permanence or through the stilling of motion, as in Yi-Fu Tuan's widely cited description of space as motion and place as pause, far less stable visions of place operate in the poetry examined in this chapter.[2] Spahr's, Gander's, and Osman's explorations of forms of mobility, change, interchange, and exchange that define current experiences of place are illuminated by the groundbreaking work of Doreen Massey, also a geographer, who reconceived place as something in process in which the global and local interact, as lacking fixed boundaries, as necessarily involving multiple identities and multiple ongoing stories. While Massey, as I will explain below, challenged monolithic notions of time-space compression by emphasizing social diversity, Spahr, Gander, and Osman add to her perspective an emphasis on ecological processes and ongoing environmental degradation as crucial contributors to a globally interactive sense of place and space.

A MOBILE AND TRANSLOCAL SENSE OF PLACE

In American ecocriticism the poets most invoked in the discourse of place are Gary Snyder and Wendell Berry, key figures in any examination of American environmental literature and twentieth-century environmental thought. Not surprisingly, Lawrence Buell selects as an epigraph to his chapter "Place" in *The Environmental Imagination* (1995) the following passage from Snyder's *The Practice of the Wild:* "I describe my location as: on the western slope of the northern Sierra Nevada, in the Yuba River watershed, north of the south fork at the three-thousand-foot elevation, in a community of Black Oak, Incense Cedar, Douglas Fir, and Ponderosa Pine."[3] And the first person quoted in the body of the essay is Berry, remarking on the importance to responsible stewardship of a complex knowledge of one's place. Similarly, Robert Hass begins his more recent introduction to Ann Fisher-Wirth and Laura-Gray Street's *The Ecopoetry Anthology* (2013) with the following early poem of Snyder's:

burning the small dead
    branches
broke from beneath

> thick spreading
> > whitebark pine.
>
> > a hundred summers
> snowmelt   rock   and air
>
> hiss in a twisted bough.
>
> > sierra granite;
> > > Mt. Ritter—
> > > black rock twice as old.
>
> Deneb, Altair
>
> windy fire[4]

Extending the poem's emphasis on local particularity, Hass then provides some "facts" about whitebark pines' adaptation to the highest elevations in the Sierra Nevada and about the geological origins of those mountains before pursuing a meditation on the history of the knowledge that makes "this location of Snyder's poem possible."[5] Berry and Snyder, champions of agrarianism and watershed-based activism respectively, represent a powerful strain of American thought that, as Ursula Heise observes, emphasizes "the local as the ground for individual and communal identity and as the site of connections to nature that modern society is perceived to have undone."[6]

Connection to and caring for one's local place, then, has been widely understood as a form of resistance to the environmental and social degradations of modernity. The places associated with this vision of place-attachment are usually either rural—like Berry's organic farm in Henry County, Kentucky—or wild—like the foothills of the Sierra where Snyder built the home he dubbed Kitkitdizze, the Miwok name for an evergreen shrub that grows only on the western slopes of the Sierra Nevada range at altitudes between two thousand and seven thousand feet. While the stars Deneb and Altair mentioned in his poem are visible as points in the Summer Triangle, indicating a hemispheric or possibly global scale, along with a galactic context, and while Snyder's thinking is deeply influenced by his years living in Asia and his extensive study of Chinese and Japanese philosophy, his sense of place nonetheless remains firmly rooted in the Sierra granite and what grows on it. In setting up her own contrasting project, Ursula Heise observes, "Snyder's underlying assumption seems to be . . . that cultural identities will be shaped and reshaped by whatever place one

chooses to live in, rather than that cultural migrations will in any fundamental way unsettle the terms of local inhabitation." This kind of locally
specific writing, so precisely grounded in its ecosystems—and in the case
of Berry and Snyder, practiced by people invested in living sustainably off
the land, minimizing their participation in the global capitalist economy—
has often been illuminated through Heidegger's notion of dwelling, which
idealizes a rootedness associated with ancient local traditions of rural folk
life.[7] It has also frequently been discussed in terms of bioregionalism—
the biogregion being, as Greg Garrard explains, an "eco-political unit that
respects the boundaries of pre-existing indigenous societies as well as the
natural boundaries and constituencies of mountain range and watershed,
ecosystem and biome." That approach is particularly well suited to Snyder's
politicized interest in watersheds, with their "ethnically and economically
diverse stakeholders," as geographically and ecologically sensible units for
effective environmentalist mobilization.[8]

The literature that comes from deep knowledge of a single locale or
from focused attention to a particular bioregion continues to support environmentally concerned perspectives in the self-conscious Anthropocene,
as it can illuminate ecological interdependence while connecting readers to
the aesthetic and spiritual sustenance that may be found in less disturbed
environments. While some have represented Snyder's and Berry's work as
anachronistic, such critiques risk mistaking space for time by identifying
alternative ways of living with earlier moments on a trajectory of industrial
development falsely assumed to be inevitable. When Berry in his essays
urges urban dwellers not to be "industrial eaters," for instance, he hopes
to create a different future than the one we seem to be headed toward but
does not imagine it will replicate the agrarian past.[9] Nonetheless, his poetry,
like much popular environmental writing on place, does generally bracket
the translocal and global forces that so powerfully shape current lives on
all continents and so crucially determine present environmental problems
across the globe. The poets I will focus on in this chapter have chosen otherwise; their writing about place deliberately foregrounds awareness of global
social and environmental transformations and often confronts politically
charged issues of migrancy, travel, and tourism and of the ongoing social
and environmental effects of colonial history.

Ideas Doreen Massey developed in her important essay "A Global Sense
of Place" illuminate these poets' representations of place.[10] Massey challenges widespread understandings of postmodern "time-space compres-

sion" as lacking sufficient social differentiation. That term, introduced by David Harvey, denotes the increased speed of contemporary social life—the elision of spatial and temporal distances—resulting from widespread changes in communication technologies and in the mode of capitalist economic production and consumption.[11] She responds by seeking a sense of place that is adequate to this era of movement and intermixing, one that is not reactionary but "progressive, not self-enclosing and defensive, but outward-looking." Massey begins by critiquing some aspects of Harvey's concept, pointing out that it ethnocentrically represents a Western, colonizer's view, while its focus on capital fails to acknowledge the many determinants, such as race and gender, affecting how people experience space. She identifies an overlooked "power geometry of time-space compression," according to which "different social groups and different individuals are placed in very distinct ways in relation to these flows and interconnections." Not all those who are moving are powerful and prosperous, for instance; refugees and undocumented migrant workers move without being "'in charge' of the process," while others stay put but are nonetheless exposed to social, political, and environmental influences from around the globe. Believing in the importance of a sense of place but wanting to avoid notions of place that involve turning inward, drawing boundaries, or cultivating a "romanticized escapism from the real business of the world," Massey looks to the example of her own neighborhood in London. Tracing a walk down Kilburn High Road and the evidence there of myriad links to the wider world, she argues that "while Kilburn may have a character of its own, it is absolutely not a seamless, coherent identity, a single sense of place which everyone shares."[12]

Because a large proportion of the relations, experiences, and understandings that now construct a place "are constructed on a far larger scale than what we happen to define for that moment as the place itself, whether that be a street, or a region or even a continent," Massey argues that places can be "imagined as articulated moments in networks of social relations and understandings. . . . And this in turn allows a sense of place which is extroverted, which includes a consciousness of its links with the wider world, which integrates in a positive way the global and the local." This progressive sense of place she would like to see cultivated is not static; it doesn't "have boundaries in the sense of divisions which frame simple enclosures"; and it is understood to be full of internal differences and conflicts. For globalization does not entail simply homogenization; its uneven development can produce or exaggerate differences. In Massey's approach, place specificity is retained but is not understood to result from some long, internalized history (as it is in Heideggerian thinking); specificity in a globalized era derives from each place being "the focus of a distinct *mixture* of wider and more local social relations" that may "produce effects which would not have happened otherwise." She concludes that a progressive sense of place "is a sense of place, an understanding of 'its character', which can only be constructed by linking that place to places beyond. A progressive sense of place would recognize that, without being threatened by it. What we need, it seems to me, is a global sense of the local, a global sense of place."[13]

An ecocritic is likely to hear in that conclusion anticipations of Ursula Heise's important *Sense of Place and Sense of Planet: The Environmental Imagination of the Global* (2008), and Heise does refer to Massey's work of this period once in her study. Heise's book responds critically to "the insistence on individuals' and communities' need to reconnect to local places as a way of overcoming the alienation from nature that modern societies generate, as well as the long-standing ambivalences about the global [that] are two of the most formative and characteristic dimensions of American environmentalism." Seeking to bring the insights of cultural theories of globalization to U.S. environmentalist and ecocritical discourse, Heise emphasizes two concepts: deterritorialization, "understood as the weakening of the ties between culture and place," and cosmopolitanism, as a way of "thinking about environmental allegiances that reach beyond the local and the national." Modeling the "eco-cosmopolitanism" she advocates, Heise provides readings of works of literature and film that "frame localism from a globalist environmental perspective."[14] While much indebted to Heise's thinking and sympathetic with her call for a more global environmentalist perspective, my analysis here will not invoke deterritorialization or cosmopolitanism, in part because the poets under discussion remain keenly interested also in the differences between places and their cultural and ecological determinants. Moreover, attunement to the problematic residues of colonialism evident in the works I'll examine by Spahr and Gander militates against embracing cosmopolitanism, which is too readily associated with privileged travel and the view of the colonizer.

In this context Massey's work—particularly *For Space* (2005)—again proves useful, now for confronting the issues of colonialism that regularly attend discussions of global place, travel, and cosmopolitanism. She opens *For Space* with a striking "rumination" that juxtaposes two culturally in-

formed imaginations of the same event: the arrival of Cortéz and his sol-
diers at the Aztec city of Tenochtitlán. Having established the very different
perspectives first of Moctezuma's people and then of the Spanish, Massey
observes that we Westerners tend to treat space as "something to be crossed
and maybe conquered," making space seem like a surface, continuous and
given. This "unthought cosmology" continues to carry social and political
effects. Imagining other places, people, and cultures simply as phenomena
on this surface, we deprive them of their own histories and trajectories
(which her imagination of the Aztec perspective brought to life), making
it difficult to see in our mind's eye the histories others have been living.
Pointing to the project of her book, she asks, "If instead, we conceive of a
meeting up of histories, what happens to our implicit imaginations of time
and space?" A second rumination involving world trade negotiations during
Bill Clinton's presidency reveals how Euro-American ways of conceiving
of globalized space tend to turn space into time. That is, producing narratives of the ineluctability of neoliberal capitalist globalization, we do not
imagine the cultures of other places as having their own trajectories "and
the potential for their own, perhaps different, futures" and instead position
them as occupying an earlier stage of what we regard as the only possible
narrative. Massey concludes that rumination by asking what would happen
to our conceptions of space and time and their relation if we allowed for a
multiplicity of trajectories.[15] The poetry examined in this chapter is invested
in using the powers of the imagination to animate multiple trajectories
within places and to complicate a Western tendency to see "foreign" places
from the flattening or exoticizing perspective of the privileged traveler. In
what follows I will return periodically to Massey's formulations because
the poets' works seem to me to produce the socially attuned, nonstatic,
and nonmonolithic global sense of place Massey called for. While Massey's
works demonstrate an awareness of environmental issues, to my knowledge
she did not attempt any thorough integration of environmental concerns
and ecological processes into her theorizing of place.[16] These poets add to
her emphasis on "networks of social relations" a penetrating awareness of
dynamic networks of ecological relations.

   Before turning to work by the three poets I've named, I'd like to observe
this chapter's understanding of poetic place in motion as it's enacted in Ed
Roberson's "Urban Nature," from *City Eclogue*. For like Snyder's "Burning
the Small Dead" and unlike other works I'll discuss, Roberson's sonnet
describes a fixed and bounded place, though in destabilizing terms that em-

phasize migration. The opening lines distinguish the poem's setting from the conventional visions of desired local places represented by rustic New England landscapes, midwestern farmland, or upscale seaside retreats of "some Hamptons garden / thing," and insist this place does not offer the kind of natural beauty we conventionally imagine as spiritualized and uplifting. What Roberson is describing is "just a street / pocket park" in a moment of "simple quiet." Implicitly refuting the anti-urban bias still prevalent in much environmental literature, he emphatically distinguishes this kind of quiet from a vision of blighted nature like that offered by Keats in "La Belle Dame Sans Merci" ("The sedge has wither'd from the lake, / And no birds sing") and taken up by Rachel Carson, who used Keats's lines as an epigraph to *Silent Spring*.[17] This is a quiet "not the same as no birds sing, / definitely not the dead of no birds sing." Here's the closing sestet that follows:

> The bus stop posture in the interval
> of nothing coming, a not quite here running
> sound underground, sidewalk's grate vibrationless
> in open voice, sweet berries ripen in the street
> hawk's kiosks. The orange is being flown in
> this very moment picked of its origin.[18]

The poem resists thinking of nature and its valued places simply in terms of pristine landscapes or locales apart from human habitation; sweet berries ripen in the street, not just in the wilderness where Wallace Stevens gorgeously positioned them in "Sunday Morning." (The oranges, too, allude to Stevens's poem in which the leisured woman in her peignoir daydreams over coffee and oranges.)[19] Roberson challenges the tradition of Romantic nature writing that so often situates its solitary speaker in a relatively undisturbed natural setting. His quiet spot is so only at intervals, and even then his speaker is aware, without distress, of the machine sounds and vibrations that will shortly intensify. In the scene's urban ornithology, the birds are street hawks and airplanes.

The social and environmental costs of forced migration are not dwelt upon here, but they are suggested in that resonant closing phrase "picked of its origin." The street hawk is probably not a Native American whose forebears were indigenous to this place; the person calling out his or her wares is likely to be, if not a recent immigrant, then one descended from an earlier immigrant generation, perhaps someone whose ancestors were "picked" from their African roots by slave traders. Yet, just as berries will ripen in city sun essentially as they do on the vine, and just as the imported orange (and the fossil fuel required for its transportation) needs to be understood as part of this decidedly unfixed urban nature, so does the "imported" person. This treasured place in urban nature, then, is not defined by intact ecosystems of native flora and fauna like those Snyder lovingly observes, or by the kind of tradition-derived practices of land-use celebrated by both Snyder and Berry and embraced in Heidegger's "dwelling," or by cultural continuity and ethnic homogeneity. Instead, its complex syncretism—a phrase I take from Spahr that speaks to the sense of place developed by all three poets discussed in the rest of this chapter—is produced by various kinds of on-going trans-spatial mobility and mixing.

THE "THERE" OF JULIANA SPAHR'S *WELL THEN THERE NOW*

The opening poem in Juliana Spahr's *Well Then There Now* (2011) offers a formally experimental presentation of the mobile and translocal twenty-first-century version of place-based writing I have been outlining, as the method of its construction enacts the processes of place-formation-in-movement that is one of the poem's central concerns. *Well Then There Now* is very consciously a book about place. Signaling this even before the first poem, Spahr expands the usual list of acknowledgments into a section of "Acknowledgments and Other Information" that records the address where each piece was written: "at 5000 MacArthur Boulevard, Oakland, California 94613," for instance, or "at 3029 Lowrey Avenue, Honolulu, Hawai'i 96822." Three different Hawaiian addresses, from the period between 1997 and 2003 when Spahr taught at the University of Hawai'i, appear there, along with several California Bay Area addresses and one in Brooklyn, New York. In addition, as with "Unnamed Dragonfly Species" discussed in chapter 1, each poem is preceded by a simple silhouette map of a state or island on which the specific place of the poem's composition appears as a target-like spot, with the latitude and longitude of that location inscribed on the facing page above the title. These details of presentation indicate that the place-perspective of a piece of writing matters; one's location shapes one's awareness of and responses to the social, political, and environmental forces operating in the self-conscious Anthropocene.

The title of the volume's opening poem, "Some of We and the Land That Was Never Ours," alludes to Robert Frost's "The Gift Outright," which he recited at John F. Kennedy's inauguration in 1961 as the first poet to be invited to participate in an inauguration ceremony. That sixteen-line poem about U.S. history and Americans' relation to the land begins:

> The land was ours before we were the land's.
> She was our land more than a hundred years
> Before we were her people. She was ours
> In Massachusetts, in Virginia,
> But we were England's, still colonials,
> Possessing what we still were unpossessed by,
> Possessed by what we now no more possessed.[20]

The speaker's blindness to the ways in which the English who settled the American colonies were themselves colonialist forces displacing indigenous people is striking, as is the propertied whiteness of his "we" and his thinking of land in terms of possession. Spahr's poem refutes those perspectives; it speaks of "the land that was never ours" and "never to be owned," while its use of "we" where proper grammar requires the pronoun's objective case, "us," defies any objectification of those who do not possess power or land. In response to Frost, "Some of We and the Land That Was Never Ours" develops an alternative narrative about the complex and never-settled relation between land and its occupants, particularly its settler colonials—a narrative that highlights the power differentials important to Massey's thinking about space. The poem's four page-long sections (written in prose and followed by an italicized note explaining the circumstances and method of the poem's composition) rely heavily on progressive repetition and permutation that bring to mind Gertrude Stein's modes of insistence. This near-repetition that produces continual variation suggests multiple trajectories and perspectives within the unfolding of historical change, an instability that also opens future possibilities.[21]

Spahr's poem begins with an emphasis on the existence—and the perspective—of those who are "small," who are united by their common engagement in mundane activities like eating:

> We are all. We of all the small ones are. We are all. We of all the small ones are. We are in this world. We are in this world. We are together. We are together. And some of we are eating grapes. Some of we are all eating grapes. Some of we are all eating. We are all in this world today.[22]

The rest of the page continues to focus on we small ones eating grapes together "in this place" today, conveying a sense of community among those who are not powerful, with some attention also to wine and the sensory character of grapes: "In the world of the grapes. In this world. In the grapes. In the grapes. In taste. In the taste. In fermentation. In fermentation. In wine. Out of the wine. In fresh tight skin. In the fresh tight skin. In seed" (*WTTN* 11). The second page responds directly to Frost, emphasizing labor on the land and different classes' differing relations to the land; it questions established ideas of land ownership and possession while emphasizing how the production and consumption of food binds us to the land. Thus in the middle of the page: "Some of we were to settle. Some of we were to arrange. And the land was never ours. And the ground was never with us. And yet we were made by the land, by the grapes. We were eating the leaves of the land. The grapes of the land. The green of the land. The leaves. Sheets. And we were the land's because we were eating and the land let some of us eat." As the page continues, the emphasis on exclusions from the privilege of land ownership and on alienation from the land intensifies: "And yet the land was never some of ours. But the ground was never sure with us. Is never some of ours. Be never certain with us. Never will be rightly some of ours. Be correctly never certain with us. Never to be owned" (*WTTN* 12). The third page introduces a Saint Francis–like scene of sparrows eating grain out of "our hand" in ways that make the we of "the small ones" include birds, hands, and grains; its language of flying, flying at, pecking, and pecking back suggests social hierarchies and the struggles of those "down on the ground." The fourth page opens, "What it means to settle. What means it arrangement" and explores, again with lots of repetition in simple but often slightly torqued syntax, not only the possible arrangement of words but the arrangements of "we" in this world and the challenges we face not as a unified entity but as various small ones together who are in different relations to power and to the land (*WTTN* 13–14). Some eat grapes, some plant or pick them.

The key challenge posed by the poem emerges in the following passage that expands the discourse of relation to land to consider social and political change more broadly:

> How to move. How to move from settle on top to inside. How to move stabilization on the top inside. To embrace, to not settle. To embrace, not to arrange. To speak. To speak. To spoke. With the spoke. To poke away at what it is that is wrong in this world we are all in together. To push far what is with it is incorrect in this world which all the small ones are us in the unit. (*WTTN* 14)

Spahr seeks a changed relation to place that involves embracing what is there rather than claiming possession, dominating, and attempting to control; she seeks a shift from dominion ("on top") to participation and nonhierarchical belonging ("inside"). This is tied to a desire to use language for political and social transformation that benefits the (human and other-than-human) "small ones" of the biosphere.

How geographical movement figures in all this becomes clear in the concluding explanatory note, which begins by describing the scene in a park in France where Spahr and her mother were tourists and from which the poem's details emerge—including information that the person feeding sparrows was "making them perch on the thumb and eat out of the hand if they wanted any food," though the sparrows "preferred to eat on the ground." The poem's mentions of grapes gain context as Spahr further explains:

> *I was thinking about a story I had heard about a French grandfather who left early in my father's life, moved to Canada, and died by falling off a horse. I thought about the vines that grew in France, then came as cuttings to California, then went back to France after a blight. I thought about who owned what. And divisions . . . I came home and used a translation machine to push my notes back and forth between French and English until a different sort of English came out: this poem.* (WTTN 15)

Her compositional method, then, imitates the movement back and forth between continents that enabled her to witness people in France eating grapes—grapes that grow in France only because their predecessors had been transported to America and then returned to Europe. Movement of people and plants has shaped places and will continue to do so. Spahr's use of a translation machine generates forms of linguistic strangeness that call attention to the conventions of syntactic arrangement and naming peculiar to different languages. "Sheets," for instance, is introduced through translation of "leaves," both of which can be referred to as *feuille* in French. It also highlights linguistic hybridity and the interactive ongoing processes of language change, suggested by the integration into the otherwise English text variants of the French, *picoter,* meaning "to peck."

"Some of We and the Land That Was Never Ours," then, is a poem written in Honolulu about a scene in France observed by a person of French ancestry who came from the continental United States and responds in part to a poem about the United States, a settler colonial nation, seen as a former

British colony; it is written in a version of English produced by shuttling translations between French and English in ways that reenact the transcontinental movement of people and plants. The place registered in this poem is a generalized world we all occupy together, where our proximity and interconnection are more notable than any particular ecological context, but also where "our" perspectives on the place we occupy will be affected by our species (humans and sparrows have different relations to the ground), by our nationality (*picoter* also means to tingle or prickle, meanings a French reader would hear and ponder), and especially by our social class and occupation (do we pick grapes, own vineyards, or purchase grapes to eat?).

Juliana Spahr's six years living in Hawai'i had a great impact on her awareness of place and of what attention to place—to specific plants and birds, street names, posted signs, arrangements of buildings and walkways—may reveal about history, social power structures and dynamics, ecology, and environmental change. As is evident not only from her poetry but also from her prose memoir *The Transformation,* she was intensely conscious of having come to Hawai'i from a very different environment and as part of a history of colonization that implicates her, however unwillingly, in the "arriving and making different" that has preceded her.[23] That making-different involved introducing nonnative plant and animal species and consequently, if unintentionally, eliminating native species; it involved deliberately transforming the landscape for development and for the production of the colonial and neocolonial wealth. This ongoing process has made Hawai'i, though it remains a place of extraordinary beauty, "a site of huge ecological catastrophe." The opening poem of the "Sonnets" series in *Well Then There Now* concludes:

> We tried not to notice but as we arrived we became a part of arriving and
>   making different.
> We grew into it but with complicities and assumptions and languages
> and kiawe and koa haole and mongooses. [species introduced into
>   Hawai'i]
> With these things we kicked out certain other things whether we meant
>   to or not.
>
> Asking what this means matters.
> And the answer also matters.   (*WTTN* 19)

Much of the book pursues the answer.

In "Sonnets," that pursuit involves reconsidering the role of individual awareness and personal speech, partly by juxtaposing meditations on, for instance, the relation of the individual to collectivities or of takers to those whose land has been taken with facing pages displaying statistics of Spahr's own blood work—for example, "glucose at 111 milligrams per deciliter / creatinine at 0.9 milligrams per deciliter / . . . rapid plasma reagin titer at 1:2 / flourescent treponemal antibody, absorbed at nonreactive" (*WTTN* 26). This intimate information, registered via "norms and abnormalities and their percentages," defines Spahr as a bounded singular entity and functions as a kind of parodic version of the confessional lyric. "Things should be said more largely than the personal way" (*WTTN* 23), Spahr asserts, so the final pages abandon the bloodwork and gesture beyond an enclosed notion of personhood. Speaking of a "we" that includes earlier generations of arrivants, Spahr explains the psychology of "our response" to a lush landscape where "this growing and this flowing into all around us confused us" as "we couldn't tell where we began and where we ended with the land and with the others" (*WTTN* 28). In this context the idea that the land was never ours resonates specifically with the situation of the settler colonials:

> And because we could not figure it out bunkering was a way for us
> to claim what wasn't really ours, what could never really be
> ours and it gave us a power we otherwise would not have had
> and we believed this made the place ours.
> But because we were bunkered, the place was never ours, could
> never really be ours, because we were bunkered from what
> mattered, growing and flowing into.   (*WTTN* 29)

A better if still compromised relation to the colonized place is achieved by "some of we" arrivants who let the place "grow in our own hearts, flow in our own blood" (*WTTN* 29), where, unlike levels of antigens or minerals, it is presumably an unmeasurable yet crucial presence. More bounded notions of personhood, then, are linked to a more environmentally damaging, immobile understanding of place (not grasping its growing and flowing) and a tragically restricted response to it.

The essay that follows, "Dole Street," records what Spahr learned about this place by walking up and down the street on which she lived and worked, integrating researched history with what she herself observed as she moved through it, paying particular attention to stickers displayed on cars and to street names. A public sculpture by George Segal, *Chance Meeting*—notably inappropriate because of its "inattentiveness to the local"—which realistically represents three "haole" (Caucasian, foreign) people "dressed for late fall on the east coast" provides one center for her meditations on the connections that form a place. As Spahr sees it, "three haoles never meet by chance in Hawai'i," while other details of the street and the haole names of the streets intersecting Dole point to connections that underscore deliberately established lines of power. Speaking in terms that echo Massey's ideas about power-geometry, Spahr characterizes Dole Street around the university, where no buildings are named after Hawaiians, as "a closed system of sorts, one that illustrates how power clusters in close patterns on top of geography" (*WTTN* 41). Her use of "on top" recalls the challenge to settler colonials of "how to move from settle on top to inside" posed in "Some of We and the Land That Was Never Ours." Identifying the figures behind each successive street name yields a history of how nonnative people and plants have taken over the island, transformed its landscape and ecology, drastically lowered its water tables, and altered the lives of its people.

Like Massey, Spahr is keenly aware that a place has multiple identities for its diverse inhabitants. She several times uses the figure of the contour lines on a topographic map to communicate her sense of the non-intersecting place identities that "swirl" within a single locale, along with a more dynamic image of the various biological systems that energize the mammalian body:

> While the story of Dole and Wilder and Spreckels is not my story, I am part of Dole Street's swirl of connection whether I like it or not. A swirl that is like the system of the separate lines on the topographic map that are inside each other but are not a spiral and never really meet. Like the systems that circulate fluids and energy throughout the body but never mix. (*WTTN* 47)

The final section of "Dole Street" considers and rejects simple syncretism as a way to conceptualize places like this where multiple cultures, nationalities, and species from different ecosystems have interacted (and continue to interact) in complicated ways: "Simple syncretism has been used again and again in Hawai'i to erase the power dynamics that make it a colonial state" (*WTTN* 48). Like Massey, Spahr is committed to recognizing the very different experiences of different participants in the "unchance meetings" in Hawaiian history and geography. The challenge, then, is to contribute to a complex syncretism that is nondamaging culturally and environmentally:

I need to think about Dole Street's history because I am a part of Dole Street as I walk up and down it. I came to it as part of this history. As a stereotypical continental schoolteacher, I need to think about how to respect the water that is there, how not to suck it all up with my root system, how to make a syncretism that matters, how to allow fresh water to flow through it, how to acknowledge and how to change in various unpredictable ways. (*WTTN* 49)

In closing she offers as a model of such complex syncretism the image of the artist Kim Jones who (as Mudman) constructed a large boxy nest of loosely tied sticks and mud, an apparatus that "looks like the land," which he carried around on his back—a striking contrast, one might note, to the "simple oneness" and rooted order of Heidegger's ideal Black Forest farmhouse. "Nests," Spahr concludes, "draw things together and have many points of contact. They swirl into a new thing. All sorts of items end up in them. I found one the other day on Dole Street that was full of twigs and leaves and feathers and gum and plastic string" (*WTTN* 50). Place, then, becomes an energetic aggregate of multiple distinct experiences that are nonetheless touching one another, made from the materials of one locale, which turn out to be materials from a vast range of places.

The dependency of sense of place upon one's cultural positioning, and the interaction of different groups' relation to place, is explored quite differently in the poem that follows, titled "Things of Each Possible Relation Hashing Against One Another." As she did in "Some of We and the Land That Was Never Ours," Spahr offers at the end of this poem a clear explanation of her sources and compositional process—a process that, again using a translation machine, itself enacts some of the dynamics being examined. Reading, one first has the unsettling experience of a text that doesn't quite make sense, but in which certain preoccupations are clear. Later, one receives information that adds to and clarifies some aspects of that reading experience, but does not erase its strangeness, its foreignness. Without knowing anything about the poem's generation—that is, as one reads for the first time—one can readily discern its preoccupation with "the problems of analogy," which suggests the inability to see something for what it is when one insists on seeing it in terms of likeness to something else one already knows. In the Hawaiian context, that presumably includes the desire to make Hawai'i more like places familiar to those coming from elsewhere, so that, unable to see and respect what was there already as a complete and well-functioning social and ecological system, settler colonials not only introduced the plants and animals they knew, but also imposed "western concepts of government, trade, money." "The problem of analogy" may also refer to the way in which introduced plants were biologically enough like native ones to take over their ecological niche, and sufficiently not alike to wreck havoc on the ecosystem, producing "great and extremely fast modification." One gleans these things from a text that seems nonetheless chaotic, in which syntax is often incomplete and disturbance is palpable:

> what we know is like and unalike
> whereas one continues being diverse formed assemblies
> whereas the problems of the analogy
> whereas the sight of the sea
> whereas the introduction of tree of heaven and cow
> also continue being like the way of the aʻo
> then again the sight of the sea
> again a series of great and extremely fast changes
> what us knows is like and unalike
> as we continues to be the various formed assemblies
> as the sight of the sea
> as the introduction of exotic, alien plants and animals   (WTTN 57)

The text gives its readers a visceral experience of disruption, not unlike the kind of disruption produced by "the arrival to someplace differently."

With the explanation at the poem's end, much becomes clearer, while the reader's experience of linguistic displacement remains. Readers learn, for instance, that the repeating phrases, "the view from the sea" and "the view from the land," derive from ethnographic historian Greg Dening's argument that these two views define the Pacific—the former being "the view of those who arrived from elsewhere" and the latter of "those who were already there" (WTTN 71).[24] These views are essentially the two perspectives Massey brought to life in the opening gambit of For Space. "These poems," Spahr explains, "are about the hashing that happens as these two views meet."

As a foreigner come to Hawaiʻi, Spahr knew little of the native perspective: "I knew that when I looked around anywhere on the islands that most of what I was seeing had come from somewhere else but I didn't know where or when. I was not yet seeing how the deeper history of contact was shaping the things I saw around me" (WTTN 70). Attempting to gain further knowledge and understanding of the place she had come to live in—that is, attempting to get closer to the Hawaiian view from the land rather than the colonials' view from the sea—she enrolled in an ethnobotany course. She also consulted books and websites, which she lists, about Hawaiian plants and their traditional uses, traditional Hawaiian agriculture, literature, and language. In Massey's terms, such readings help one appreciate the vibrant alternative trajectories within Hawaiian history. Spahr incorporated text from the material she was reading into the drafts of this set of poems, which "open with the view from the sea and end with the view from the land and are about the hashing that happens" when they meet. To register that hashing (not unlike the "duplicitous negotiation, miscalculation, bloodshed, rout, retreat, and readvance" Massey describes as the process of Cortéz's conquest),[25] she also incorporated a quote: "The introduction of exotic (alien) plants and animals as well as Western concepts of government, trade, money, and taxation began a series of large and extremely rapid changes."[26] Spahr put her drafts through the machine that "translated [her] English words between the languages that came to the Pacific from somewhere else: French, Spanish, German, and Portuguese." She subsequently wove together parts of those multiply translated versions according to "patterns from the math that shows up in plants" or according to her own perceptions of "the shapes of things" around her (WTTN 71). Such a compositional process attempts to convey place as a dynamic construction resulting from the complex interaction of differentially empowered cultures and from the constant movement of human and other-than-human populations.

The writing that emerges constitutes Spahr's deliberate alternative to nature poetry, which she criticizes for tending to include too little context—the same complaint that Massey levels against the nonprogressive sense of place. Spahr explains that she had been

> suspicious of nature poetry because even when it got the birds and the plants and the animals right it tended to show the beautiful bird but not so often the bulldozer off to the side that was destroying the bird's habitat. And it wasn't talking about how the bird, often a bird which had arrived recently from somewhere else, interacted with and changed the larger system of this small part of the world we live in and on.

This work she produced instead was in what she came to understand as "the tradition of ecopoetics," which she defines as "a poetics full of systematic analysis that questions the divisions between nature and culture" (WTTN 69, 71).

While Spahr creates a dynamic sense of place that renders any locality also a place of global connections and interactions, local specificity of the kind that is cultivated by, say, Snyder still retains an important place in her work. The volume's closing poem, "The Incinerator," aptly demonstrates how Spahr's project is concerned with quite specific places, even as these lead into the larger contexts of the transnational global environmental and social issues those places may epitomize; as one refrain in that poem has it, "As I write this other stories keep popping up" (WTTN 139). The first section of "The Incinerator" personifies the southern Ohio town where Spahr grew up, Chillicothe, so that the speaker has sex (she uses a cruder term) with what is ambiguously a person and also a specific place with a particular geography that includes unglaciated and glaciated areas, hills and flatlands, with named rivers and geological features—the Scioto, Swiger Knob. (Its geographical specificity is comparable to the biological specificity of the animal and plant species cataloged in the immediately preceding poem, also about her Ohio childhood, "Gentle Now, Don't Add to Heartache.") In subsequent sections of "The Incinerator," details of Spahr's family situation, such as her father's precarious employment at a radio station owned by an upper-class woman who kept an eye on her employees through the station's bathroom window, emerge via disjunctive bits. That situation, however, serves to anchor a broader interrogation of what social class means in the United States, where Chillicothe is part of the impoverished region, Appalachia, and of how being of the working or middle class there relates to levels of poverty and prosperity in the rest of the nation and in other parts of the globe. Like place, class emerges as relational, so that the class position of those in one town or region can't be considered apart from the larger context: "For if," Spahr declares late in the poem, "we were middle class on the block, and lower class in the nation, we were upper class in the world, or in other words, the terms were so relationally slippery they were hard to define" (WTTN 151). She expresses worry about categorization and the way in which generalized identity categories, such as those of gender, may exaggerate commonalities while obscuring differences: in the context of international trade agreements like NAFTA, she tries "to think about" women of different nations engaged in various forms of labor, but "the categories were not equal: working class US women and then just any woman from the global south, as if these categories had any relationship between them" (WTTN 152). Local particulars matter—it is at the local level that distinctions can be most sensitively registered—but because alone they are insufficient for understanding a place or one's place in the social or eco-logical fabric, the focus of Spahr's poems is never restricted to a stable and bounded locality. Fractured by the multiple planes of its power geographies, "there" in *Well Then There Now* is a mobile, expansive, heterogeneous, and highly relational place.

"FOREIGN" PLACES IN FORREST GANDER'S *CORE SAMPLES FROM THE WORLD*

Spahr's concern with specific places gives to *Well Then There Now* a docu-mentary cast that is shared by Gander's *Core Samples from the World,* to which I will turn momentarily. In "Dole Street" and "2199 Kalia Road," Spahr even includes snapshots that document observations she makes about the places she describes, supporting her exposure of the social and environmental underbelly of the paradisal visions of Hawai'i's tourist literature. Notably, Spahr understands the tradition of documentary in which she works as itself highly mobile. This becomes evident through the several allusions in the epilogue that concludes both "The Incinerator" and the volume to Muriel Rukeyser's powerful documentary poem from 1938, also about Appalachia, "The Book of the Dead." The opening of Spahr's epilogue, "These are the roads we take," alludes to the investigative journey Rukeyser introduces in her opening line, "These are the roads to take when you think of your country." Spahr also incorporates Rukeyser's closing line, "seeds of unending love," into her own final lines.[27] Spahr's epilogue revisits the geography of the opening section of "The Incinerator," moving again over the particular landforms and place names around Chillicothe and blending them into a more expansive animated vision suggesting the flows and move-ment of globalized space: "Streams going off in all directions. / Going off in all directions, / the road" (*WTTN* 155).

A mobile documentary impulse is strong in Forrest Gander's *Core Samples from the World* (2011) as well, and here photography plays a more central role, as it allows access to places neither the poet nor the reader may have visited in the flesh. *Core Samples* is another volume concerned with traveling (literally as well as imaginatively) to other continents and cultures, generat-ing through "the roads you take" another version of a global sense of place. For while we think of place most often in association with "home base or home range,"[28] the place sense acquired by those who visit places even briefly may yield environmentally sensitive place-based writing. Visitors' writing can reflect superficial or inaccurate understandings of a place and its ecological and social networks—hence Spahr's disparagement of tourists' "747 poems"—but environmental historian Kate Brown rightly points out that "traveling is not always an appropriation . . . traveling can be a form of negotiation, an unraveling of certainties and convictions and a reassembling of the past, aided by strangers who generously open their doors to reveal histories that are in play, contingent, and subjective."[29] Of the eight extended series in *Core Samples*, four recount journeys taken by Gander as an internationally known poet and translator. These pieces whose titles identify the place visited employ the originally Japanese form haibun, a combination of prose and haiku that, appropriately, was often used for travel journals and has spread to many languages and cultures. The other four poems employ various forms of free verse lyric, often with repetition of lines or phrases, in response to evocative documentation of particular places and the communities or families living there by three fine-art photographers from the United States and Mexico, Raymond Meeks (whose work is the basis for two poems), Graciela Iturbide, and Lucas Foglia.

Less concerned than *Well Then There Now* with the guilty burden of colonial history, *Core Samples from the World* investigates what one can understand of culturally distant places one visits, either in person or through the mediation of documentary art. A note in the front matter announces, "The book comes about as unprecedented human movement leads, here as elsewhere, to conflicts, suspicions, and opportunities to reconsider what is meant by 'the foreign,' by 'the foreigner.' It is also a very personal account of negotiations across borders (between languages and cultures, between one species and all the rest, between health and sickness, between poetic forms, and between self and others)." As in Massey's thinking, borders here are not enclosures; they are potentially permeable sites of negotiation and exchange. The relational condition of foreignness is itself a kind of border, understood as a trafficked location of possible exchange: "The foreign, a crossing place of languages and codes."[30]

Gander is trained in geology, a field in which core sampling illuminates multiple aspects of geological history; analyzable changes in sedimentation register variations of climate and species over time, as well as geological upheavals and transformation. The book's title implies that each poem or each visit offers only a limited sample, a tiny specimen from one location on the globe, but it also suggests that such small snippets may nonetheless prove sources of useful understanding. Gander follows through on this core sampling metaphor by opening each of the book's four sections with a one-page "Evaporation," composed of juxtaposed bits from distinct layers of experience. Evaporation methods are used with soil cores to determine water retention and unsaturated hydraulic conductivity. In a book where many of the landscapes are desert or desertified, the emphasis on loss of moisture itself may be meaningful, but the figure is also a reminder of flows and changes of state that are ongoing processes, even if invisibly so, in any place.

In part, the book concerns what one learns of oneself through travel, and that aspect of the volume will remain in the background here as it's less directly relevant to my focus. However, *Core Samples* also investigates ideas of place-in-motion, as Gander explores ways of representing and documenting the dynamic nonhomogenization of both physical places and the people or cultures that inhabit them—ways that avoid being merely exoticizing or appropriative. Not that the two central concerns of the book, knowledge of self and knowledge of "foreign" places, are really separable; as Gander writes, "Of course, every place is equally exotic and numbingly familiar, and our distance from others, as Edmond Jabès notes, is exactly that of our distance from ourselves" (*CSW* 48). The places depicted in this book seem removed from the kind of globalization associated with "time-space compression"; linguistic and cultural particularities appear intact. Yet local and global clearly intersect and interact, much as they do in Massey's Kilburn. Take, for instance, the following description of a market visited by an international group of poets who, after gathering at Beijing, are given a tour into western China's Xinjiang Autonomous Region:

Abdul announces the next stop, the famous Kashgar Market, where *everything but milk of chicken* is sold. A labyrinth of stalls that display ancient Chinese and Roman coins, Pashmina wraps and scarves, dry toads wide as umbrellas, bins of walnuts and ripe cherries, cheap Pakistani suits, traditional Uyghur hats made in Italy, bolts of striped silk, jars of saffron, pelts common and exotic, and fragrant peaches. There are hanging carcasses harassed by flies at butcher stands one beside another and, at every corner, pomegranate vendors beside marvelous juice-presses ornamented in silver and wood.

Men at the edge of

their shops, spitting on fingertips

to seal the deal.   (*CSW* 14)

Many of the social relations that compose this place are "constructed on a far larger scale than what we happen to define for that moment as the place itself."[31] There is no romanticized fixing of this market as a display of ancient local traditions; rather, the specificity of the place derives from particular social relations that weave together at this moment. That includes the suits and "traditional" hats brought to Kashgar through world trade networks and international corporate development, along with the culturally distinctive juice presses, food items, and shop-owners' gestures. The notably local materials are not presented nostalgically; Gander does not convey the error Massey critiques in *For Space* of imagining the geography of globalization in terms of Westerners going out and finding, not contemporary stories, but the past.[32]

Even so, how comfortable is the reader likely to be with the visitor's stance? Is the word "marvelous" in the passage just quoted—potentially patronizing and exoticizing at once—a misstep on the part of the privileged visitor? Possibly, yet it would be an ethnocentric blindness not to acknowledge the marvelousness of this ornamentation of the ordinary, an example of the artfulness valued in cultures where craftsmen produce objects that in more thoroughly industrialized places would be produced by machines. That Gander's language evokes some discomfort in the reader seems appropriate to the complex mobility of place-sense here, given that few of the people the foreigners visit can themselves afford voluntary world travel. Like the traveler, the reader is invited to open her or himself to other trajectories through a process that may yield unsettling perspectives. Approaching an unfamiliar place as a privileged, cosmopolitan outsider sets up a tricky dance, as is evident, for instance, from a conversation between "the foreigner" and a Tsotzil shepherdess in "The Tinajera Notebook":

Have you been to France?
I have.
How do they live?
Like everywhere.
They have sheep?
Sure.
How many might one shepherd have?
I don't know, thousands.
How could they be counted?
You've got me.

What did you say?
I said I'm not sure.
And what took you there?
I was looking for bonds. I wanted to break a mirror. I wanted
to render myself accessible, available. I wanted to borrow eyes
from another language. I was looking for words to come.
And now?
And now what?
And now that everything in your life has changed?   (CSW 31)

The traveler who seeks a way beyond his own reflection, a breakthrough
into others' ways of seeing (think Massey, Dening, and Spahr), could indeed be profoundly changed by his contact with another place—though
his experience of the place might be just a fantasized misunderstanding
produced by impenetrable differences in languages and cultures. That Gander's speaker apparently has little more comprehension of industrial agriculture than does his indigenous Mayan interrogator who has never before
contemplated such scale of production signals a further complication and
instability in the notion of "foreignness," as does the surprising intimacy of
the shepherdess's final question. What one expects to be familiar is strange,
and vice versa. The foreigner's experience of unexpectedly encountering a
collection of anamorphoses—"those distorted paintings that, viewed in a
convex mirror or from a certain perspective, suddenly resolve into natural
proportions" (CSW 47)—perhaps provides an image for this manner of
witnessing otherwise withheld aspects of oneself and one's usual place-
sense through the surprising lens of what is spatially distant and culturally
unfamiliar. Tellingly, the moment in the volume when the traveler feels that
he is at last "in rhythm with the local, at home, that the foreign has rendered
itself accessible and his life is taking place in real time in the place where he
has arrived" occurs when his vision is distorted, in this case by alcohol. At
that moment, "the space in the room is contracting, expanding," and the
next thing he knows, he finds himself kneeling alone on the cobblestones
in the alley outside the "throbbing, roaring cantina" (CSW 93). Like this
scene, the book's narratives suggest that one's understanding of "foreign"
places one visits (and this may apply also to the "familiar" places one usually
inhabits) necessarily remains shifting and partial; only from particular, perhaps chancy perspectives experienced in ephemeral moments will a full and
proportional view emerge.

As a counterpoint to the works in *Core Samples* highlighting a global sense of place grasped, however fleetingly or partially, via international travel, "Moving Around for the Light, a Madrigal" evokes the lives of Americans who deliberately try to live independently of the globalized economy and to create a relation to their place somewhat like that experienced in nonindustrialized societies. Photos taken by Lucas Foglia in outsider communities where people live off the grid and off of the land provide documentary grounding for text that arranges and rearranges snippets of speech from community members. (Foglia recorded hundreds of hours of interviews from which Gander "drew out phrases.")[33] The piece exposes how largely invisible places may be carved out within larger social or national spaces—in this case, places where independently minded people, even those "too independent to listen to each other," seek to "move in a way that's more connected" to what they regard as "the natural order of things." Some of the speakers are preparing for postapocalyptic survival after the banks and modern systems of provision fail: "When / others won't, we'll make it" (*CSW* 59). Their remarks highlight the us-versus-them mentality of the saved and the damned that often accompanies apocalyptic thinking. Others quoted are simply wanting "to lose that feeling of being a foreigner and find / a sense of being at home" (*CSW* 57) by living with like-minded people and growing, foraging, or hunting their own food, consuming roadkill or wild game including owl, heron, rabbit, and squirrel. The photographs convey the cultural distance of such communities from the world of time-space compression; the people shown wear minimal or no clothing, and their dwellings are made of bark held in place by bent and lashed saplings (fig. 10).[34] Presumably, those who drive through the mountains and produce the roadkill that these people salvage have no clue that they are passing near such communities drawn together by powerful shared beliefs and aversions: "Nobody comes in, / nobody leaves" (*CSW* 54). "Moving Around for the Light," then, underscores the multiplicity of places and place-perspectives that may coexist in one region or nation. It also demonstrates that (as Massey teaches and Berry and Snyder know well) the way most of us Westerners inhabit the places we live and the high carbon footprint associated with it—a way that we perhaps tell ourselves is dictated by global corporations and established infrastructures—remains in fact a choice, one trajectory among many currently possible trajectories.

A final aspect of place in *Core Samples from the World* that has particular significance for the self-conscious Anthropocene is that many of the descrip-

Figure 10. People living off the grid in the United States, in Forrest Gander, *Core Samples from the World*, 56. (Photographs by Lucas Foglia; courtesy of Lucas Foglia)

tions that seem least exotic and that tend least toward cultural distinctness depict sites of anthropogenic environmental degradation. Mining and its damage to landscape and communities recur again and again, as if they are becoming near universals. Repeatedly in *Core Samples*, landscapes are dry, forbidding, eroding, full of airborne dust. A little research into the haunting photographic series by Raymond Meeks that underlies Gander's "A Clearing" reveals that the photos come not from one region but from several removed ones: they depict the Burmese mining industry and also American aggregate pits and desolate quarries.[35] Yet the two come together seamlessly; a reader may not be able to distinguish between the unpeopled Burmese wastelands and the American ones in the photos, and the Burmese miners might be taken for people from several continents. The opening of "A Clearing" may be read as suggesting the difficulty of determining where one is or where one comes from precisely because of this kind of pervasive environmental damage that renders geographically distant places more and more alike:

> Where are you going? Ghosted with dust. From where have you come?
> Dull assertiveness of the rock heap, a barren monarchy.
> Wolfspider, size of a hand, encrusted with dirt at the rubble's edge.
>
> What crosses here goes fanged or spiked and draws its color from the
>   ground.
> Xanthic shadow at the edges.
> Where are we going? Ghosted with dust. From where have we come?
>
> Stretcher loaded with clods by a spavined work shed.
> What does it mean, a cauterized topography? (*CSW* 5)

The stretcher loaded with dirt clods turns out a few pages later to be a literal reality; a photo shows men carrying it (fig. 11). But the idea that the land itself is in a kind of health emergency is carried through in the verbal image of "a cauterized topography," as if there has been an attempt to seal off a wound on the surface of the land, which in the photo appears parched, cratered, without plant life. The homogenization that seems most deadly here is that of environmental degradation due to resource extraction: the destruction and erosion of the soil, the poisoning of land, water, air, and of human and nonhuman health.

Related indirectly to the homogenization of built "nonspaces" like airports and malls that is commonly associated with time-space compression,

Figure 11. Burmese miners, in Forrest Gander, *Core Samples from the World*, 8.
(Photograph by Raymond Meeks; courtesy of Raymond Meeks)

this transformation of place that produces nonbuilt nonspaces is something Gander particularly attends to. Here's a passage in which an activity that is memorably "foreign" is upstaged by the environmental consequences of China's globalizing development:

> Then they are whisked by van to the desert to witness the Kyrgyz version of a polo match, played with the decapitated carcass of a goat. Those who can ride are given mounts from which to survey the tumultuous competition, men grappling from the saddles of their galloping horses for a hold on the carcass. Behind the yipping riders, in the distance where a new mining facility squats in the Haoshi Bulak ore field and where the rocky plain, plowed and abandoned, lies denuded, a stupendous dirt cloud rises, mixing with

the dark purple sky. One competition framing another. The riders have not given up, but the storm is barreling theatrically toward them, their clothes snapping in wind like a fire. (*CSW* 18)

That fast-moving cloud, carrying topsoil and perhaps mining tailings, is, unfortunately, one version of place-in-motion, and an increasingly common one around the globe.

If anything differentiates these desiccated and degraded nonplace landscapes from one another, it is the varied forms of pollution that in the final poem add colors to the scene. In a section of "Chile: Pigs of Gold" set in "Andacollo: haunted by the ghosts of miners and gritty with tailings that blow from buzz-cut and beveled mountains," Gander observes, "The river is dry, a depository of bulging green plastic bags and noisome litter." He also witnesses, "In cratered flats, tarry, / orange-fringed chemical / pools glisten" (*CSW* 85). Even the gold of the title becomes visible in association with toxic pollution. The traveler observes the owner of a failing wildcat mining operation that has struggled on after the mines have played out—a man whose appearance indicates mercury poisoning—using that highly toxic heavy metal to mine gold:

> In the sear of afternoon sun, one miner is crushing stone, another scooping the pieces into a rudimentary wooden sieve. The owner steps under a tin roof where sieved gravel is swirled in large washtubs. From his pocket, he takes a vial and pours several beads of quicksilver, mercury, across the life-line of his palm. He smears this against a tin plate he attaches to the washtub. After swishing the muddy water with a paddle, he removes the metal plate, flecked now with gold precipitate. This he wipes into a cloth filter, again with his bare hand. (*CSW* 88)

By focusing on this man, Gander again makes evident something Massey insists upon: that place is differently perceived and differently experienced by people in differing social positions. Higher social and economic standing sometimes offers protection from environmental dangers; in this scene, however, the financial investment of the owner makes him, perhaps unknowingly, assume more environmental risk than his employees. Yet, viewed on a global scale, the lack of environmental protection for both owners and workers in this "developing" country is a manifestation of environmental injustice typical of global capitalism. The contrastingly privileged tourists from the industrialized world are not really threatened by the "apocalyptic pastoral" landscape the speaker observes and in their short stay are unlikely to inhale or otherwise absorb significant amounts of mercury. While Massey recognizes that the time-space compression involved in producing the lives of those comfortably well off in the global North "may entail environmental consequences . . . which will limit the lives of others before their own,"[36] Gander's work, like Spahr's, adds to Massey's analysis of the power geometry and social differentiations within space-time compression a more developed awareness of the ecological and environmental justice dimensions of global place.

PLANETARY AND INTERPLANETARY PLACES IN JENA OSMAN'S "MERCURY RISING"

In "Toxicity and the Consuming Subject," historian Nan Enstad identifies a "broad-based new anxiety about globalization and its perils" emerging around the toxic debris that is deposited in human bodies from transnationally circulating commodities. Toxic chemicals, Enstad observes, "move silently with a giddy freedom from place to place" aiding their ready absorption by our permeable bodies. As toxicity manifests "the global 'within us,'" it has ramifications for our spatial categories of global and local. It also, as Mel Y. Chen elaborates, alters our notions of selfhood—"toxicity becomes us, we become the toxin"—along with our understandings of what is and is not animate.[37] The final work I will discuss in this chapter, Jena Osman's "Mercury Rising (A Visualization)," imaginatively creates a vision of the global place that is formed through the mobility of toxins by rendering nearly indistinguishable varied interacting scales of place—the scales of the individual human body, the town, and the planet. In so doing, she highlights the damage to human and environmental health caused by anthropogenic uses of mercury and of nuclear weapons. In the context of this chapter, Osman can be seen as extending Gander's use of art to expose the nonplaces that are resulting from human exploitation of "natural resources" around the globe and as bringing home the personal impact such environmental destruction may have.

"Mercury Rising" concludes Osman's volume *The Network* (2010), a collection much concerned with place that elsewhere shows little concern with what we readily recognize as environmental issues. The book, which the back cover blurb situates "at the intersection of conceptual and documentary poetics," offers fascinatingly woven explorations of etymological and American history exploring such subjects as the sugar industry, the Franklin party, and, in the longest poem, the history of New York's financial district. "Mercury Rising" is parenthetically labeled "a visualization," and at multiple points it presents breathing instructions like those of a meditation technique meant to direct and calm one's mind. The poem is staged as a three-part visualization, in which each part has three sections. These shift between physical locations—in particular, between the closed town of Mercury, Nevada—which is located in an area where mercury was formerly mined and situated within the Nevada Test Site (now more euphemistically designated the Nevada National Security Site)—and the imagined planet Mercury.[38] The town was constructed by the U.S. Atomic Energy Commission to house personnel during the period when A-bombs and their effects were tested in the Nevada desert—above ground between 1951 and 1963, underground until 1992 (with, Osman informs us, some "subcritical" testing since). After that, most of the facilities in Mercury were abandoned. The poem shifts, too, among different versions of mercury: the town built by the government in the 1950s; the closest planet to our sun; the highly toxic, silvery heavy metal; the Roman god of travelers, thieves, messengers, and poetry; and the comic book figures for which the god is prototype. Here, to demonstrate how the text moves in space, time, and reference, is the opening of part 1B:

> there will be three parts that lead to others. pay attention to your breath. breathe deeply, in through your nose, out through your mouth. hold it. then release. you are northwest of las vegas. when you breathe out, your breath is like a vapor that lifts back up and you inhale it through your nose like a circle. you are 36 million miles from the sun, small and singular. study the explosion clouds of bombs in the height of the cold war. this place is not really a place, just housing. you are on an empty street and the light is bright and hot. no atmosphere to ward off or soften impact. you pass a movie theater, a bowling alley, both now closed. you notice that one side of the street is unbearably hot and the other side has ice in its corners. the eccentric orbit rotates three times for every two revolutions. twenty newspaper boxes. you stop for a moment and listen to the air and it streams around the debris. dust carried by solar wind. hot enough to melt lead. there are voices in the distance and you walk toward them and the fluorescent lights above. a group of VIPs sit on bleachers. they watch the desert floor crater like the moon in the wake of over 900 explosions. where the surface is fractured is called "weird terrain."[39]

As details shift from abandoned town to lifeless planet, it's hard to tell which one is being described; elements of fantasy blend them, as sides of a street, for instance, take on the traits of sides of the planet. Sometimes particular details might describe both locales—dust, for instance, or (seemingly or literally) unbearable heat. The absence of capitalization allows sentence demarcations to blur and makes the distinctions even harder to sustain. This seems to me precisely the point: when we subject an area to nuclear blasts, we turn that part of earth into a cratered wasteland hardly distinguishable from the surface of the planet Mercury. The solar wind "hot enough to melt lead" would be experienced on the planet Mercury, which on its day side has temperatures up to 801 degrees Fahrenheit, while lead melts at 621 degrees. Far higher heat occurs in nuclear explosions; the surface temperature of the Hiroshima fireball was 10,830 degrees Fahrenheit. The poem may implicitly situate us in the places of those lead-melting events as well. Neither the uninhabitable planet nor the guarded, empty town "is really a place" in that neither is a site of human place-attachments, but at the same time the two nonplaces are truly one in the all too real Nevada testing grounds.

Buell has emphasized that fantasy, as a form of place imagination, is one resource for putting people in touch with place, and Osman's piece is partly mytho-fantastic.[40] It begins with a journey reminiscent of crossing the mythic river Styx; its journeying "you" walking on forest trails speaks with oracle-like animals and magically locates a key that unlocks "your" dream house, your most secure place; at times the world "you" walks is that of Marvel comics, where there are "crystal shards of terrigen mist," and so forth. And of course, Hermes or Mercury, the messenger god, god of "boundaries, travelers, shepherds, poets, commerce, etc." and "the intermediary for any kind of exchange, transition, or crossing over" including the crossing of dead souls to the underworld, is also a mythic creation.

But the transformation of "you" into a quicksilver-contaminated being—someone with "silver skin" and mercury-impregnated breath who experiences what the reader may recognize as symptoms of mercury poisoning such as tremors, sleep disturbance, and memory loss—is not so fantastic. Thus, the final sections of Osman's poem, again suggesting documentary poetics, offer more and more straightforward factual information about mercury. Readers learn that while half the mercury in our atmosphere comes from volcanic eruptions, the other half is produced "primarily by power plants (particularly those that combust coal), hazardous waste incineration, and gold mining" (*TN* 114). Osman provides information about the heavy metal's movement up the food chain from spiders and small fish, accumulating "greater power" as it goes. A primary way in which mercury is absorbed into the body, however, is through the respiratory tract and from there into the circulatory system. Knowing this gives a gradually accumulating resonance—and horror—to the visualization's emphasis on the breath. Breathing should bring vitalizing oxygen to blood and, in exhalation, cleanse the body of waste and toxins, but by the end of "Mercury Rising" it is mercury that "goes in through the nose and out the mouth in a circle" (*TN* 114). The piece closes with a journey back across the river: "When you reach the other side you get out of the boat. You close your eyes and take a deep silver breath. You very slowly open your eyes and you are here, in this room, with the light as it is" (*TN* 115). That light, of course, exposes real-world mercury pollution and other forms of environmental degradation.

I find this a powerful piece of toxic discourse, and its power rests on a keen sense of interacting imaginary, locally specific, global, and interplanetary places. It's a commonplace that forms of environmental pollution don't respect the boundaries humans impose on place; it's also evident that particular places and their inhabitants (such as the Chilean gold miners Gander observes) inequitably bear the brunt of the worst forms of environmental contamination. But those discomforting realities are ones from which we often turn away. By prompting the imagination of the planet Mercury alongside that of a specific closed town in a toxified area of the United States, Osman draws readers into both an overview and a particularized perspective on the vulnerable, changing spaces of our miraculously and precariously habitable earth.

Several decades ago Buell observed: "Seeing things new, seeing new things, expanding the notion of community so that it becomes situated within the ecological community—these are some ways in which environmental writing can reperceive the familiar in the interest of deepening the sense of place."[41] Osman's piece that combines documentary information with sci-fi fantasy and pastoral nostalgia (in the visualized walk through the forest) manages—like the other, very different works I've introduced here—to perform such re-perceptions in ways that enhance a sense of space whose multidimensional interactivity is crucial to the environmental dynamics of the self-conscious Anthropocene. "Mercury Rising" invites us to "see" often invisible toxins and register how their translocal dispersal alters the places and bodies we inhabit; it prompts us to understand ourselves as members of ecological and toxicological communities at once local and global. Like the perspectives of Spahr and Gander, Osman's is sensitive to the complexly mobile social constructions of contemporary places and to their startling ecological instabilities.

Environmental Justice Poetry of the Self-Conscious Anthropocene

The dramatic environmental changes of the post–World War II "Great Acceleration" have not been produced by a monolithic humankind, as the term Anthropocene might seem to suggest. Consequently, although the concept of the Anthropocene has great potential value in bringing together various kinds of environmental change so that their interrelations can be considered and their collective impact addressed, not all environmental scholars embrace it. Anthropologist Anna Tsing, for instance, observes: "This 'anthropo' blocks attention to patchy landscapes, multiple temporalities, and shifting assemblages of humans and non-humans: the very stuff of collaborative survival."[1] A more common complaint is that summarized by Jennifer Wenzel: "To many ears, Anthropocene species talk is a troubling new universalism that disregards the highly uneven roles that different groups of humans have played in the transformation of the planet, and the uneven distribution of risk and resilience in confronting this human-made world. Newfound interest in geological stratification threatens to displace attention to social stratification."[2] Rob Nixon rightly describes the Anthropocene as "a shared geomorphic story about increasingly unshared resources."[3] Recent changes to the global environment have been disproportionately produced by the industrialized nations where lifestyles have a particularly large carbon footprint and by the transnational corporations that enable and profit from those lifestyles. Numerous communities, micro-minorities, and even nations (if one leaves aside their ruling elites) in the less developed parts of the world live in ways that have contributed relatively little to planetary changes arising from fossil fuel consumption.[4] Impoverished populations outside the global North who contribute to global environmental change as laborers in resource extraction involving mines or oil fields, or in sweat shops and factories, do so largely without experiencing the improved standards of living—including, for example, ready access to electricity, clean running water, or modern medical care—that industrial development can make possible. Instead, they suffer disproportionately the effects of water and air pollution, soil erosion and degradation, and health problems caused by environmental toxins. Much of the highly toxic e-waste of the developed nations is dumped in the developing world. Within the developed nations, too, the costs and benefits of industrialization are unevenly borne: in the United States, for instance, dumps, dirty factories, and power plants tend to be located near minority and working-class neighborhoods; minority and impoverished populations are significantly more likely than the white middle class to live in areas where air and water are less clean and where there are more environmentally linked health hazards; in the workplace as well, disadvantaged populations are often exposed to toxic substances that pose health risks. Brought to wide public attention by Pope Francis's encyclical from 2015, *"Laudato Si',"* these are issues of what in the United States is widely termed environmental justice and also referred to, usually in a more global context, as the environmentalism of the poor.[5] This chapter examines poems by Ed Roberson, Mark Nowak, and Myung Mi Kim that address current issues of environmental justice linked, respectively, to urban redevelopment in the United States, coal mining in the United States and China, and displaced or refugee populations of Korea and other countries.[6]

The seventeen Principles of Environmental Justice were drawn up in 1991 at the First National People of Color Environmental Leadership Summit in Washington, D.C. Communities of environmental justice activists adopted as their accessible definition of the environment: "where we live, work, play, and pray."[7] The social focus of the environmental justice movement evident in that definition did not coordinate comfortably with the nature-focused protectionist and conservation concerns of mainstream (largely white) environmentalism, or of ecocriticism as it had been developed (almost entirely by white scholars) into the 1990s.[8] After decades of concerted efforts to move beyond anthropocentrism to ecocentrism, some environmentalists and ecocritics alike were reluctant to embrace visions of environmentalism that foreground among their concerns issues of human workplace health and safety, human access to clean air and water or healthy food, and human freedom from various kinds of environmental toxins including lead paint in homes or mercury in edible fish. As recently as 2005 Lawrence Buell observed that despite their shared vision of personhood being defined by environmental entanglement, "It remains to be seen just how far the discourses of urbanism and environmental justice can be coordinated with the discourses of nature and the protectionist agendas they tend to imply."[9]

More than a decade later, however, as the rift between rich and poor across the globe widens while changes to the earth's waters, surfaces, and atmosphere intensify, increasing numbers of scholars in the environmental humanities are recognizing an urgent need to bring together our perceptions of the crisis posed by "the Great Acceleration" of the Anthropocene with the current crisis of human inequality for which Nixon, an eloquent spokesperson for this perspective, adopts Timothy Noah's term "the Great Divergence."[10] Recognizing the extraordinary earth-altering power of a very few and the radically inequitable distribution of the benefits and harms generated by those alterations, Nixon and others like him call for responses to our environmental problems that also address the associated social problems and don't amount to "adaptation by the rich for the rich."[11]

The poetry to be discussed here attends to social justice issues that have foundations in Anthropocene changes to the earth's surface arising from urbanization, resource extraction, and military conflict. Notably, its social focus does not entail leaving aside attention to traditional nature. This work does reject aestheticized visions of nature as something apart from human habitation and use, and it critiques hierarchies that value wild and rural over urban or industrial environments. But these poets demonstrate concern for the nonhuman, nonbuilt nature that is valued by conservationists. As they bring the discourses of nature and conservation together with the discourses of environmental justice, Roberson, Nowak, and Kim expand the scope, power, and relevance of both. Roberson's insistence that nothing exists outside of nature, communicated partly by figuring human culture and the built environment in terms of nonhuman nature, functions also as a critique of social forms of exclusion and racial segregation. In Nowak's volume, photos of mining country and rare glimpses of landscapes undamaged by extraction speak especially clearly to the entwining of environmental degradation with wretched human impoverishment, adding important dimensions to the tragedy of mining accidents and mining company negligence the text exposes. In Kim's *Penury*, the inseparability of political and environmental sources of the suffering and displacement of human populations is clear in her disjunctive spare writing's refusal to distinguish the consequences of military oppression from the results of mining and industrial processing or the impact of natural disasters including anthropogenic climate change. All three poets respond to the damaging, if not the decimation, of human communities, and each understands human communities as themselves relational ecosystems that are woven into the battered natural ecosystems of their locales.

The poetry considered in this chapter enacts a distinctive take on environmental justice in that the poets don't approach the environment as being *only* where we live and work, though that is crucially important. They are also thinking of natural ecosystems and nonhuman beings—of nature, which humans are part of and in which human communities are embedded. Here, for instance, is Ed Roberson's characterization of the importance of nature to his urban poetics: "In my own poems I try to show our social nature in and as the growth of our cities and city culture. Our technology, however, is more likely to conserve, regenerate, and nourish the limiting and exclusive resource base of capitalism than our larger human or Earth/Nature. Restoring this larger Earth to urban poetry, embedding city life within a living Nature focuses on an interrelation that should keep us sensitized to exploitative relationships which could cut us off, cut us out of life."[12] Because of their interest in keeping "this larger Earth" in view in their environmental justice writing, these poets do not discard the pastoral tradition, despite its association with some of the dichotomies they reject. Instead, they redeploy its resources. Refusing the split Buell observed between environmental justice and conservation discourses, Roberson, Nowak, and Kim both modify and capitalize upon inherited discourses of nature and wilderness, marshaling the resources of the pastoral among the rhetorical strategies available to promote their inclusive visions of environmental concerns.

"A HIGHWAY THROUGH TO SOMEONE ELSE'S POSSIBILITY": ED ROBERSON'S *CITY ECLOGUE*

The title of Ed Roberson's volume *City Eclogue,* a ringing challenge to those who would see the two words in oxymoronic relation, indicates his desire for an encompassing understanding of nature that incorporates the spaces of human culture and habitation and expands rather than rejects poetic traditions of the pastoral in which the eclogue is prominent. The title poem, "City Eclogue: Words for It," prepares for the volume's exposure of the racialization of space and the inequities that have accompanied it by linking dominant understandings of nature and its beauty with issues of social stratification and, implicitly, of racial segregation. Roberson suggests, then, that while received understandings of nature—often associated with pastoralism and its opposition of city to country—need not be discarded, they need to be substantially recast.

The poem begins by contrasting the "actual" way in which trees are planted in the city with common ideas of their reproduction in nature, ideas that are filtered through romanticized visions of the pastoral's *locus amoenus:*

> Beautifully flowering trees you'd expect
> should rise from seeds whose fluttering to the ground
> is the bird's delicate alight
> or the soft petal stepping its image
> into the soil
>   but here come the city's trucks
> bumping up over the curb dropping
> the tight balls of roots in a blueprint out
> on the actual site in the street
> someone come behind with a shovel will bury.[13]

In Roberson's view, "man can't be outside of Nature; our life exists as an act of Nature."[14] Thus, cities that humans have produced as their habitat are part of nature, which makes the planned planting of saplings along city streets a natural phenomenon. Succeeding passages of this poem argue (though with characteristically complicated syntax that can often be read several ways) that the contemporary city exists in a context of censorship and deceit that includes misrepresentation of what is "natural"; it's a place where people "lie" in saying

>   that this shit is not the flowering,
> that shit off the truck and not the gut
> bless of bird and animal dropping isn't somehow
>
> just as natural a distribution
> as the wild bloom.   (*CE* 16)

Aestheticized and idealized visions of nature that imagine seeds being dispersed by graceful fall to the earth, rather than via either bird and animal droppings or deliberate human cultivation, foster perspectives that distort the real, messy processes of nature and deny the nature of cities. Roberson links these attitudes with attempts to regulate proper speech and control language change (which would deny the order and logic behind "dirt mouth curse and graffiti") and, further, with efforts to separate different social classes. He suggests that attempts at segregation generally—whether dividing off the natural from the supposed unnatural or separating the upper classes conscious of their social propriety from the supposedly indecorous and sinful lower classes—are proving increasingly irrelevant as they are being overpowered by larger hybridizing forces of nature and history. "The idea of the place" (I take him to refer to the city)

> tramples up its rich regenerate head
> of crazy mud into the mutant's changling potion.
> Committee cleanliness and its neat
> districts for making nice nice and for making sin
> may separate its pick of celebrant monsters:
> > but which it is now is
> irrelevant as the numbered street sequence
> to archival orders of drifting sand.   (CE 17)

The emerging future Roberson looks to involves an urban nature that diverges from the tidy districting imposed by city planners as well as from the anti-urban visions of a nature unsullied by human intervention. He offers in closing a fragmented vision of something already in motion that is less beautiful and less easy than either: "the stinking flower / the difficult fruit bitter complex." Its composting action integrates processes of nonhuman nature with historically determined social realities and complicates the neat divisions previous approaches to nature and to cities have imposed:[15]

> > > > > > —all
>
> | on the clock | on the tree rings' clock |
> | history's | section cross cut |
> | portrait | landscape |
> | | it already |
> | knows | composts into ours the |
> | | grounds for city.   (CE 17) |

The environmental injustices that have followed from imposed orders of separation or segregation come into focus particularly in the section of the volume titled "The Open." Within a U.S. context, environmental injustice often emerges as an extension of environmental racism; in other parts of the world, where race and class are not so significantly aligned, this is less true. Roberson, who is African American and has lived most of his life in cities—especially Pittsburgh, Newark, and Chicago—has a keen sense of what American environmental justice scholars talk about as the spatialization of race. He's well aware that those "districts for making nice nice" tend to be white neighborhoods that the powers that be would keep separate from the black neighborhoods they disparage as full of sin. His poem "The Open" develops from an all too familiar narrative of the racialization of space in which the white power structure routes a highway through a poor black neighborhood for the convenience of commuters, driving out the inhabitants and making the land available for developers who get rich by gentrifying the area and opening it to prosperous whites. Roberson conveys the devastating effects on the residents of a black neighborhood of razing its buildings in order to make way for such a highway.

In this grieving and angry poem, a human community has been destroyed with the destruction of the buildings in which its members lived: "People [had] lived where it weren't open," and the opening of space resulting from the bulldozing of their homes has left them "drowned in exposure." The poem's first lines depict the residents choking as much on their losses as on the dust produced by turning their homes into rubble:

> Their buildings razed.   they ghosts
>   their color that haze of plaster dust
>
> their blocks of bulldozed air opened to light
>   take your breath as much
>
> by this kind of blinding choke as by the loss felt
>   in the openness
>
> suddenly able to see
>   as if across a drained lake from below
>
> a missing surface: (CE 63)

Roberson, who has extensive outdoor experience as a climber and an explorer of remote areas of the globe, introduces here a figure of speech that likens this community's experience of loss to the kind of loss that would upset conservationists: the draining of a lake. He then extends the conceit of the drained lake with language that puns on schools of fish or, in the following lines, on the catch of a fisherman: "the way   the neighborhood // a village packing up and leaving raises you with / the catch // out in the open." Such a catch, of course, would not be harvestable—it would quickly rot. Roberson makes clear that habitat destruction is as much of a threat for certain human populations as it is for nonhuman species. Prompted by thinking of schools of fish to consider human schooling, Roberson plays on the purportedly African proverb, "it takes a village to raise a child," a popular phrase among educators after Hillary Clinton used it as a book title. What's been lost is precisely the kind of community a village provides: "some common // immersion schooling you" that contrasts with the awful empty space of exposure. Roberson's use of natural figures in this poem is not simply a rhetorical strategy that will work on the environmentalist sympathies cultivated by our pastoral traditions. Nor does the likening of humans to stranded fish animalize those humans in a degrading way. Instead, here as elsewhere in Roberson's writing, depicting humans and built nature in terms of the nonhuman is a way of positioning the human within nature and insisting that nothing human is outside nature.

As we move further into "The Open," it's worth noting how much Roberson's depictions of the racial dynamics of urban redevelopment correspond with those of urban sociologists. Many of the ideas Michael Bennett draws from such scholars in his essay "Manufacturing the Ghetto: Anti-Urbanism and the Spatialization of Race" could be drawn equally well from Roberson's poem. Bennett has called for an urban ecocriticism that will help put an end to racist public policy by confronting "the ecological devastation being wreaked upon inner cities and the ideologies that underlie this assault." His essay, which presents the American ghetto as an "internal colony" or the "Third World within," explains the social barriers constructed by the "coded racism" of public policies that concentrate urban poverty in poor black neighborhoods and result in the spatialization of race. Bennett comments on how anti-urban sentiment "provides an alibi for the cyclical process of disinvestment and gentrification by building 'a symbolic construction of "white places" as civilized, rational, and orderly and "black places" as uncivilized, irrational, and disorderly'"[16]—Roberson's "districts for making nice nice and for making sin" in "City Eclogue: Words for It." The alignment of Roberson's social analysis with that of Bennett and the social scientists he cites is particularly clear in this passage from "The Open":

a people whose any beginning is disbursed
    by a vagrant progress,

whose any settlement
  is overturned for the better

of a highway through to someone else's
  possibility.

A people within a people   yet whose link
  we lived in a distant separation as if

across the low valley we never knew
  our ward flowed through

or knew the downtown was as close to
  as the gold dome on the new municipal

horizon. (*CE* 64)

Close to wealth only in geography, this colonized "people within a people" can now see the full extent and depth of the segregation that has been there all along—what Bennett speaks of as "urban apartheid"—but is only now dramatically exposed. Lines in a later section of the poem emphasize that the destruction of the community is not just collateral damage incurred in urban development; it's a deliberate economic strategy: *"Destruction is a hidden real investment: / nurture loss in value, mine what's left"* (*CE* 72). Identifying the same dynamics, Bennett explains that "the problem with gentrification . . . is that it actually begins with the process of disinvestment that clears the land and makes it available to up-scale developers," and, as part of his description of government "assault on urban areas," lists "building highways that destroyed housing and sealed off most people of color from the suburbanizing white middle class." Such projects, Bennett notes, transform "many black communities into pockets of unremitting poverty. . . . [T]he combined effects of anti-urbanism and the spatialization of race have been built into current public policy, which leaves a majority of African Americans in communities deprived of adequate education, employment, health care, housing, and overall social capital."[17] Roberson's poetry, we observe, can compress into a few lines or even single words the insights of pages of scholarly analysis: the verb "mine" in the italicized lines just quoted equates what are considered disposable human communities with "natural resources," both ripe for exploitation by the powerful.

  This reference to mining clarifies how Roberson's figurative depiction of urban space as part of nature serves the anti-humanist dimensions of his environmentalism. When Roberson attacks developers who dehumanize disenfranchised populations by comparing those oppressed people to exploited natural resources, he does not then defend those people by defending their humanity. The profundity of the developers' wrong is instead evident in the figure that indicates their greedy violation of the earth. Given that humans and all of human civilization are simply part of nature, for Roberson no one is human in the anthropocentric humanist sense that positions humans at the pinnacle of creation. His natural figures equalize the human and the nonhuman, just as they thwart a privileging of the nonbuilt over the built. When he speaks in "The Open" of "poor pride-kept and neat / stands of // old houses mown down" as if they were carefully tended orchards or forest preserves felled by a heavy mower and of "vacant lots of garbage lawn" now "fallowing," his metaphor reminds his readers that city spaces are as loved and precious as their rural counterparts and that human communities are ecologies that themselves warrant protection. By presenting violations of human rights in environmental terms, Roberson represents the situation he depicts as specifically one of environmental injustice. Elsewhere in the volume the geography of the city is also naturalized in what we might generalize as pastoral terms, its streets a "hive grid," or a "high plateau," the skyscrapers "peaks downtown," the bulldozer a "bulldozer-beetle" with its ball of dung, and the crowds rhythmically flowing through the crosswalks as "oceans" (CE 26, 132, 131, 44); such language works to counter in readers anti-urban attitudes that, as Bennett persuasively argues, enable such injustice.

Those in power, however, have no such sensitivity. When it comes to razed neighborhoods, they are waiting only for "the dead to clear   and the air / to smell of the scrub of money" before they take over this space for their own uses (CE 65). In a later section of "The Open," where the severance of these people from what had been their home and their place of connection to others is dramatized through the image of a cut-off phone line, Roberson conveys the scale of the power the developers wield when he compares what has happened to this neighborhood to the transformation wrought by a glacier tearing up the land and bringing cold: "as plowed earth up as // by a glacier   as by erasure changed to this / house of dead connection of no warm answering // on the lines / held frozen in our hands" (CE 66). The members of this (former) community march in protest, but effectively it's too late: a vital and meaningful place has been turned into a meaningless open space: "not even a place anymore // can't even walk it as / a street!" (*CE* 67). Again, he uses figures from nonhuman nature to convey what has gone wrong in the human world and thereby points to their essential unity. That unified realm is not idealized, however; nonhuman nature can be brutal and predatory, and human society can be brutally unjust. Thus, another poem describes the neighborhood's garbage collection after the city subcontracts with the mob using imagery of predatory animals:

> Brakes howling wild as a thing possessed
> loose in the alleys, the city's garbage truck
>
> lopes house to house, street to street, the wolf—
> in that hour before light— to the sleepless.
> It has our scent. It has our fucking jobs.

> ───────────────────────

> when the city tore down   like shooting
> all the houses living   on our street
>
> we couldn't even get the job
> of hauling
>
> away
> our dead   (*CE* 56–57)

It's widely acknowledged that aspects of nature figuring in literature are differently inflected according to a people's history as well as their culture; for instance, large trees in works by African Americans are more likely to suggest lynching than a shady bower. Notions of "the open" have generally positive meanings for white America, particularly in connection with nature, where the open is associated with individual freedom and the possibilities of the unfenced, unbounded frontier. For black Americans, however, in Roberson's representation, the open is a threatening space of isolation and dangerous exposure, where the protection of community is lacking, where those with dark skins experience potentially deadly vulnerability. This sense of vulnerability derives partly from America's racialized past. Invoking the image of core sampling in "The Open," Roberson examines "the fine segregations / taken as a core from our society" (*CE* 68). The civil rights struggles ("fire / hoses // run people off down the pavement") and the urban riots of the late 1960s are figured as another kind of opening, envisioned possibly as the "phoenix re-invention / of the nation" but resting on terrible African American sacrifice, the most horrifying of atmospheric pollutions: "God's strange rope spinning things open out of sky, / up in smoke // our tornado   our lynched / black pillar of light" (*CE* 69).

A less horrific but still grief-filled vision of the open—this time as a space of aimless drifting—emerges in the later sections "12" and "13," which return to the scene of "a flattened sea of housing brick rubble," "vacant block after block," to focus on an isolated, nearly naked man, a "just wakened" squatter, seen at the window of "the last building standing" as if both together are the lone survivors of a deadly battle (*CE* 70). No champion, however, the man seems closer to an embodiment of Agamben's "bare life"—a vulnerable figure stripped of political significance.[18] Though positioned as if on the prow of a "ghost ship," the lone figure "hanging out / of his shorts" where previously so many people were "hanging out / of windows" talking from floor to floor, is "keeping it open" only in an uninhabited ghost world where what's left of people's home furnishings—"the twisted / chrome-less tubing of cheap kitchenettes"—assumes forms reminiscent of rusted chains that once bound African slaves (*CE* 73–4).

In a poem later in the volume titled "Open / *Back Up! (breadth of field)*" Roberson makes clear that even the notion of "open field poetics"—one formulation for the projectivist poetics with which his highly visual arrangements of text might seem aligned—can't have the positive resonance for him as an African American male as it can for a white writer. The poem's opening announces that the "most recent open field [he's] crossed" is a long block on campus where "Black people get stopped regularly" by police in cars "to show they have university / I.D."—a far cry from the meadow ("so near to the heart, / an eternal pasture folded in all thought") to which Robert Duncan's mind gratefully returns.[19] The first few stanzas of Roberson's poem use regular left-hand margins, but lines broken and spaced to allude with grim irony to open field poetics end the poem as follows:

<blockquote>

Nature

life and limb gone through divestiture
of place from point
           reads to the lie
of open
        breasts of field   Elysian,
nor the narrow badge number of the gun.   (*CE* 88)

</blockquote>

What might seem evidently true for white Americans proves a stark lie for Americans of color because of the historical and continuing vulnerability of black bodies. The threat to life and limb African Americans experience in open spaces—an issue of environmental justice—has invalidated for them the "Elysian" meaning of the open.

Although Roberson's multiple books of poetry demonstrate extensive knowledge of and loving attention to nonbuilt nature, in *City Eclogue* he warns that bounded and aestheticizing perspectives on the natural world can too easily overlook social and economic realities. As one poem puts it, "Watching too much sunrise warms the breast / but often clouds the hands' / emptiness and the [nearly empty] pocket you're not facing // up to" (*CE* 33). It's the phrase "too much" that is key, for ultimately Roberson's thinking about nature is not dichotomous; he's not suggesting that one need give up sunrise appreciation (or the hope it symbolizes) altogether. Rather, he consistently emphasizes that, like the damaging division of black from white or past from present, thinking that divides urban and built nature from nonbuilt nature, or separates environmental damage from harm to human communities, results in a false positioning of humankind in relation to the planetary systems that sustain us.

While he clearly sees consequential distinctions between the powerful and the disempowered, and while *City Eclogue* starkly exposes violent oppression of African Americans, Roberson refuses to think of the human as divided in separatist terms. That this refusal is rooted in his response to America's awful history of racial division is evident in "Sit In What City We're In," which depicts the black civil rights activists of the 1960s and the white segregationists who viciously opposed them as ultimately mirrored versions of each other—"our one // long likeness" endlessly reflected in the lunch counter mirrors of the Greensboro, North Carolina, Woolworths. In one passage he imagines the barriers of difference dematerializing as those mirrors transmute to transparent glass and then "thin air":

> finally, us with no you nor I
>   but being
> —with all our world—   inside the other;
> but there only in   our each part yet having
>   no displacement of the other,
> just as each wishes   the self not lost, shared
> being in common in each other   being

> as different as
> night and day still   of one spin. (*CE* 31)

The difference between night and day suggests dark and light skin, but in this vision of what's possible, they coexist in all their fullness while occupying the same place in the natural order and following the same natural laws. Roberson's analogous vision of the oneness of urban and non-urban nature emerges in the close of the poem's first section, which extends the lunch-counter mirroring into all of the built and nonbuilt natural world of which humans are part:

> The oceans, themselves one,   catch their image
>   hosed by riot cops down the gutter into
> The sphere surface
> river
>   looked into   reflects
>   one face.   (*CE* 27–28)

The political challenge we face, at once social and environmental, is to honor that oneness and seek the equity and justice that is its ethical demand.

"LESSON[S] PAID FOR IN BLOOD": MARK NOWAK'S *COAL MOUNTAIN ELEMENTARY*

While Ed Roberson's vision ultimately reaches the global scale where humankind, like the planet's oceans, is a single entity transcending the divisions culture imposes, the environmental justice issues that concern him in *City Eclogue* are firmly centered in the United States and its racial fractures. In contrast, poet-activist Mark Nowak is among the North American poets whose environmental justice concerns take an international perspective. Nowak, who is the founder and director of the Worker Writers institute, has led poetry workshops for workers and trade unions in several European countries and in South Africa. His blog continually updates notices of mining disasters around the globe.[20] Nowak's *Coal Mountain Elementary* exposes the workplace hazards of coal mining along with some of its costs to the natural environment by bringing together documentation on American and Chinese mining disasters. The volume contains no original text; instead its "remix poetry" (Nowak's term) interweaves five sets of documents: (1) verbatim statements, set in boldface, that Nowak culled from 6,300 pages of transcribed testimony by rescue workers and miners who survived the mine explosion in January 2006 in Sago, West Virginia, that for two days trapped thirteen miners, twelve of whom died; (2) Nowak's color photographs of West Virginia mining towns, including Sago, mostly in winter; (3) chronologically arranged passages from English-language newspaper reporting on mining disasters in China over the two-and-a-half-year period between mid-February 2005 and late August 2007, printed in italics; (4) alternating with Nowak's photos, color photographs of Chinese miners and mining towns taken by the Malaysian-born British photojournalist Ian Teh; and (5) excerpts, which Nowak lineates as poetry, from three of the coal mining–related lessons for school children that appear on the American Coal Foundation website. When listing that last source in the volume's "Works Cited," Nowak quotes from the website: "The American Coal Foundation (ACF) was created in 1981 as a 501(c)(3) organization to develop, produce and disseminate, via the web, coal-related educational materials and programs designed for teachers and students. The ACF does not engage in lobbying."[21] A visit to the site casts doubt on that statement's suggestion of a distance from politics. The home page I encountered in May of 2014 announces in bold colorful lettering, "America has the world's largest coal supply— enough coal to power us for 200 more years," setting those words next to a photo of upscale apartments at dusk, with warm light glowing from cozily lit interiors.[22] The site's page where Nowak found the information about the 501(c)(3) organization (indicating it's officially a charitable organization to which donations are tax deductible) announces the foundation's links to the coal industry: "Support for the ACF is provided by coal producers and manufacturers of mining equipment and supplies. In addition, electric utilities, railroads, and organized labor have supported the work of the Foundation over the years. The ACF Board of Directors, comprised of industry executives, manages the operation of the Foundation." That same page goes on to explain that "ACF staff members work closely with outside educational partners to develop credible and effective educational materials for distribution to teachers."[23] Of course, although coal has the highest carbon content of all fossil fuels, this website makes no mention of the tremendous contribution coal burning makes to global warming. In fact, in 2012 CO_2 emissions from coal were responsible for 24.5 percent of U.S. greenhouse gas emissions.[24] As of 2014, although U.S. dependence on coal has been declining with the increased use of natural gas, coal-fired power plants were producing about 30 percent of the total fossil fuel–related emissions in the

United States. The nation with the largest CO_2 emissions is China, producing 30 percent of all global emissions in 2014—the United States is second, at 15 percent—and in 2014 coal consumption was responsible for about 83 percent of China's CO_2 emissions.[25] Nor does the ACF website acknowledge that burning coal is a leading cause of smog, acid rain, and multiple kinds of toxic air pollution. It does not mention that coal mines are associated with a host of public health problems because they are a huge source of mercury pollution, they introduce multiple carcinogens into regional drinking water, and their sludge and slurry ponds contaminate groundwater. And there is no mention of lives lost in mining.[26]

I don't want to give the impression, however, that Nowak has simply provided a crudely ironic, easy contrast in setting educational materials designed by a pro-coal organization beside evidence of the terrible danger coal mining poses to miners, their families and communities, and the natural environments where mines are situated. The juxtaposed materials speak to each other in a variety of ways so that he creates something that is clear in its politics yet also rewardingly complex.

The book's bold-faced pages take the reader through the excruciating tale of a single American disaster in minute detail via the painstaking testimony of those who were there and most closely involved, including men in a second cart who experienced the blast but were able to escape from the tunnel, a dispatcher, and rescue workers who found the victims and retrieved their bodies. The story slowly unfolds over the entire 176-page volume, its pieces separated by the other documentary threads; the vivid and peculiarly selective details of personal memory force the reader to participate in the horrors and suspense of this experience through a close-up, almost slow-motion, perspective. The use of multiple first-person speakers recreates the immediate uncertainty, confusion, and desperation of the men at the scene. The narrative also traces an excruciating error that the reader unfamiliar with the story of the Sago disaster only gradually discerns: a false report of twelve survivors circulated to the mining families three hours before the accurate report of twelve deaths reached them, so that they were wrenched from fear to ecstatic hope and then to doubly agonizing loss. This polyphony of male voices ends with the attempts to remove the body bags from the scene in a respectful way. The points at which the retrospective speakers stumble or fail to complete their sentences eloquently convey the ongoing trauma of the experience.

In contrast to the slow unfolding of a few hours' events at Sago, the italicized pages of reporting from China provide an almost panoramic overview, as one disaster follows another—60 dead here, 21 there, 122 dead another place, 148 in another, at least 62 somewhere else—without let-up, despite government officials repeatedly proclaiming the need for greater safety in the mines, even as descriptions of desperate and grieving widows left without means to support themselves and their children recur again and again. Here the book's length has a different impact, producing not a sense of moving along a course with the inevitability of a Greek tragedy, but of stagnation in a hellish realm where bodies just keep accumulating and the multiple mine explosions or mine floods become virtually indistinguishable from one another. Because the two narratives are juxtaposed, the reader is always aware that behind the generalized reporting from China lie suffering individuals like those whose first-person voices bring us close to Sago, and that those who keep on mining may be victims of future accidents.

A third kind of time is evoked in the lessons, where activities are imagined by the ACF as readily circumscribed into neat units; an exercise might be specified to take two one-hour periods, for instance. This vision of time that is easily divided and controlled is undercut by both the Chinese and American mining narratives, where orderly schedules and lives have been completely and irreparably disrupted.

Some significant differences between mining conditions in the two countries are discernable. In Sago, for instance, the miners know procedures to follow underground in emergencies, and each carries oxygen—neither of which is true in the Chinese disasters, where the miners seem often to be peasant farmers who enter the mines without training in order to supplement their inadequate agricultural incomes. Additionally, mining disasters are far more frequent and tend to involve far more deaths in China, where corruption is also more blatant (e.g., mining companies send bodies elsewhere in order to reduce accident body counts or bribe bereaved families hoping to suppress news of disasters). But in many ways the two kinds of text present the same story told in different time frames. Presenting the photos without captions yields a similar sense of sameness; a scene might be from Sago or from another American mining town, and sometimes—particularly because in Teh's pictures coal dust and smoke or miners' lights and movements partly obscure the figures, while Nowak's photos often show rusty mining structures—it's not obvious whether an image is from China or the United States. Extending this impression, a journalistic piece in which a massive open-pit mine in China is identified as founded by an

American industrialist signals that the two threads are part of the same system of multinational corporations (*CME* 136).

What's clear is that both nations' narratives and the accompanying images reflect major violations of the fundamental environmental justice principles originally affirmed at the 1991 First National People of Color Environmental Leadership Summit, most notably "the right of all workers to a safe and healthy work environment, without being forced to choose between an unsafe livelihood and unemployment," but also: "the right to be free from ecological destruction," "the right to ethical, balanced and responsible uses of land and renewable resources in the interest of a sustainable planet for humans and other living things," and the call for "universal protection from . . . extraction, production and disposal of toxic/hazardous wastes and poisons . . . that threaten the fundamental right to clean air, land, water, and food."[27] In an interview, Nowak approvingly repeats the following statement from Maurice Manning's review of *Coal Mountain Elementary* that brings together environmental and economic concerns: "Coal mining is the same everywhere. Most mines are located in remote places with little economic diversity, leaving local workers and their families vulnerable to the only game in town. Despite being tucked away in rural areas, however, many mining operations function on an unimaginable scale: The combined area of mountaintop-removal sites in West Virginia and Kentucky, for example, will be as big as Delaware by the end of the decade; an open-pit mine in Wyoming is visible from space."[28] The capitalist system underlying this sameness is exposed in the second of the three ACF curricular units that structure the book (all of which are still among the lessons on the website in May of 2016)—and this is where the book's juxtapositions are most heavily ironic. In an exercise using cookies from which chocolate chips are mined, elementary school students are supposed to simulate "the costs associated with the mining of coal." These costs are exclusively financial and include the purchase of property, tools, and labor, and also the price of environmental remediation. Nowak's context for these excerpts calls attention to the ACF's failure to include loss of human lives among the costs.

ACF does consider environmental costs—as the industry is mandated to do—but not, Nowak suggests, with sufficient integrity. The notion of environmental remediation is introduced just after a page on a disaster that killed at least 138 people, which *"came as the nearby city of Harbin was struggling to recover from a toxic spill [of benzene] in a river that forced the government to cut off water supplies for five days"* (*CME* 73). That is, it enters the text along-

Figure 12. Billboard image of green mountains in front of barren brown land-scape of Chinese mining region, in Mark Nowak and Ian Teh, *Coal Mountain Elementary,* 79. (Photograph by Ian Teh; courtesy of Ian Teh)

side evidence of aspects of industrial development besides coal extraction that similarly damage the environment and human health. A forceful dis-play of the impossibility of true remediation is provided a few pages later by Teh's photograph that shows a huge billboard set up in front of a line of low brick-and-stone buildings on a bleak brown hillside scarred with what appear to be open-pit mines; the billboard depicts bucolic farm fields and graceful mountains that perhaps approximate what one used to see at this spot (fig. 12; *CME* 79). The image creates an effect that eerily evokes a few of Magritte's surrealist paintings such as *Call of the Peaks* or *The Human Con-dition,* in which an easel supports a painting of exactly the scene behind it; there, the landscape and the representation are distinguishable only because of the easel. In Teh's photo the contrast between the representation and the landscape could hardly be more stark.

The fields in the billboard are bright green and yellow, the sky blue with white puffy clouds; it's a scene of perfect pastoral fertility and freshness that contrasts painfully with the local reality. Text from the elementary school lesson subsequently explains that:

> Coal companies
> are required by federal law
> to return the land they mine
> to its original, or an improved, condition.
> This process, known as reclamation,
> is a significant expense for the industry.   (*CME* 94)

Teh's photo makes obvious the impossibility of such a return. Its difficulty is perhaps implied in the ACF instructions for the students doing reclamation with cookies, but their pretense is that there need be no residual damage to the environment. (I suspect, however, that no child would mistake his or her chip-less reformed cookie for an undamaged original):

> have students
> restore their property
> to its original condition,
> within the drawn circle
> on the grid paper.
> This "reclamation"
> should also be timed
> (no more than three minutes)
> and students may only use
> their tools, not fingers.
> After time is up,
> collect additional
> reclamation costs
> ($) for each square covered
> outside the original outline.   (*CME* 118)

As this school lesson about making a profit unfolds, the juxtaposed Sago narrative follows first the false news of rescue and then the discovery of a dozen dead miners. Nowak's juxtapositions point to analogies between the industry's overlooking of environmental costs and its discounting of human ones. The ACF materials teach children how to cover up environmental damage and how to treat that damage as merely a "($)" cost, not a tragedy; at the same time, those materials fail to acknowledge human costs and tragedies. It could hardly be clearer that both tolls are being obscenely underestimated.

That the human costs of coal mining cannot be restricted to the immediate period of the accident is underscored by the book's coda, the only newspaper reportage connected with Sago that Nowak includes. It's an article from September 2006 that reports on the suicides of two "miners whose jobs included watching for safety hazards" inside the mine before the deadly explosion; one seems to be the dispatcher whose voice we heard earlier. He was seen by another miner after the explosion as "real nervous and he was trying to figure out what was going on, what we needed to do and who we needed to call and—" (*CME* 40). He's apparently the one who recounts his own ineffectual attempts to call this person and that one (when the superintendent, the maintenance superintendent, and the safety director were all "underground"), trying with his wife's help to locate people's numbers in the phone book and leaving messages on answering machines an hour and a half after the explosion, when he had been instructed to get in state and federal emergency teams (*CME* 45, 48). Some of the responsibility for this bungling may well have been his own, yet it also appears that the company had inadequately prepared the systems that would enable its employees to respond effectively to such a disaster. The other suicide was the person who cleared the mine as safe before the two carts of miners entered it. These deaths highlight the problematic invisibility of the corporate and economic structures that are most profoundly responsible for mining disasters—rather like the invisibility of the mines in Nowak's photo of a wooded area closed off for "active coal mining" (*CME* 100)—even as they point to individuals' complicities with larger systems. Occurring nine months after the accident, they reinforce the words of a Chinese taxi driver following a mining tragedy: *"what has happened will continue to haunt us for years to come"* (*CME* 92).

The environmental costs of extraction, too, are long lasting, and Nowak relies on pastoral tropes and values to communicate this. The dramatic contrast between the bucolic panorama of the billboard and the landscape against which it's seen, for instance, makes clear how terribly long full recovery of the land would take. Anthropogenic change happening over time is evident in Nowak's photos of rusted mining facilities or of abandoned home appliances in front of a crumbling shack; the striking absence of pastoral beauty in these dreary images conveys the severity of the environmental degradation as well as the poverty level of mining areas; there will be no quick fixes. How far these visual images fall short of the pastoral beauty our culture has taught us to value enforces readers' sense of the losses imposed by coal mining.[29]

Like Roberson, however, Nowak also seems wary of narrow visions that idealize or sweeten people's ideas of nature, though his critique is directed at class-marked condescending perspectives on quaint rural folk rather than the romanticization of rural landscapes. This emerges particularly in his presentation of the first lesson, on the "historic craft" of coal flowers. The ACF materials instruct teachers to explain:

When mining families had
little money
to buy decorations
or purchase toys,
they used
common household products
and coal to make
beautiful crystal flowers.
It was entertaining to watch
the crystal flowers grow,
because the changes took place
in a relatively short period of time.
Coal flowers were sometimes used
as Christmas decorations
because they resemble
snowflakes. (*CME* 32)

Although the miners' coal flowers were white, today's students—who can buy the necessary laundry bluing online from Martha Stewart (*CME* 25)—"will use / food coloring to enhance / the beauty of their coal flowers" (*CME* 37), suggesting that what was "entertaining" for these simple folks is insufficient for those who study them. How this relates to ideas of nature and the natural is suggested by the assessment page for this exercise:

Place the experiment
in its historical context
by discussing why
this activity might be
a natural one
for coal mining families
in the late 1800s
and early 1900s. (*CME* 50)

Are students being invited to regard being too poor to buy toys as a "natural" condition for miners? Convenient assumptions about what is natural for others can blind us to social and economic inequities and their consequences. The immediate commitment of what Nowak calls his "social poetics" is to social justice, yet he demonstrates a keen understanding of the thorough intertwining of social and environmental ills.[30] Some readers have failed to see the environmental concerns woven into *Coal Mountain Elementary*. Don Featherston, for instance, asserts, "Although Nowak documents the costs of the coal industry in human life and livelihood, he does not address the costs to the environment."[31] Such readings demonstrate the continued critical tendency to impose a separation between environmental and social justice.

Although infrequently introduced, miners' longings for remembered green landscapes and the associated pleasures of clean water and fresh air provide a crucial emotional counterpoint to *Coal Mountain Elementary*'s otherwise unrelenting presentation of suffocating air and gas-filled tunnels, deadly explosions, dead bodies, blackened, rubble-filled, and toxified landscapes. In the final section involving the lesson called "Coal Camps and Mining Towns," Nowak includes several passages of journalism in which Chinese people recall with pastoral nostalgia beautiful farmland and streams one could drink from, fish from, or swim in where now *"mountains of coal waste"* are piled and streams are poisoned (*CME* 136). In one of these passages, reference to blood invites the reader to connect what has happened to the land with what happened to the bodies of the trapped miners who died of carbon monoxide poisoning:

> *Some residents later talked about the village's founding myth, an old fable about how the beautiful village was founded in ancient times with a small lake in its center. But one day, according to the fable, a smart man from southern China came and stole the village frog, bringing ruin to Shangma Huangtou. "I don't believe this myth," Mr. Lin, the village chief, said. "I believe there's no water because of the coal mines. The earth is like the human body. And the water is like the blood in your veins. But now there's no water; no blood."* (*CME* 140)

Here's how an earlier passage in the Sago testimony described the mechanism by which carbon monoxide kills:

As it gradually builds, you have side effects, nausea, headache. Then at some point in time it gets to the point to where your respirations

aren't effective, because carbon monoxide binds to your red blood cells more higher, more affinity—what we call affinity to your red blood cells than pure oxygen does. So when your red blood cells are transporting oxygen, they're not really transporting oxygen, they're transporting carbon monoxide, which cannot be used. And that cycle stays. And it's a very hard bond to break between the carbon monoxide and the red blood cells. (*CME* 129)

The association between the two passages (recalling also the Chinese prime minister's description of a mining tragedy as a *"lesson paid for in blood"* [*CME* 5]) underscores the severity and likely irreversibility of the damage done to the earth in this mining area, where the earth is rendered effectively dead. It serves, too, as a reminder of the inseparability of human and environmental health, both of which are profoundly threatened by the Great Acceleration in which China, through its pursuit of American-style industrialization and economic growth, now participates.

"MINIMUM HUMAN SUBSISTENCE EXPERIMENT": MYUNG MI KIM'S *PENURY*

Nowak's work connects to that of Myung Mi Kim through the two poets' use of formal structures and techniques that reflect awareness of language's limitations and its potential distortion under political, social, or emotional pressure. The verbatim transcripts in *Coal Mountain Elementary* are full of places where speakers stumble or break off, unable to find adequate words, particularly around traumatic moments like the discovery of the bodies and the single survivor in the Sago mine: "**and there they were, all—all— Jim's working on McCloy, because he's alive, you know, he's—and I go directly to the opposite side of him and start checking for pulse and—you know, any breathing on the guys**" (*CME* 119). The very first newspaper reportage in the volume closes with a Chinese miner's widow announcing, "*I have no language for my feelings. . . . And there's no way anybody else can understand it*'" (*CME* 2). On the next page, however, the American speaker recalls being troubled by the unseasonable January thunderstorms that may have sparked the mine explosion; uncomfortable with the weather, this person longed for the reassurance of an explanatory "old wive's tale," feeling, "there's got to be a tale of some sort, you know." By constructing a book that works via juxtaposition and without added words, but that does tell stories nonetheless, Nowak respects both the need for "a tale of some sort" and the inability of language's denotative range to reach extreme emotions or experiences.

Myung Mi Kim pushes further toward the limits of verbal expression and what Joan Retallack has discussed as an "unintelligibility" perhaps necessary if poetry is going to reach beyond conventional understandings and ideologies.[32] Kim employs extremely pared-down fragmented language and large spaces of visualized silence as if she can only gesture toward all her words are to convey. Her formal experimentalism attempts to produce something that addresses "the problem of [the presupposition of] [there already exists] a language for" what she needs to say—that is, it strives to register "what is excluded in the sociohistorical index" and "that which is emergent [irreducible] in the cultural order."[33] In addition, much of the language Nowak and Kim use is lifted from media reporting—or, in Kim's case, at least sounds as if it comes from journalism or from legal and military documents—so that each volume implicitly acknowledges how mediated our approach to understanding other people's experience, "what passes for the actual," has become.[34] In a work about penury—extreme poverty, privation, or lack—Kim's always minimalist forms assume particular mimetic power.

Kim, who emigrated from Korea with her family when she was nine, writes often of the difficulties encountered by those displaced from their homelands and native languages. In her 2009 book *Penury*, as in her other volumes, the ways in which traits of speech mark one as a foreigner and subject one to prejudice and economic restriction are a recurrent concern. However, more directly related to the environmental justice issues that are my focus here are the portions of the text that suggest refugees' struggles for subsistence and evoke the effects on human survival of environmental damages wrought by industrialization and by warfare. I say "suggest" and "evoke" because in Kim's pared-down and space-filled writing a single word often has to do the work that might conventionally be done by a paragraph or stanza. Her words are like those that float up as one turns the Magic 8-Ball, mysterious, promising, weighted with significance. Or to offer a more aural analogy, appropriate to work in which sound is important: the reader is like someone leaning in to listen closely when a large choir sings at the level of a whisper, able to catch only suggestive bits of the lyrics, suggestions of a scene or situation. Particularly in the early sections of the volume, those situations often involve people on the deprived side of "the Great Divergence" as Kim explores the sources of dire poverty, famine, and want, particularly among displaced populations.[35] Militarization figures among them, including torture and strategies that involve such weapons as deliberate starvation though destruction of cropland and crops. Other environmental factors that might or might not be anthropogenic, like extended drought, also come in. In Kim's work, it's not always clear whether people are displaced because of war, or because of environmental devastation, or because driven by economic need. This conveys how the three are in fact so often intertwined, just as anthropogenic and non-anthropogenic environmental changes in a particular region often reinforce each other. (Farming techniques and deforestation, for example, may exaggerate the consequences of drought.)

The situations alluded to in *Penury* might speak to Korean history in particular—for instance, as Angela Hume has noted, the famines endured in North Korea in the 1990s and again in recent years.[36] Yet the generalizable language suggests that these situations are widespread. Here, for instance, are three pages within the section titled "fell (for six multilingual voices)" where military occupation and tools of torture figure, as do bits suggesting mass migration by poor women to find work as housemaids, a situation in which many are abused:

: | Measure streets by the number of uniforms

: | It's the pitch of the cry that carries

: | Hunger noise thirst noise fear noise

: | Inside acts conducted outside

: | Decades of continuous drought

: | Weapon and deed

: | Whether the house has windows, whether the windows have glass

: | The dirt air

: | Of the tens of thousands of women who leave each year

: | Electric baton   rifle butts

: | Fifty cents more and we go there

: | Calculated withholding of food   *(P* 51–52)

. . .

: | The epidemic phase of famine

: | Sea surface temperature   urban heat island

: | Stripped bark from pines and boiled it—and swallowed it

: | Housemaids elsewhere

: | Sacrifices to the Altar of Land and Grain

: | Foreign Employment Bureau *(P* 54)

The passages suggest multiple circumstances that might be producing what Laura Westra, among others, has termed "ecological refugees," a category that in her use encompasses environmental refugees—those who migrate because of a marked environmental disruption or deterioration that jeopardizes their existence or seriously degrades their quality of life— along with the more recent category of climate refugees, and those fleeing industrial and chemical hazards.[37] The people in Kim's poem who are re- duced to eating boiled pine bark are clearly starving, perhaps because of the decades of drought. The drought may be caused by global warming ("sea surface temperature urban heat island"), though one can imagine other factors unmentioned by Kim that might contribute to crop failures or desertification. The famine may have been intensified by military tac- tics involving "calculated withholding of food" (an earlier poem speaks of "withholding . designed to starve the whole region into submission"

[P 7]). Regardless of the specific causes, environmental disruption contributes to people's misery and to their seeking employment abroad. Attempts
to track the cultures and places from which Kim draws her cultural details
point all over the globe and even back in time to the myths and practices
of the earlier Aztec and Taino people. The marks that precede each line
on the pages I quoted—a colon followed by a space and a vertical line [: |
] suggest, as C. J. Martin has noted, the musical repeat sign;[38] I take that as
an indication that the things listed are recurring phenomena rather than
singular occurrences. What Kim offers are fragments of specific examples
that speak to worldwide problems. Significantly, lines early in the volume
echo the "Universal Declaration of Human Rights" adopted by the UN
General Assembly in 1948; "freedom of residence / freedom of movement"
(P 10) are rights affirmed in Article 13.1, "Everyone has the right to freedom of movement and residence, within the borders of each state." Kim's
minimalistic lines quietly insist that violations of these universal rights are
pervasive.

That such violations now involve specifically environmental injustices is
reinforced by later lines on that same page: "as history knows / what justice
looks like // industry's station / street by street // smelting is in progress"
(P 10). Smelting, the fiery, energy-intensive process by which metal is ex-
tracted from ore, tends to be highly polluting, releasing hydrogen fluoride,
sulfur dioxide (the source of acid rain), oxides of nitrogen, along with a
range of heavy metals (lead, mercury, cadmium, arsenic, and so on), often
carried in dust that pollutes soil and surface waterways. Sulfuric acid and
contaminant-containing slag are also byproducts. Smelters for iron, zinc,
lead, copper, aluminum, and other metals are located around the globe,
from Arizona to Australia, Bahrain to Sweden, Ghana to India, and numerous health problems are associated with the chemicals they release. At a
later point in the volume, Kim probably points to the health hazards posed
by smelters when she mentions "nitrogen oxides, heavy metal (mercury) de-
posits" (P 73) and on the next page presents lines that might be spoken by a
health worker treating someone suffering heavy-metal poisoning: "Do you
eat berries, mushrooms, fish, and game? / Most likely how it entered your
body." Toxins are often concentrated high in the food chain, as in fish and
game, while mushrooms readily absorb heavy metals and other chemical
pollutants (and in some cases, break them down, contributing importantly
to bioremediation).

Mention of these wild foods that one might hunt and forage and which in a nontoxic region would provide a very healthy diet points to the role that pastoral elements play in this volume. As was the case in Nowak's volume, allusions to pastoral landscapes and versions of the *locus amoenus* in Kim's book provide resonant contrasts to the degraded landscapes of the present on which the poet focuses. As in *Coal Mountain Elementary,* in *Penury* evocations of the pastoral are infrequent and not much attached to the present. Nonbuilt nature, when mentioned, tends to be clearly disturbed or else threatening. A stranded cow bellows; there's mention of the largest rat ever and of a canary yellow rock that's probably carnotite, a radioactive uranium-venadium ore. One line describes a massive fish die off: "When the fish die all at once and appear on the bank all at once" (*P* 43); there's mention of extensive land cleared for military tank traffic. On one page where a pastoral scene appears—"Rolling country small poplar bluffs"—the context suggests the property is being transferred to someone powerful in exchange for the release of prisoners. And, as we've just seen, eating "berries, mushrooms, fish, and game" is mentioned in connection with toxicity. By and large, pastoral pleasures seem drastically attenuated if not inaccessible. Jonathan Bate has drawn attention to Raymond Williams' insight that "the better life is always just behind us, 'over the last hill.' . . . Williams portrays rural nostalgia as an escalator reaching further and further back into the past" and ultimately back to Eden. In this sense, Kim's presentation exaggerates a trait of all pastoral. Such myths "of the natural life which exposes the ills of our own condition," Bate notes, are "necessary imaginings": they may help check anthropocentric "instincts" toward what he calls "self-advancement."[39]

Very occasionally, a few words denoting nature in the (presumed) present and without unpleasant associations do appear in *Penury,* as in the lines "tree frog toads" (*P* 58) or "a ripple | birched / alyssum"—the latter example perhaps providing relief from a woman's "weeping work" (*P* 22). The solace associated with traditional ideas of a pure, relatively undisturbed nonhuman nature has not, then, been eradicated despite the "scorched earth tactics" (*P* 58) and famine that fill these pages; hints of pastoral landscapes appear as precious alternatives to the living conditions of the disenfranchised. In this book, we should note, degraded or corrupted living conditions are not evidently urban, as they have been in conventional pastoral writing. The environmental refugees and forced laborers whose suffering is sketched here inhabit camps or desertified landscapes or "makeshift shelters." So the urban versus rural or urban versus natural dichotomy that Roberson challenged is not reestablished here. Rather, its terms are shifted and expanded to acknowledge environmental degradation caused by phenomena like war or the extraction industries that support industrial development and the consumerism of the developed nations.

The thread in Kim's volume that reaches back toward pastoral scenes associated with less damaged ecosystems reaches also toward traditions and ceremonies that suggest more intact cultures than those subject to military occupation, environmental disruption, and diaspora. The single scene in which "sumptuous blossoms and fresh herbs" are joyfully evoked begins, "Near one, do you recall," as if the speaker is trying to prompt in a relative a shared memory of the distant past. The scene exists as a treasured remembrance of a traditional ceremony "celebrated by a family for the welfare of all belonging to it"; there's no suggestion that such rituals are still practiced by the speaker or the person addressed. On the volume's final page, where Kim, I think, suggests the possibility of something positive emerging when people start from scratch, turning the space of destitution and emptiness into a space for future abidance, she employs the kind of imagery that one might find in a nature poem written before the self-conscious Anthropocene:

> Radiant falcon
> Scattering acacias
>
> The recitation of acacias
> A grove of riverbeds
>
> Residence of years' repose

The imagery also has links to traditional Korean culture, where acacia and other thorny branches have been used to chase away bad spirits from homes. The genus of acacias, however, is heterogeneous, suited to varied habitats and climates. This passage may invoke cultural as well as ecological recuperation, but more generally it gives embodiment to the hope of again experiencing political freedom (figured in the falcon's flight) accompanied by belonging in and to a land healthy enough to sustain human and non-human life.

The politics and priorities of those concerned with social justice issues and those concerned with environmentalism do not always align. Yet the three poets discussed here understand social justice as environmental justice, and see justice as inseparable from traditional environmentalist concerns. In addition to understanding the spaces where people live and work as part of "the environment," they integrate into their environmental justice writing attention to the well-being of the habitats and nonhuman creatures long recognized as part of nature. Both the discourses of nature and those of environmental justice benefit: environmental justice writing broadens its appeal by locating in the pastoral, modified in varying degrees, a center of value. Current discourses of nature gain ethical force from their incorporation into the writing of environmental justice.

Coda

Writing the Self-Conscious Anthropocene

The chapters of this book have been organized around specific issues so that particular volumes of poetry have been examined in terms of single environmental concerns. This structure has enabled me to intervene, chapter by chapter, in distinct critical conversations and also to highlight the poetry's contributions to particular environmental discourses of the self-conscious Anthropocene. The first chapter, on scale—a key issue for scientists considering, for instance, the scalability of particular ways of producing or distributing food or energy—foregrounds psychological and perceptual dimensions of scalar thinking, explored in works by Spahr, Gander, and Roberson, that must also be taken into account if society is to meaningfully address the environmental issues of the Anthropocene. The poetic treatments of plastics examined in the second chapter demonstrate art's crucial ability to explore complex issues in ways that respect conflicting claims and ambivalence. Reilly in *Styrofoam* and Dickinson in *The Polymers* celebrate plasticity and playfully display the marvels of plastics' multifunctionality while stressing the costs, downplayed by industry and insufficiently addressed by policymakers, of these accumulating toxic materials to human and environmental health. The third chapter's examination of current apocalyptic discourse in Graham's *Sea Change* and Reilly's *Apocalypso* reveals how resourcefully poets are revising an ancient rhetoric some have thought exhausted so as to both call attention to the entanglement of human fate with that of other species and provide pleasures that make bearable confrontation with potentially devastating risks. The poets discussed in chapter 4, a.rawlings, Gladding, and Skinner, daringly experiment with the visual and aural resources of poetry in order to learn about and from nonhuman animals; in ways that honor interspecies differences, they model versions of the human/animal indistinction some animal studies theorists have championed. In the fifth chapter, on how the self-conscious Anthropocene has affected ecopoetic representations of place and place-attachment, Spahr, Gander, and Osman demonstrate poetry's ability to represent place as translocal in ways appropriate to this era of globalized movement of trade, pollutants, and information, as well as people and other bioforms. In the final chapter, analysis of Roberson's *City Eclogue,* Nowak's *Coal Mountain Elementary,* and Kim's *Penury* reveals possibilities for bringing together discourses often at odds— the nature-based discourses of environmentalism and the socially based discourses of environmental justice—partly by refurbishing the ancient literary resources of the pastoral.

This issue-based approach has been fruitful. Yet such an organization obscures a key aspect of the self-conscious Anthropocene: the multiple environmental issues that come together in its awareness. The widespread concern about human impact on planetary systems that defines the self-conscious Anthropocene has been produced by myriad environmental transformations that together justify the dramatic claim that, rather than inhabiting the Holocene, we now live in the Anthropocene. While each of the issues I have foregrounded is crucial to our time, their intertwining is also essential to how poets and readers experience the Anthropocene. The multiplicity of anthropogenic transformations now taking place and their frequent interaction prove crucial to the difficulty they pose for both personal response and public policy.

In this book, work from one volume has occasionally been featured in more than one chapter—as with *Well Then There Now,* treated in chapters 1 and 5—or different volumes by one poet have figured in separate chapters—as has been the case with Roberson, Gander, and Reilly. In those ways I have gestured toward the range of concerns on the writers' minds. Yet the works under discussion were selected in part because of their relevance to a particular focus, when in fact a good deal of contemporary ecopoetry draws attention to multiple, sometimes intertwined environmental issues. Additionally, environmental concerns so saturate consciousness in the self-conscious Anthropocene that writing on a surprising array of subjects assumes an ecopoetic cast. To more fully acknowledge the intertwining of multiple environmental concerns that increasingly characterizes environmentally conscious poetry—or that informs work one might not regard as obviously ecopoetic—I will by way of brief conclusion examine a poem by Brenda Coultas that demonstrates the mix of environmental anxieties or problems, and their convergence with social and political issues, typically acknowledged in current North American poetry. This poem's weaving together of digital technology and social media with fossil fuel consumption and global warming, the diminution of potable water, the environmental impacts of fracking, and the relation of corporate power to land rights, water rights, and genetic manipulation conveys the complexity of our environmental circumstances.

Like several works examined in previous chapters, "A Gaze," from Coultas's fourth poetry collection *The Tatters* (2014), is a generic hybrid that uses prose and relies heavily on parataxis to generate meaning. Its epigraph from the Halliburton website might be a clue to the poem's anti-fracking stance: "*Shale is incredibly complex. When it comes to finding the shale sweet spot and unlocking it in a cost-efficient manner, no one has more experience than Halliburton.*" However, fracking is only one of many concerns raised in "A Gaze." More generally, the epigraph identifies a context for that array of concerns in a set of attitudes toward the natural world and a set of values operating in corporate capitalism: the complexity of the earth's sedimentary geology is acknowledged but taken as a challenge for human ingenuity; humans (rightly, from the website's perspective) use the technologies they have developed to triumph over that complexity while insuring the financial profit served by cost efficiency.

Further into the poem one comes to understand the anger and politicized energy behind it, but that is not immediately evident from its matter of fact, observational mode, in which environmental and social preoccupations intertwine. The opening lines seem to contemplate human striving for interpersonal connection as much as they observe people's obliviousness to the connections between their technology-dependent lifestyles and global warming:

A man texts a photograph of his meal, but to who? Himself or others?
Others too, texting in a crowd on 1st Avenue as glaciers recede.
They do not feel the fading cold of the ice. Only the heat of the
key strokes.

A man texts crystal water glass pixels to quench real thirst.[1]

Observing our failure to connect physically or emotionally to the environmental consequences of the way we live, the poet may suggest contemporary social media prevent us from making those connections. Overreliance on technology remains a preoccupation as the speaker recounts being on the top of a mountain "where only small mammals live" and recognizing that she does not belong where the air is so thin, "though I can drive there." She describes using her phone's camera "as an extension of [her] eyes" in the gift shop on the glacier and then admits she sometimes forgets she's "not an extension of the machine" until burning her palms on a pot hot from the stove reminds her that she needs to protect her flesh. Implicitly, less attachment to our machines would enhance our perception of how dangerously we are heating the world.

Simultaneously, a cluster of thematic threads involving water is developing as well. Introduced by the man texting an image of his water glass, water recurs as the speaker "texted forward a rumor of siphoned great lakes water to China. A / Chinese bureaucrat texts images of fresh lake water to billions at home." Soon a preoccupation with water—with the preciousness of clean water, with our wasting of it, with who has rights to it, and with the extraction industries polluting it—comes to dominate the poem. Strikingly, even as Coultas returns repeatedly to receding glaciers, she doesn't, despite her attention to water, mention consequent rising sea levels, which would keep the focus on global warming. This bears upon my argument about the conglomeration of concerns that burden the self-conscious Anthropocene. Instead of focusing readers' minds exclusively on the consequences of anthropogenic melting of the world's glaciers, Coultas is raising questions about the purity and availability of drinking water or the diversion of water for hydro-fracking, and she is contemplating ancient sea beds that are now dry land, the corpses emerging from melting glaciers, or the deceptive labels of water bottles that suggest the contents come from pure mountain steams when "you know the source is a corporate tap of public water" (*TT* 17). Coultas even gestures toward issues associated with industrial agriculture: "Fertilizer runs off into our family well. . . . Even though people spoke of the well running dry, ours magically replenished itself under the blanket of Monsanto crops" (*TT* 17). The reader of this poem, while considering several versions of the line, "The last glass of water sits before you, how fast or slow will you drink it?"—a puzzle both literally and in its metaphorical resonances—is asked to keep in mind issues ranging from digitally generated alienation to private satellites in public space to monopolist genetic engineering.

The poem's second part looks at water through the lens of fantasy, prompted apparently by the phrase "water table," here imagined as a table on which one would eat, the underground location of "a banquette of the last supper." This event "we" attend is initially an elegant one—"the clear plates as detailed as a sea monkey's anatomy or the vulvas of Judy Chicago's dinner party. // A centerpiece of lilies welcomes us. A waiter comes with his crystal water pitcher" (*TT* 18)—but apparently we are not invited guests, and, with a dreamlike shift, the scene loses its "diamond-worthy" elegance and becomes threatening:

> We sit down before the guards can catch us.
> Wastewater, its chemicals pass through the tablecloth, and infect it
> with radiation. Inside pantry doors, mining deep into the cabinet, the
> heavy minerals are stored in the far reaches of the cupboard and on the
> top shelf out of reach
>
> Who holds the crystal-clear machine guns?
> Who fires the shocks of the invisible fence?
>
> We gaze at the fence of ownership
> Once set for us
> Then set against us (*TT* 19)

The next line finds the speaker taking shelter in the watershed, imagining it "untouchable, such / a treasure, Catskill pure." But her description invokes a part of New York City's water history that makes clear such places are far from untouchable. She shelters "in a house that once sat in a place now underwater, a house meant to be drowned under the Ashokan." Between 1907 and 1914 the Ashokan Reservoir was constructed to provide New York City with clean water. In the process two thousand people were relocated, as four towns and thousands of acres of farmland were submerged and eight additional towns relocated. "Theft of water from Bishop Falls / Greatest heist of all / Starts the flow downstream," Coultas observes, referring to one of the lost towns and a famous landmark, now under 180 feet of water at the deepest part of the reservoir.

The next set of lines begins "Marcellus Shale" and speaks of "Shalenlaires, farmers made wealthy overnight" by selling their lands to companies extracting natural gas. (The Marcellus Shale formation runs beneath New York, Pennsylvania, Ohio, and West Virginia and, as of 2015, yielded over 36 percent of the shale gas produced in the United States.) Coultas doesn't say anything about water, but its relevance is obvious: according to the U.S. Geological Survey, fracking a well in the Marcellus Shale requires on average 4.5 million gallons of water. Fracking is known to contaminate wells, and chemical spills of fracking fluid can leak into the water table.

Coultas's juxtaposition of the Ashokan dam project's "theft of water" with the extraction of natural gas from Marcellus Shale is no more subtle than the poem's closing lines: "They use private forces against us / Weapons to keep us away from our water." The lines' crude us-versus-them dichotomy doesn't do justice to the kinds of widespread if not always conscious complicity in environmental degradation suggested in the work's opening depiction of people texting while glaciers melt or in the speaker's early admission, "Sometimes, the tap runs while I brush my teeth and empty bathwater down the drain." Yet Coultas is not without justification: "experienced" corporations like Halliburton have been subject to far weaker controls and far less accountability than environmentally minded citizens believe prudent for the protection of America's potable water (as well as protection from the health problems associated with frack-sand mining, or even from earthquakes thought to be prompted by widespread subterranean injection of fracking solutions). People have reason to regard such powerful corporations and the political lobbies that support them as a terrible other, a "they," opposing citizens' rights and environmental health. The last glass of water that Coultas invites us to imagine sitting before us may be the last because anthropogenic global warming has eliminated the glacial sources of clean water, but it could equally well be the last because human activities have lowered water tables and poisoned aquifers. In the self-conscious Anthropocene, one necessarily thinks in terms of multiple, often interacting developments shaping the environment.

With her closing phrase, "our water," Coultas seems to mean the people's water, as opposed to the corporations' or the government's. But the phrase returns us to the key challenges of the Anthropocene and the power of humans it acknowledges. This is, after all, the planet's water, on which the entire biosphere depends. The environmental future rests in large part on the "we" we think and act with: Will it include nonhuman species? Will it include the people of the global South, or the impoverished populations of the global North? And will "we" adequately recognize the limits of human understanding and human powers (humans may "start the flow downhill," but it is gravity that carries the water down) along with the likelihood of unanticipated consequences to our actions? The work of ecopoetics in the self-conscious Anthropocene includes fostering such inclusive perspectives while making vivid the multifaceted damage humans are doing to what we like to think of, whether in hubris or humble stewardship, as our Earth.

Notes

INTRODUCTION

1. Pope Francis, *"Laudato Si'*: Encyclical Letter of the Holy Father Francis on Care for Our Common Home."

2. Lewis and Maslin, "Defining the Anthropocene."

3. Boes and Marshall, "Writing the Anthropocene," 66; N. Clark, *Inhuman Nature*, xiii.

4. Boes and Marshall, "Writing the Anthropocene," 66. Gabriele Dürbek "proposes the term *Anthropocene literature* . . . to characterize literary texts that reflect on the human condition in the face of fundamental human transformations of the planetary surface on a global scale" ("Ambivalent Characters and Fragmented Poetics in Anthropocene Literature," 112). Her term might have been useful for this book had her definition been less narrow. Reflecting on more than the human condition, the artists I consider explore the conditions of many parts of the biosphere, often attempting to shift the focus away from humankind. Dürbek takes into consideration only works of prose fiction, so that many traits of Anthropocene literature she observes involve plot, narrative, and protagonists, all of which have little relevance for ecopoetics.

5. There is not yet consensus about the meaning of "ecopoetry." Some use it to identify all environmentally engaged poetry of any period, including nature poetry. In a chronologically restricted version of that position, Ann Fisher-Wirth and Laura-Gray Street use "ecopoetry" as an umbrella term for poetry since 1960 that responds to environmental crisis; within that they locate subcategories of nature poetry, environmental poetry, and ecological poetry (*The Ecopoetry Anthology*, xxviii–xxix). Some reserve "ecopoetry" for recent work that diverges from traditional nature poetry in being formally and linguistically experimental (what Fisher-Wirth and Street call "ecological poetry"). Using the term in distinction from traditional nature poetry, I join those who apply it to poetry that approaches environmental writing with an interest in the intertwining of nature and culture.

6. See, for example, Asafu-Adjaye et al., "An Ecomodernist Manifesto."

7. Crutzen, "Geology of Mankind," 23; the piece published in 2000 is Crutzen and Stoermer, "The 'Anthropocene.'"

8. Crutzen, "Geology of Mankind," 23; Steffen, Crutzen, and McNeill, "The Anthropocene," 614, 618–20.

9. Autin and Holbrook, "Is the Anthropocene an Issue of Stratigraphy or Pop Culture?," 61.

10. Zalasiewicz, Williams, et al., "The New World of the Anthropocene," 2230–31.

11. Zalasiewicz, Cearreta, et al., "Response to Autin and Holbrook," e21.

12. Lewis and Maslin, "Defining the Anthropocene."

13. Nixon, "The Anthropocene: Promise."

14. Haraway, *Staying with the Trouble*, 49.

15. Elder, *Imagining the Earth*; Scigaj, *Sustainable Poetry*; Bate, *The Song of the Earth*. The traditions of nature writing on which anglophone writers draw go back to the classical Greeks and works like the *Georgics*, and there are important developments in English nature writing before Romanticism. However, the tradition of the Romantic nature lyric (with its assimilated earlier influences) is most formative for twentieth- and twenty-first-century poets.

16. Raymond Williams, *Problems in Materialism and Culture*, 79–81.

17. Wordsworth, *Wordsworth's Poetry and Prose*, 66.

18. Bate, *The Song of the Earth*, 245, 64, 247.

19. L. Buell, *The Future of Environmental Criticism*, ch. 1; Scigaj, *Sustainable Poetry*, 28, 27.

20. Silliman et al., "Aesthetic Tendency and the Politics of Poetry," 263.

21. Skinner, "Editor's Statement," 7, 6; Corey and Waldrep, *The Arcadia Project*; Fisher-Wirth and Street, *The Ecopoetry Anthology*; Dungy, *Black Nature*; Rasula, *This Compost*; Iijima, *Eco Language Reader*.

22. Cronon, "The Trouble with Wilderness," 71, 81.

23. Crutzen and Schwägerl, "Living in the Anthropocene"; Purdy, "Losing Nature."

24. Morton, *Ecology without Nature*, 1; Morton, *The Ecological Thought*, 7, 9; Heise, review of *Hyperobjects*.

25. L. Buell, "Ecocriticism," 94.

26. Berry, *The Selected Poems*, 30.

27. Wordsworth, *Wordsworth's Poetry and Prose*, 67, 403.

28. Kumin, "Intimations of Mortality."

29. Oliver, *House of Light*, 18.

30. Slovic, *Seeking Awareness in American Nature Writing*, 18.

31. Arguably, the category "environmentalist" now includes those, like the noted evolutionary biologist E. O. Wilson, who are championing the idea of "half earth"—of avoiding a cataclysmic extinction event by setting aside half the earth for nonhuman species (*Half-Earth*). The "ecomodernists" or "ecopragmatists," too, are committed to shrinking human impact on nature, and in fact to reinforcing the division between the human and the rest of nature, by "decoupling human development from environmental impacts" (Asafu-Adjaye et al., "An Ecomodernist Manifesto"). The "ecomodernists" are techno-optimists whose thinking in many ways diverges from mainstream environmentalism.

32. The quoted phrase comes from Oliver's "Nature." The poem describes a nighttime scene of an owl hunting and ends with tree branches tossing "the white moon upward / on its slow way / to another morning / in which nothing new // would ever happen, which is the true gift of nature, / which is the reason / we love it" (*House of Light*, 55).

33. Spahr, *Well Then There Now*, 69.

34. For more extended analysis of the poem, see Keller, "The Ecopoetics of Hyperobjects."

35. Reilly, *Styrofoam*, 27. From now on, this work will be cited parenthetically in the text as *S*.

36. Reilly, "Eco-Noise and the Flux of Lux," 257.

37. Ibid., 261.

38. Ibid.

39. Morton, *The Ecological Thought*, 28, 29, 31.

40. See Retallack, *The Poethical Wager*, where this concept recurs, esp. 25–26, and "Poethics of a Complex Realism," 196–221.

41. Purdy, "Losing Nature."

42. Grubisic, "Instructions for Building the Arc."

43. Blackie, "An Interview with Jorie Graham."

44. Bate, *The Song of the Earth*, 64.

45. Retallack, "What Is Experimental Poetry?"

46. L. Buell, *The Environmental Imagination*, 285; Nordhaus and Shellenberger, "Apocalypse Fatigue"; F. Buell, *From Apocalypse to Way of Life*.

47. Kimmerer, *Braiding Sweetgrass*; Plumwood, *Environmental Culture*; Gander and Kinsella, *Redstart*, 11.

48. Schellnhuber et al., "Earth System Analysis for Sustainability," 12.

1. "IN DEEP TIME INTO DEEPSONG"

1. Worster, "Second Earth." This talk was an early version of material that Worster develops in his 2016 book, *Shrinking the Earth*.

2. Some cultures have recognized human insignificance in ways that Judeo-Christian cultures have not, since Christian teaching situates humans as the pinnacle of creation and gives humans dominion over the rest of creation. Recognition of human insignificance requires more of a conceptual change for some populations than for others.

3. Gee, *In Search of Deep Time*, 31, 26.

4. Woods, "Scale Critique for the Anthropocene."

5. Chakrabarty, "The Climate of History," 201, 204–7, 213.

6. Ibid., 216, 220.

7. Chakrabarty, "Climate and Capital," 3.

8. The three rifts Chakrabarty discusses are (1) "the various regimes of probability that govern our everyday lives in modern economies and which now have to be supplanted by our knowledge of the radical uncertainty of the climate"; (2) "the

story of our necessarily divided human lives having to be supplemented by the story of our collective life as a species, a dominant species, on the planet"; and (3) "our inevitably anthropocentric thinking in order to supplement it with forms of disposition towards the planet that do not put humans first" (ibid.).

9. Ibid., 9.

10. Chakrabarty, "Brute Force."

11. Woods, "Scale Critique for the Anthropocene," 133, 136.

12. T. Clark, "Scale," 148–50.

13. Woods, "Scale Critique for the Anthropocene," 134.

14. T. Clark, "Scale," 152.

15. Woods, "Scale Critique for the Anthropocene," 139.

16. There is controversy about the scientific status and the appropriateness of "tipping point" warnings in connection with climate change. The term signals a critical threshold, a point where rapid and irreversible shifts in large systems are triggered. James Hansen used it in a presentation to the Geophysical Union in 2005, and the term now appears with some frequency in scientific literature concerning climate change. However, its initial popularity in the discourse around climate change came in popular media and public debate; scientists may be using it as a "generative metaphor." For an analysis of the term's use, see Russill and Nyssa, "The Tipping Point Trend in Climate Change Communication."

17. Spahr, *Well Then There Now,* 6–7. From now on, this work will be cited parenthetically in the text as *WTTN.*

18. Butler, *Gender Trouble,* 32.

19. Nixon, *Slow Violence and the Environmentalism of the Poor.*

20. T. Clark, "Scale," 150.

21. For another reading of this poem, focusing on the refrain, see Chisholm, "On the House That Ecopoetics Builds."

22. Margaret Ronda, in "Mourning and Melancholia in the Anthropocene," argues that another poem from *Well Then There Now,* "Gentle Now, Don't Add to Heartache," mimics conventional elegy but repeatedly points to the incompleteness of mourning. Some of the same arguments could be applied to "Unnamed Dragonfly Species."

23. Franzen, "Carbon Capture"; italics in original.

24. Gander and Kinsella, *Redstart,* 5. From now on, this work will be cited parenthetically in the text as *RS.*

25. Roberson, *To See the Earth Before the End of the World.* From now on this volume will be cited parenthetically in the text as *TSEB.*

26. Keller and Wagstaff, "An Interview with Ed Roberson," 412.

27. Stevens, *Collected Poetry and Prose,* 56.

28. Heringman, "Deep Time at the Dawn of the Anthropocene," 57.

29. As the poet Giovanni Singleton pointed out to me, his title alludes to the lyrics of jazz musician, Sun Ra, "It's after the end of the world. Don't you know that yet?" In the context of Sun Ra's worldview, the lines suggest the foolishness of anxi-

ety focused on anticipated disaster. Roberson dedicates a later poem in the collection, "Sight Read on a Couple Stars," to Sun Ra.

30. For an interesting discussion of the translation of that passage from Marx and Engels, see Menely, "Anthropocene Air," 97.

31. Shakespeare, *The Riverside Shakespeare*, 1608.

2. TOXICITY, NETS, AND POLYMERIC CHAINS

1. Reilly, "Eco-Noise and the Flux of Lux," 258.

2. Beck and Chalmers, "Risk Society and the Provident State," 27.

3. Beck, "Living in the World Risk Society," 338; Beck and Chalmers, "Risk Society and the Provident State," 28.

4. Beck and Chalmers, "Risk Society and the Provident State," 29; Beck, *Risk Society*, 163, 162; italics in original.

5. Alaimo, *Bodily Natures*, 2, 18.

6. Ibid., 16.

7. Reilly, "Eco-Noise and the Flux of Lux," 261.

8. Reilly, *Styrofoam*, 9. From now on, this work will be cited parenthetically in the text as *S*.

9. Freinkel, *Plastic*, 10; Gourmelon, "Global Plastic Production Rises, Recycling Lags"; Parker, "Ocean Trash." According to an article published in 2012 by the Earth Institute of Columbia University, "today Americans discard about 33.6 million tons of plastic each year, but only 6.5 percent of it is recycled and 7.7 percent is combusted in waste-to-energy facilities, which create electricity or heat from garbage" (Cho, "What Happens to All That Plastic?").

10. Micro- or nano-plastics are a growing concern for scientists. Because they do not figure prominently in the two books under discussion, I will not address the dangers they pose. However, I recommend the overview provided by Tamara S. Galloway in "Micro- and Nano-Plastics and Human Health."

11. Langston, *Toxic Bodies*, 6. According to Langston, whose study focuses not on plastics but on the hormonally active chemical DES, researchers in the 1950s found that "small doses of DES could be more effective at inducing cancer than larger doses, just as lower doses of DES were more effective at inducing weight gain in the cattle," its intended purpose (78). There was also research "showing that chronic, low-dose exposure to estrogens had induced cancer in mice even though intermittent high doses had not. Putting DES in the food supply . . . had resulted in precisely this continuing, chronic, low-dose exposure in humans that had caused cancer in mice" (79). Because most endocrine-disrupting chemicals are fat soluble and get stored in body fat, they do not flush out readily and instead bio-accumulate up the food chain. Very low levels of a chemical in the air, water, or soil may lead to high levels in carnivores and omnivores.

12. Partly for this reason, I have chosen not to invoke the structures of toxic discourse that Lawrence Buell has outlined. However, aspects of his description are

certainly pertinent, particularly his observation that "the nature that toxic discourse recognizes as the physical environment humans inhabit is *not* a holistic spiritual or biotic economy but a network or networks within which, on the one hand, humans are biotically imbricated (like it or not), and within which, on the other hand, first nature has been greatly modified (like it or not) by *techne*" (*Writing for an Endangered World*, 45.)

13. Dickinson, "Pataphysics and Postmodern Ecocriticism," 134; Duncan-Cole and Bosley, "The Great Canadian Writer's Craft Interview."

14. Dickinson, "The Weather of Weeds," para 2, para 9.

15. Dickinson, "Pataphysics and Postmodern Ecocriticism," 147.

16. Ibid., 133, 135.

17. Queyras, "In Conversation."

18. Dickinson, *The Polymers*, 25. Subsequent quotations from this work will be cited parenthetically in the text as *TP*.

19. Poems in this vein bring to mind Harryette Mullen's punning verbal substitutions in her work of the 1990s. Dickinson has written about her *S*PeRM**K*T* as an example of "ambient" pataphysical poetics that explores contemporary consumption of petrochemical products while challenging conventional assumptions about distinctions between inside and outside ("Pataphysics and Postmodern Ecocriticism").

20. Both poets under discussion are drawn to languages of the World Wide Web that are transmitted through plastic (or plastic-coated glass) fibers. Reilly imitates domain name punctuation (pointing to nonlinear organization of information) as she lifts text and images from the Internet, while Dickinson practices a proceduralist mining of what Joshua Clover has identified as the "junkspeech" of the Internet. See Clover, "Generals and Globetrotters."

21. See "List of Coalition Military Operations of the Iraq War"; "Stupid Facts— License Plate Slogans."

22. "Habitat (disambiguation)." Accessing this Wikipedia page in 2015, I find Habitat 67 and Habitat for Humanity still among the entries, but not the others Dickinson lists. The two companies for blinds and insulating foam still exist, however, and both are Canadian.

23. Duncan-Cole and Bosley, "The Great Canadian Writer's Craft Interview."

24. My essay "The Ecopoetics of Hyperobjects" considers in more depth the relation between Reilly's work and two concepts of Morton's: the ecological mesh and hyperobjects. While that essay duplicates some of the material here, it analyzes more fully the workings of her collage as well as Reilly's citational practices.

25. Reed, *Nobody's Business*, 87.

26. Reilly, "Eco-Noise and the Flux of Lux," 257.

27. FPPG is now PFPG, the Plastics Foodservice Packaging Group, which, according to their website "creates programs to educate the public about the importance and benefits of plastic foodservice packaging. PFPG members include major resin suppliers as well as manufacturers, also known as converters, of plastic foodservice products" ("The Plastics Foodservice Packaging Group (PFPG)"). A few years ago, I could find online what Reilly quotes in italics here, but I can no longer locate

those entries on thriftyfun.com. The PFPG website now makes lots of claims for the environmental benefits of their products.

28. Reilly's capitalization of SEA turns this literary usage into the acronym for Strategic Environmental Assessment, a directive by which the European Union has attempted to ensure decisions that are more environmentally responsible.

29. Yang et al., "Most Plastic Products Release Estrogenic Chemicals," 989.

30. James Watt patented his steam engine in 1781; Coleridge's poem was first published in 1798 and Melville's novel in 1851.

31. Coleridge, *The Complete Poems*, 170.

32. Melville, *Moby-Dick*, 256.

33. On March 15, 2012, when I accessed this Wikipedia entry, the list of examples and their illuminance did not include an LCD screen, though it did mix office lights and family living room lights with various situations of natural light ("Lux"). Reilly's line "that which fallsoutside.thespectrum" may come from the statement on that entry, "The luminosity function falls to zero for wavelengths outside the visible spectrum."

34. Melville, *Moby-Dick*, 264.

35. Reilly, interview. Sarah Dimick and I conducted this filmed interview for the benefit of our introductory literature students on September 11, 2014, in Madison, Wisconsin.

36. M. Brown, *Goodnight Moon*.

37. Nixon, *Slow Violence and the Environmentalism of the Poor*, 6.

38. Garrard, *Ecocriticism*, 16.

39. Roger Williams, *A Key into the Language of America*; Waldrop, *A Key into the Language of America*.

3. "UNDER THESE APO-CALYPSO RAYS"

1. F. Buell, *From Apocalypse to Way of Life*. For Buell on Beck's *Risk Society*, see 192, 204.

2. Reilly, "The Grief of Ecopoetics," 323.

3. Beck, *Risk Society*, 22; italics in original.

4. L. Buell, *Writing for an Endangered World*, 35.

5. L. Buell, *The Environmental Imagination*, 295.

6. Morton, *The Ecological Thought*, 130. In *Hyperobjects*, Morton significantly expands the term so that it might designate the biosphere or the solar system or global warming. I find more useful his narrower definition in *The Ecological Thought* where it seems limited to specific materials like Styrofoam.

7. Heise, *Sense of Place and Sense of Planet*, 140.

8. Ibid., 141.

9. Ibid., 142.

10. Nordhaus and Shellenberger, "Apocalypse Fatigue"; Simms, "Apocalypse?"; Knefel, "Apocalypse Soon"; Mukerjee, "Apocalypse Soon"; Altucher and Sease, *The Wall Street Journal Guide to Investing in the Apocalypse*.

11. L. Buell, *The Environmental Imagination*, 285. The quote is from Al Gore.

12. Ibid., 285, 308; Veldman, "Narrating the Environmental Apocalypse"; Garforth, "Green Utopias," 398.

13. Berger, *After the End*, 5; Heise, *Sense of Place and Sense of Planet*, 122; L. Buell, *The Environmental Imagination*, 44, 40; Garrard, *Ecocriticism*, 104–7.

14. Garrard, *Ecocriticism*, 93.

15. Stewart and Harding, "Bad Endings," 290.

16. Killingsworth and Palmer, "Millennial Ecology," 41, 22; L. Buell, *The Environmental Imagination*, 284; Kunkel, "Dystopia and the End of Politics."

17. Garrard, *Ecocriticism*, 87–88.

18. Ibid., 87.

19. Ibid., 88.

20. Veldman, "Narrating the Environmental Apocalypse," 4; Garrard, *Ecocriticism*, 99; Graham, *Sea Change*, 32–34.

21. Garrard, *Ecocriticism*, 107; italics in original.

22. F. Buell, *From Apocalypse to Way of Life*, 177. It is more widely acknowledged now than it was in 2004 that "across diverse geopolitical and biopolitical locations, the present moment increasingly imposes itself on consciousness as a moment in extended crisis" (Berlant, *Cruel Optimism*, 7). Lauren Berlant, for instance, tracks the affective consequences of "crisis ordinariness."

23. F. Buell, *From Apocalypse to Way of Life*, 202–3, 206.

24. Berger, *After the End*, 6.

25. Graham, *Sea Change*, 3. From now on, *Sea Change* will be cited parenthetically in the text as *SC*.

26. Further biblical echoes sound in "I am inclining my heart toward the end," which recalls Proverbs 2:2, "Incline your heart to understanding." Quotations from the Bible come from the *New American Standard Bible*. I have also used the version comparison available through BibleGateway.com, "New American Standard Bible (NASB)—Version Information."

27. Wengen, "Imagining the Unimaginable."

28. F. Buell, *From Apocalypse to Way of Life*, 205.

29. Wengen, "Imagining the Unimaginable."

30. Ibid.

31. Stevens, *The Collected Poems of Wallace Stevens*, 68.

32. Heise attributes the influence of apocalyptic narrative in the environmental movement to its having "often implicitly or explicitly relied on pastoral as the template for alternative scenarios." Wanting to foster forward-looking planetary perspectives and large-scale changes through environmentally oriented cosmopolitanism, Heise finds it problematic that "such pastoral residues manifest themselves variously in longings for a return to premodern ways of life, 'detoxified' bodies, and holistic, small scale communities" (122).

33. L. Buell, *The Environmental Imagination*, 300–301.

34. Daniel 7:10 provides another apocalyptic antecedent to this image: "A river of fire was flowing and coming out before him."

35. L. Buell, *The Environmental Imagination*, 41–42; italics in original.

36. Marx, "Pastoralism in America," 56–57.

37. Reilly's perspective aligns with Donna Haraway's in *The Companion Species Manifesto* and may have been influenced by Haraway's meditations on technobiopolitics. The realm of "significant otherness" that Haraway wants to cultivate may productively include the cyborg and the biological animal; she presents the cyborg as a companion species (21). Neither Haraway nor Reilly takes an anti-technological stance, but ultimately they find the realm of animal interactions more promising for the environmentally beneficial, ethical enactment that Haraway calls "significant otherness-in-connection" (51).

38. Byron, *Lord Byron*, 19–206; Johnson, *Harold and the Purple Crayon*.

39. Reilly, *Apocalypso*, 29. From now on this work will be cited parenthetically in the text as *A*.

40. Reilly, "Eco-Noise and the Flux of Lux," 260–61.

41. Reilly, "Environmental Dreamscapes."

42. Reilly, "The Grief of Ecopoetics," 320–21.

43. Ibid., 321.

44. Ibid., 322–23.

45. Blanciak, *Siteless*.

46. L. Buell, *The Environmental Imagination*, 300.

47. She has additional criticisms: she points to the brutal power dynamics established among humans in Revelation, "allowing those with the seal / upon their foreheads / to torture the rest / for a numerologically important / number of months and years" (*A* 101). Those lines call attention to an aspect of biblical apocalypticism infrequently addressed in environmental apocalyptic discourse: its creation of an insider/outsider dynamic in which the apocalypse will mean heaping the blessings of God on the saved, but heaping destruction and dire punishment on all others. Elsewhere she critiques Revelation from a feminist standpoint: she wants to "unblot" the name of the whore of Babylon "in the book of life," clothing her in innocent white and designating her "a victim of privilege screen / comfort mechanisms" (*A* 89)—a reference to patriarchy's turning of women into (pornographic?) objects whose function, whether as angel or whore, is to serve male desires.

48. L. Buell, *The Environmental Imagination*, 303–4.

49. Reilly, "The Grief of Ecopoetics," 322.

50. Ibid.

51. Creeley, *The Collected Poems of Robert Creeley, 1945–1975*, 132.

52. David Zimmerman, who astutely critiqued a draft of this chapter, cautions that, historically, the focus of Christian apocalyptic doctrine on a blessed future for the saved has not interfered with the use of apocalyptic rhetoric in sermons and jeremiads to urge immediate action and reform. See Bercovitch, *The American Jeremiad*; University of Virginia Library Online Exhibits, "Red, White, Blue and Brimstone." In my understanding, Reilly's wariness of a focus on transcendence reflects her concern particularly with the association between her chosen genre, poetry, and transcendence—a linkage especially strong in Romanticism and its legacies. Despite her

mockery of the tangled language of apocalyptic prophesy, I don't think she would suggest that all Christian futurism is irresponsible.

53. Reilly, "The Grief of Ecopoetics," 323.

4. UNDERSTANDING NONHUMANS

1. One could label such work "zoopoetics." I have not done so, however, because the emphases of Aaron Moe's book *Zoopoetics* don't entirely fit the work I discuss or the approach I take. Like Moe's zoopoetics, the works I discuss here assume animal agency and are interested in animals' ability to make signs. His emphasis is on how animal bodily *poesis* or making catalyzes poetic intelligence, on how "human poets continue to imitate animals throughout the process of making their poems" (7); his work explores "the places where the gestures of poetic form depend on, mine, or play with the gestures of animals" (24). More explicitly ecocritical, my own emphasis is on how environmentally conscious poets use the making of poems to generate fuller understanding of animals and to encourage altered animal/human relations.

2. Retallack, "What Is Experimental Poetry?"

3. Derrida, "The Animal That Therefore I Am," 394; italics in original.

4. Ibid.

5. For an engaging overview, see Kolbert, *The Sixth Extinction*.

6. Haraway, *When Species Meet*, 19–21.

7. Haraway, *The Companion Species Manifesto*, 50.

8. Haraway, *When Species Meet*, 22.

9. Skinner, "Slow Listening."

10. Haraway, *The Companion Species Manifesto*, 51.

11. Calarco, "Identity, Difference, Indistinction," 42, 48, 51, 54, 56.

12. Coetzee, *Elizabeth Costello*, 80, 96.

13. Nagel, "What Is It Like to Be a Bat?," 439, 442.

14. Soper, "Humans, Animals, Machines," 105, 101.

15. Higgins, "Words on Stone, Eggshells, Feathers, Etc."

16. Little, "Jody Gladding, *Translations from Bark Beetle*."

17. Gladding, *Translations from Bark Beetle*, 7. This work will be cited parenthetically in the text as *TBB*.

18. Braidotti, *Metamorphoses*, 137.

19. Plumwood, *Environmental Culture*, 167.

20. Abram, *Becoming Animal*, 3.

21. Soper, "Humans, Animals, Machines," 100.

22. Skinner, "Countersong."

23. Plumwood, *Environmental Culture*, 142, 132–134, 142, 177, 190.

24. Calarco, "Identity, Difference, Indistinction," 58.

25. Kimmerer, *Braiding Sweetgrass*, 53, 49.

26. Ibid., 55–56. Mel Y. Chen's valuable *Animacies: Biopolitics, Racial Mattering, and Queer Affect* exemplifies the growing interdisciplinary interest in the concept of animacy. Chen extends the linguists' sense of animacy—"the grammatical effects of

the sentience or liveness of nouns" (2)—to help theorize "current anxieties around the production of humanness in contemporary times." The Potawatomi notion of animacy differs in not being centered on humanness. However, in harmony with Kimmerer's perspective, Chen's study demonstrates that "animacy has the capacity to rewrite conditions of intimacy, engendering different communalisms and revising biopolitical spheres, or, at least, how we might theorize them" (3). Chen is "leveraging animacy toward a consideration of affect in its queered and raced formations" (11); the study's important concern with the dehumanization of oppressed humans, within which animals function primarily as figures, is not my focus here.

27. Kimmerer, *Braiding Sweetgrass*, 56, 58.

28. Gander and Kinsella, *Redstart*, 11.

29. Retallack, "What Is Experimental Poetry?"

30. Coetzee, *Elizabeth Costello*, 78.

31. Daston and Mitman, *Thinking with Animals*.

32. Rawlings, "Coach House Books Asks a.rawlings."

33. Though formally more experimental than the twentieth-century poets Scott Knickerbocker treats in *Ecopoetics*, a.rawlings offers a version of what he calls "sensuous poesis," which "relies on the immediate impact on the senses of aural effects . . . and visual effects . . . even as words simultaneously invite the reflective consideration of the intellect. Such an experience is not so much prelingual as it is 'extra-lingual,' beyond semantic language" (*Ecopoetics*, 17).

34. Rawlings, *Wide Slumber for Lepidopterists*, 68–71, 98. Subsequent parenthetical citations from this book will abbreviate the title as *WS*.

35. Retallack, "What Is Experimental Poetry?"

36. This would not be the northern pearly-eye that is pictured in the text, which, unlike many butterfly species, almost never feeds on flowers. A shade-loving butterfly found in wooded areas, it feeds on sap, dung, and mud.

37. Rawlings, *PennSound: a.rawlings*.

38. In response to my questions about the production of the sound recordings I sent her after I had completed an early draft of this, Angela Rawlings wrote as follows: "To answer your questions, WSfL was imagined first as a visual object. I spent nearly six years crafting the page-bound version of the book. The performed version came once the book was published, and I spent about nine months with it (and working with a team of arts interdisciplinarists to bring the book from page to stage). We staged a 'rough draft' of the performance (an hour in length) at Toronto's Harbourfront Centre in November 2006. Beyond that, I adapted some of the more 'sound-poetry' performance strategies to the reading that I've since given probably over 300 times in the last five years. This includes the breathy, throat-singing-esque 'a hoosh a ha' and the insectile clicks and hisses and buzzes of 'xxx y zzz thorax cervix.' . . . As for the recordings on PennSound, they're comprised solely of my voice, edited using GarageBand to give an approximation of what I'd done in a few performances when working with multiple people. 'Prologue' takes the first four pages of WSfL (pp. 7–10) and overlaps them. 'Egg 0 Insomnia' features the first segment (pp. 14–17) with just a hint of 'deep slumber' (pp. 40–41) and 'bruxism' (pp. 68–71).

'Apnea' combines the prologue (pp. 7–10) with apnea (p. 24) as its centrepiece and some more ephemeral 'singing' sounds which I imagine run throughout this overall quite sound-oriented book." Rawlings, email to Keller.

39. Ibid. She continues, "I can understand a certain amount of 'false advertising' perhaps evident in the back-cover copy at this juncture (and also with the 'you, you, you' that peppers the copy when the book has been carefully written solely with 'us')." This book is hardly unusual in having the language of the back cover (e.g., "Pattern your breath on the sound of moth wings, magnified and frenzied, as you fight for sleep . . .") designed more to attract readers than to represent the text with precise accuracy.

40. My perspective here will not be shared by all readers. The other critic who has published an article on this book, Erin Gray, focuses in "'The Good Sentences of Sleep': Parasomnia and 'Pataplay in Rawlings and Legris" on the text's representation of sleep as "a sensuous practice and a source of knowledge rather than a passive state of withdrawal" (154). Our readings coincide in Gray's claim that "sleep is placed at the centre of this interspecies and interdiscursive confrontation in order to interrupt the commonly-held epistemic division between observer and observed" (156), but, unlike me, Gray reads in terms of a human-focused narrative that "illustrates the violence of sleep disturbances" (157). In my reading, the volume has less narrative coherence and is less human centered, while its violence is as much a potential inherent in language as a quality of sleep disturbance.

41. Higgins, "Words on Stone, Eggshells, Feathers, Etc."

42. Bervin, "Three Dimensions."

43. Fimrite, "Bark Beetles Ravaging Drought-Stricken Forests in California."

44. Skinner, *Chip Calls*, 25.

45. Skinner, *Birds of Tifft*.

46. Skinner, "Animal Transcriptions."

47. Ibid.; Skinner, "Poetry Animal," 99, 98, 103.

48. Skinner, "Poetry Animal," 100.

49. Skinner, "Animal Transcriptions."

50. Skinner, "Blackbird Stanzas."

51. Stevens, *Collected Poetry and Prose*, 74–76.

52. Skinner, "Blackbird Stanzas."

53. Skinner, "Slow Listening."

54. Kimmerer, *Braiding Sweetgrass*, 58.

5. GLOBAL REARRANGEMENTS

1. Cresswell, *Place*, 14.

2. Tuan, *Space and Place*, 6.

3. L. Buell, *The Environmental Imagination*, 252; Snyder, *The Practice of the Wild*, 45.

4. Hass, "American Ecopoetry," xli; Snyder, *The Back Country*, 13.

5. Hass, "American Ecopoetry," xliii.

6. Heise, *Sense of Place and Sense of Planet*, 9. Heise provides an excellent discus-

sion and critique of the persistent sense-of-place rhetoric in American ecocriticism in the early chapter of *Sense of Place and Sense of Planet*, "From the Blue Planet to Google Earth: Environmentalism, Ecocriticism, and the Imagination of the Global."

7. See, for example, Heidegger's essay, "Building Dwelling Thinking," in *Poetry, Language, Thought*, 141–160.

8. Heise, *Sense of Place and Sense of Planet*, 44; Garrard, *Ecocriticism*, 118; L. Buell, *The Future of Environmental Criticism*, 84.

9. Berry, *What Are People For?*, 146.

10. Massey foregrounds different terms in the titles of two nearly identical essays. The earlier one, published in *Marxism Today* in 1991, is titled "A Global Sense of Place"—the title used also in *Space, Place, and Gender* (1994), from which I am quoting—while the one published in 1993 is titled, "Power-Geometry and a Progressive Sense of Place." She uses the term "progressive" to counter the view that seeking after a sense of place is necessarily reactionary—a view prompted by responses to the spatial disruption of our time that include "certain forms of nationalism, sentimentalized recovering of sanitized 'heritages', and outright antagonism to newcomers and 'outsiders'" (147).

11. Harvey, *The Condition of Postmodernity*.

12. Massey, *Space, Place, and Gender*, 147, 149, 151, 153.

13. Ibid., 154–56.

14. Heise, *Sense of Place and Sense of Planet*, 28–29, 21, 9.

15. Massey, *For Space*, 4–5.

16. Massey died in 2016. Harvey, however, has devoted quite a bit of attention to how environmental concerns intersect with his own Marxist perspectives; his well-known essay "The Nature of Environment: Dialectics of Social and Environmental Change," for instance, looks for ways to bridge the antagonism between Marx's perspectives on money and community on the one hand, and Aldo Leopold's land ethic and its sense of land as community on the other.

17. Keats, *Complete Poems*, 270.

18. Roberson, *City Eclogue*, 83.

19. Stevens, *Collected Poetry and Prose*, 53–55.

20. Frost, *The Poetry of Robert Frost*, 348.

21. For an argument that Spahr uses refrains to build figurative houses, habitats, and territories whose habitability she then questions, see Dianne Chisholm, "On the House That Ecopoetics Builds."

22. Spahr, *Well Then There Now*, 11. From now on, this work will be cited parenthetically in the text as *WTTN*.

23. Spahr, *The Transformation*.

24. Dening, *Islands and Beaches*.

25. Massey, *For Space*, 4.

26. This quote is from Abbott, *Lā'au Hawai'i*, 14.

27. Rukeyser, *The Collected Poems of Muriel Rukeyser*, 73, 111.

28. L. Buell, *The Environmental Imagination*, 261.

29. K. Brown, *Dispatches from Dystopia*, 2.

30. Gander, *Core Samples from the World*, 84. From now on this work will be cited parenthetically in the text as *CSW*.

31. Massey, *Space, Place, and Gender*, 154.

32. Massey, *For Space*, 123.

33. Magee, "Paul Magee Interviews Forrest Gander."

34. In the "video-poem" version of this work available on Gander's website, many more of Foglia's photos appear and more varied communities are represented. There one sees people living in everything from brick houses to teepees and people conservatively dressed in Amish fashion or in camo or ordinary work clothes, as well as people without clothing. One sees more agriculture than in the book's version, which points more to hunting and foraging for wild edible plants. The video's images are in color, while the photos throughout the book are black and white (Gander, "Forrest Gander's Website.").

35. Meeks, *A Clearing*; Claxton, "A Clearing, Raymond Meeks."

36. Massey, *Space, Place, and Gender*, 151.

37. Enstad, "Toxicity and the Consuming Subject," 55; Chen, *Animacies*, 203.

38. Osman's introduction of another planet might bring to mind Chakrabarty's observation in "Climate and Capital" that study of other planets has been crucial to our understanding of climate change on Earth; the comparative planetary perspective, he notes, is one to which humans are incidental (23).

39. Osman, *The Network*, 107. From now on this work will be cited parenthetically in the text as *TN*.

40. See L. Buell, *The Environmental Imagination*, 266; *Writing for an Endangered World*, 71; *The Future of Environmental Criticism*, 73.

41. L. Buell, *The Environmental Imagination*, 266.

6. ENVIRONMENTAL JUSTICE POETRY OF THE SELF-CONSCIOUS ANTHROPOCENE

1. Tsing, *The Mushroom at the End of the World*, 20.

2. Wenzel, "Turning over a New Leaf," 165.

3. Nixon, "The Anthropocene and Environmental Justice," 29.

4. According to the World Bank in 2015, 1 in 7 people across the globe—1.1 billion people—live without electricity. In 2014 the average annual electricity consumption per person in the US was close to 11,000 kilowatt hours (Rowling, "One in Seven People Still Live without Electricity").

5. Pope Francis, "*Laudato Si'.*" In the United States, environmental justice often has racialized dimensions and an urban focus. Environmentalism of the poor, a phrase introduced in 1988, has been used more in reference to movements in the less industrialized world where class stratification is more central than race, and where the issues often arise from poor people's material interests in a rural or wild environment as the source of their livelihoods. There, the poor are often the majority of the population. Guha and Martínez-Alier speak of the "'full-stomach' environmentalism" of the global North and the "'empty-belly' environmentalism" of the global

South (*Varieties of Environmentalism*, xxi). Scholars such as Guha and Martínez-Alier, *Varieties of Environmentalism* (1998), and Wenzel, "Turning over a New Leaf" (2016), have proposed a convergence of environmental justice and the environmentalism of the poor; in that I am not limiting my concerns to U.S. contexts, I bring them together now, as Wenzel proposes, under the lowercase designation of environmental justice.

6. Margaret Ronda has published an insightful essay, "'Not Much Left': Wageless Life in Millennial Poetry," bringing together the same three poets. Ronda examines them as writers "turning their attention to forms of collective being subsisting at the margins of the marketplace" who attempt to restore visibility to the unemployed and poor and to investigate the representational problems their subsistence raises.

7. People of Color Environmental Leadership Summit, "Principles of Environmental Justice," 279.

8. See L. Buell, "Ecocriticism," 94, 96.

9. L. Buell, *The Future of Environmental Criticism*, 23.

10. Nixon ties the Great Acceleration to the developing plutocracy of the era; he emphasizes that "any account of human-induced planetary morphology since 1950 needs to keep neoliberalism's durable impacts front and center" ("Anthropocene 2," 46). Mark Nowak is equally emphatic about neoliberalism's responsibility for the injustices and suffering his poetry documents, while attributing to neoliberalism the institutionalization of US poetry that keeps it from engagement with a broad public including the working class (Wagstaff, "An Interview with Mark Nowak," 462).

11. Nixon, "The Anthropocene and Environmental Justice," 29.

12. Roberson, "We Must Be Careful," 5.

13. Roberson, *City Eclogue*, 16. From now on this work will be cited parenthetically in the text as *CE*.

14. Roberson, "We Must Be Careful," 3.

15. In "On the Nature of Ed Roberson's Poetics," Evie Shockley presents a reading of Roberson that coincides significantly with my own. (In revised form, the essay became a chapter in *Renegade Poetics*, a study that seeks recognition for innovative black poetry.) Developing our analyses independently and largely contemporaneously, both of us have emphasized that his writing resists the nature/culture divide and positions the human within nature. Presenting Roberson as a figure many regard as anomalous, the African American nature poet, Shockley explores the formal strategies through which he accomplishes a nuanced kind of political poetry that is also nature poetry.

16. Bennett, "Manufacturing the Ghetto," 170, 173.

17. Ibid., 182, 177.

18. Agamben, *Homo Sacer*.

19. Duncan, *The Opening of the Field*, 7.

20. Nowak, "Coal Mountain."

21. Nowak, *Coal Mountain Elementary*, 179. From now on this work will be cited parenthetically in the text as *CME*.

22. American Coal Foundation, "American Coal Foundation."

23. American Coal Foundation, "About the American Coal Foundation."

24. C2ES Center for Climate and Energy Solutions, "Global Warming Facts and Figures."

25. Olivier et al., "Trends in Global CO2 Emissions: 2015 Report," 23, 16, 18.

26. For a sobering assessment, see Epstein et al., "Full Cost Accounting for the Life Cycle of Coal."

27. People of Color Environmental Leadership Summit, "Principles of Environmental Justice," 279–80.

28. Manning, *Coal Mountain Elementary*"; quoted by Nowak in Clinton, "Chronicles in the First Person Plural."

29. Some of Teh's photos have more complicated impact, for though never pastoral, the images are often very striking. Artfully composed, and sometimes with strong reds or turquoises juxtaposed against grime and smoke, his images are discomfortingly beautiful even as they are gritty or even hellish. His defamiliarization of scenes of industrial degradation invites renewed attention to those places and those who live or work there.

30. Graves, "Spotlight."

31. Featherston, "'What Kind of Poem Would You Make Out of That?': A Review of 'Coal Mountain Elementary.'"

32. For a fuller discussion of Kim's poetics, see chapter 7 of my *Thinking Poetry.*

33. Kim, "Convolutions," 251; brackets and bracketed words are Kim's.

34. Ibid.

35. Kim, *Penury.* From now on this work will be cited parenthetically in the text as *P.* In "An Ecopoetics of the Limit," Angela Hume rightly identifies the anonymous voices of *Penury's* poem "fell" as "the abject citizen, the refugee, the immigrant."

36. Hume, "An Ecopoetics of the Limit."

37. Westra, *Environmental Justice and the Rights of Ecological Refugees.*

38. Martin, "On *Penury.*"

39. Bate, *The Song of the Earth*, 25–26.

CODA

1. Coultas, *The Tatters*, 15. From now on, this work will be cited parenthetically in the text as *TT.*

Bibliography

Abbott, Isabella Aiona. *Lā'au Hawai'i: Traditional Hawaiian Uses of Plants.* Honolulu: Bishop Museum Press, 1992.

Abram, David. *Becoming Animal: An Earthly Cosmology.* New York: Pantheon Books, 2010.

Agamben, Giorgio. *Homo Sacer: Sovereign Power and Bare Life.* Stanford: Stanford University Press, 1998.

Alaimo, Stacy. *Bodily Natures: Science, Environment, and the Material Self.* Bloomington: Indiana University Press, 2010.

Altucher, James, and Douglas R. Sease. *The Wall Street Journal Guide to Investing in the Apocalypse: Make Money by Seeing Opportunity Where Others See Peril.* New York: HarperBusiness, 2011.

American Coal Foundation. "About the American Coal Foundation." *American Coal Foundation,* 2014. http://teachcoal.org/american-coal-foundation.

———. "American Coal Foundation." *American Coal Foundation,* 2014. http://teachcoal.org/.

Asafu-Adjaye, John, Linus Blomqvist, Stewart Brand, Barry Brook, Ruth DeFries, Erle Ellis, Christopher Foreman, et al. "An Ecomodernist Manifesto," 2015. http://www.ecomodernism.org/.

Autin, Whitney J., and John M. Holbrook. "Is the Anthropocene an Issue of Stratigraphy or Pop Culture?" *GSA Today* 22, no. 7 (July 2012): 60–61. doi: 10.1130/G153GW.1.

Bate, Jonathan. *The Song of the Earth.* London: Picador, 2000.

Beck, Ulrich. "Living in the World Risk Society." *Economy and Society* 35, no. 3 (August 1, 2006): 329–45. doi: 10.1080/03085140600844902.

———. *Risk Society: Towards a New Modernity.* Translated by Mark Ritter. London: SAGE Publications, 1992.

Beck, Ulrich, and Martin Chalmers. "Risk Society and the Provident State." In *Risk, Environment and Modernity: Towards a New Ecology,* edited by Scott Lash, Bronislaw Szerszynski, and Brian Wynne, 28–43. London: SAGE Publications, 1998. http://sk.sagepub.com/books/risk-environment-and-modernity/n2.xml.

Bennett, Michael. "Manufacturing the Ghetto: Anti-Urbanism and the Spatialization of Race." In *The Nature of Cities: Ecocriticism and Urban Environments,* edited by

Michael Bennett and David W. Teague, 169–88. Tucson: University of Arizona Press, 1999.

Bercovitch, Sacvan. *The American Jeremiad.* Madison: University of Wisconsin Press, 1978.

Berger, James. *After the End: Representations of Post-Apocalypse.* Minneapolis: University of Minnesota Press, 1999.

Berlant, Lauren Gail. *Cruel Optimism.* Durham: Duke University Press, 2011.

Berry, Wendell. *The Selected Poems of Wendell Berry.* Washington, D.C.: Counterpoint, 1998.

———. *What Are People For? Essays.* 2nd rev. ed. Washington, D.C.: Counterpoint, 2010.

Bervin, Jen. "Three Dimensions: Jody Gladding on Translation, the Source of Knowledge, and How Beetles Can Speak of Longing." *Poetry Foundation,* August 20, 2014. http://www.poetryfoundation.org/features/articles/70136/three-dimensions.

BibleGateway.com. "New American Standard Bible (NASB)—Version Information." *BibleGateway.com.* https://www.biblegateway.com/versions/New-American-Standard-Bible-NASB/.

Blackie, Sharon. "An Interview with Jorie Graham." *Earthlines* 1, no. 2 (August 2012): 39.

Blanciak, François. *Siteless: 1001 Building Forms.* Cambridge, Mass.: MIT Press, 2008.

Boes, Tobias, and Kate Marshall. "Writing the Anthropocene: An Introduction." *Minnesota Review* 83, no. 1 (2014): 60–72.

Braidotti, Rosi. *Metamorphoses: Towards a Materialist Theory of Becoming.* Cambridge: Polity Press, 2002.

Brown, Kate. *Dispatches from Dystopia: Histories of Places Not Yet Forgotten.* Chicago: University of Chicago Press, 2015.

Brown, Margaret Wise. *Goodnight Moon.* Reissue ed. New York: HarperCollins, 2007.

Buell, Frederick. *From Apocalypse to Way of Life: Environmental Crisis in the American Century.* New York: Routledge, 2003.

Buell, Lawrence. "Ecocriticism: Some Emerging Trends." *Qui Parle: Critical Humanities and Social Sciences* 19, no. 2 (2011): 87–115.

———. *The Environmental Imagination: Thoreau, Nature Writing, and the Formation of American Culture.* Cambridge: Belknap Press of Harvard University Press, 1995.

———. *The Future of Environmental Criticism: Environmental Crisis and Literary Imagination.* Blackwell Manifestos. Malden, Mass.: Blackwell, 2005.

———. *Writing for an Endangered World: Literature, Culture, and Environment in the U.S. and Beyond.* Cambridge: Belknap Press of Harvard University Press, 2001.

Butler, Judith. *Gender Trouble: Feminism and the Subversion of Identity.* London: Routledge, 1990.

Byron, George Gordon, Lord. *Lord Byron: The Major Works.* Edited by Jerome J. McGann. Reissue ed.. Oxford: Oxford University Press, 2008.

C2ES Center for Climate and Energy Solutions. "Global Warming Facts and Figures." *C2ES Center for Climate and Energy Solutions.* http://www.c2es.org/facts-figures.

Calarco, Matthew. "Identity, Difference, Indistinction." *CR: The New Centennial Review* 11, no. 2 (2011): 41–60. doi: 10.1353/ncr.2012.0008.

Chakrabarty, Dipesh. "Brute Force." *Eurozine,* October 7, 2010. http://www.eurozine .com/articles/2010-10-07-chakrabarty-en.html.

———. "Climate and Capital: On Conjoined Histories." *Critical Inquiry* 41, no. 1 (2014): 1–23. doi: 10.1086/678154.

———. "The Climate of History: Four Theses." *Critical Inquiry* 35, no. 2 (2009): 197–222. doi: 10.1086/596640.

Chen, Mel Y. *Animacies: Biopolitics, Racial Mattering, and Queer Affect.* Durham: Duke University Press, 2012.

Chisholm, Dianne. "On the House That Ecopoetics Builds: Juliana Spahr's '"eco" Frame.'" *Textual Practice* 28, no. 4 (June 7, 2014): 631–53. doi: 10.1080/0950236X .2013.845600.

Cho, Renee. "What Happens to All That Plastic?" *State of the Planet, Earth Institute, Columbia University.* http://blogs.ei.columbia.edu/2012/01/31/what-happens-to -all-that-plastic/.

Clark, Nigel. *Inhuman Nature: Sociable Life on a Dynamic Planet.* Los Angeles: SAGE, 2011.

Clark, Timothy. "Scale: Derangements of Scale." In *Telemorphosis: Theory in the Era of Climate Change,* vol. 1, edited by Tom Cohen. Ann Arbor: Open Humanities Press, Michigan Publishing, 2012. http://hdl.handle.net/2027/spo.10539563.0001.001.

Claxton, Tom. "A Clearing, Raymond Meeks." *Claxton Projects.* http://www .claxtonprojects.com/books/raymond-meeks/.

Clinton, Alan. "Chronicles in the First Person Plural: An Interview with Mark Nowak." *Reconstruction* 10, no. 3 (2010). http://reconstruction.eserver.org/Issues /103/Nowak_01.shtml.

Clover, Joshua. "Generals and Globetrotters." *Claudius App: A Journal of Fast Poetry.* 2009. http://theclaudiusapp.com/1-clover.html.

Coetzee, J. M. *Elizabeth Costello.* New York: Viking, 2003.

Coleridge, Samuel Taylor. *The Complete Poems.* Edited by William Keach. London: Penguin Classics, 1997.

Corey, Joshua, and G. C. Waldrep. *The Arcadia Project: North American Postmodern Pastoral.* Boise, Idaho: Ahsahta Press, 2012.

Coultas, Brenda. *The Tatters.* Middletown, Conn.: Wesleyan University Press, 2014.

Creeley, Robert. *The Collected Poems of Robert Creeley, 1945–1975.* Berkeley: University of California Press, 1982.

Cresswell, Tim. *Place: An Introduction.* 2nd ed. Malden, Mass.: Wiley, 2014.

Cronon, William. "The Trouble with Wilderness; Or, Getting Back to the Wrong Nature." In *Uncommon Ground: Rethinking the Human Place in Nature,* edited by William Cronon, 69–90. New York: W. W. Norton and Co., 1996.

Crutzen, Paul J. "Geology of Mankind." *Nature* 415, no. 6867 (January 3, 2002): 23. doi: 10.1038/415023a.

Crutzen, Paul J., and Christian Schwägerl. "Living in the Anthropocene: Toward a

New Global Ethos." *Yale Environment 360*, January 24, 2011. http://e360.yale.edu/feature/living_in_the_anthropocene_toward_a_new_global_ethos/2363/.

Crutzen, Paul J., and Eugene F. Stoermer. "The 'Anthropocene.'" *International Geosphere-Biosphere Programme Global Change Newsletter* 41 (May 2000): 17–18.

Daston, Lorraine, and Gregg Mitman. *Thinking with Animals: New Perspectives on Anthropomorphism.* New York: Columbia University Press, 2005.

Dening, Greg. *Islands and Beaches: Discourse on a Silent Land: Marquesas, 1774–1880.* Carlton: Melbourne University Press, 1980.

Derrida, Jacques. "The Animal That Therefore I Am (More to Follow)." Translated by David Wills. *Critical Inquiry* 28, no. 2 (2002): 369–418.

Dickinson, Adam. "Pataphysics and Postmodern Ecocritcism: A Prospectus." In *The Oxford Handbook of Ecocriticism,* edited by Greg Garrard, 132–53. New York: Oxford University Press, 2014.

———. *The Polymers.* Toronto: House of Anansi Press, 2013.

———. "The Weather of Weeds: Lisa Robertson's Rhizome Poetics." *Rhizomes: Cultural Studies in Emerging Knowledge* 15 (Winter 2007). http://www.rhizomes.net/issue15/dickinson.html.

Duncan, Robert Edward. *The Opening of the Field.* New York: New Directions, 1960.

Duncan-Cole, Merlot, and Brittany Bosley. "The Great Canadian Writer's Craft Interview: Adam Dickinson." *Open Book: Toronto,* June 25, 2013. http://www.openbooktoronto.com/clelia/blog/great_canadian_writers_craft_interview_adam_dickinson.

Dungy, Camille T. *Black Nature: Four Centuries of African American Nature Poetry.* Athens: University of Georgia Press, 2009.

Dürbeck, Gabriele. "Ambivalent Characters and Fragmented Poetics in Anthropocene Literature: Max Frisch and Ilija Trojanow." *Minnesota Review* 83, no. 1 (2014): 112–21.

Elder, John. *Imagining the Earth: Poetry and the Vision of Nature.* Urbana: University of Illinois Press, 1985.

Enstad, Nan. "Toxicity and the Consuming Subject." In *States of Emergency: The Object of American Studies,* edited by Russ Castronovo and Susan Kay Gillman, 55–68. Chapel Hill: University of North Carolina Press, 2009.

Epstein, Paul R., Jonathan J. Buonocore, Kevin Eckerle, Michael Hendryx, Benjamin M. Stout III, Richard Heinberg, Richard W. Clapp, et al. "Full Cost Accounting for the Life Cycle of Coal." *Annals of the New York Academy of Sciences* 1219, no. 1 (February 1, 2011): 73–98. doi: 10.1111/j.1749–6632.2010.05890.x.

Featherston, Dan. "'What Kind of Poem Would You Make Out of That?': A Review of *Coal Mountain Elementary,* by Mark Nowak." *Jacket2,* April 4, 2011. http://jacket2.org/reviews/what-kind-poem-would-you-make-out.

Fimrite, Peter. "Bark Beetles Ravaging Drought-Stricken Forests in California." *San Francisco Chronicle,* March 28 and 30, 2015. http://www.sfchronicle.com/science/article/Bark-beetles-ravaging-drought-stricken-forests-in-6165431.php.

Fisher-Wirth, Ann W., and Laura-Gray Street. *The Ecopoetry Anthology.* San Antonio: Trinity University Press, 2013.

Franzen, Jonathan. "Carbon Capture." *The New Yorker,* April 6, 2015. http://www
.newyorker.com/magazine/2015/04/06/carbon-capture.

Freinkel, Susan. *Plastic: A Toxic Love Story.* Boston: Houghton Mifflin Harcourt, 2011.

Frost, Robert. *The Poetry of Robert Frost: The Collected Poems, Complete and Unabridged.*
Edited by Edward Connery Lathem. New York: Henry Holt and Company, 2002.

Galloway, Tamara S. "Micro- and Nano-Plastics and Human Health." In *Marine Anthropogenic Litter,* edited by Melanie Bergmann, Lars Gutow, and Michael Klages,
343–66. Cham: Springer International Publishing, 2015. https://link.springer.com
/chapter/10.1007/978-3-319-16510-3_13.

Gander, Forrest. *Core Samples from the World.* New York: New Directions, 2011.

———. "Forrest Gander's Website." *Forrest Gander,* 2012. http://forrestgander.com/.

Gander, Forrest, and John Kinsella. *Redstart: An Ecological Poetics.* Iowa City: University of Iowa Press, 2012.

Garforth, Lisa. "Green Utopias: Beyond Apocalypse, Progress, and Pastoral." *Utopian
Studies* 16, no. 3 (2005): 393–427.

Garrard, Greg. *Ecocriticism.* New Critical Idiom. London: Routledge, 2004.

Gee, Henry. *In Search of Deep Time: Beyond the Fossil Record to a New History of Life.*
New York: Free Press, 1999.

Gladding, Jody. *Translations from Bark Beetle: Poems.* Minneapolis: Milkweed Editions,
2014.

Gourmelon, Gaelle. "Global Plastic Production Rises, Recycling Lags." *Vital Signs,
Worldwatch Institute,* January 27, 2015. http://vitalsigns.worldwatch.org/vs-trend
/global-plastic-production-rises-recycling-lags.

Graham, Jorie. *Sea Change: Poems.* New York: Ecco, 2008.

Graves, Seth. "Spotlight: Mark Nowak: Sort of Uncharacterizable Interview by Seth
Graves." *Coldfront,* September 14, 2011. http://coldfrontmag.com/spotlight-mark
-nowak/.

Gray, Erin. "'The Good Sentences of Sleep': Parasomnia and 'Pataplay in Rawlings
and Legris." *Open Letter* 13, no. 9 (Summer 2009): 153–65.

Grubisic, Katia. "Instructions for Building the Arc." *The Fiddlehead,* Summer 2010.
http://www.joriegraham.com/interview_grubisic.

Guha, Ramachandra, and Juan Martínez-Alier. *Varieties of Environmentalism: Essays
North and South.* Delhi: Oxford University Press, 1998.

"Habitat (disambiguation)." *Wikipedia, the Free Encyclopedia,* May 23, 2016. https://
en.wikipedia.org/w/index.php?title=Habitat_(disambiguation)&oldid=7217
50004.

Haraway, Donna. *The Companion Species Manifesto: Dogs, People, and Significant Otherness.* Chicago: Prickly Paradigm, 2003.

———. *Staying with the Trouble: Making Kin in the Chthulucene.* Duke University Press,
2016.

———. *When Species Meet.* Posthumanities 3. Minneapolis: University of Minnesota
Press, 2008.

Harvey, David. *The Condition of Postmodernity: An Enquiry into the Origins of Cultural
Change.* Oxford: Blackwell, 1990.

————. "The Nature of Environment: Dialectics of Social and Environmental Change." *Socialist Register* 29 (March 18, 1993). http://socialistregister.com/index .php/srv/article/view/5621.

Hass, Robert. "American Ecopoetry: An Introduction." In *The Ecopoetry Anthology*, edited by Ann W. Fisher-Wirth and Laura-Gray Street, xli–lxv. San Antonio: Trinity University Press, 2013.

Heidegger, Martin. *Poetry, Language, Thought.* Perennial Classics ed. New York: Harper Perennial Modern Classics, 2013.

Heise, Ursula K. Review of *Hyperobjects: Philosophy and Ecology after the End of the World*, by Timothy Morton. *Critical Inquiry* 41, no. 2 (2015): 460–61.

————. *Sense of Place and Sense of Planet: The Environmental Imagination of the Global.* Oxford: Oxford University Press, 2008.

Heringman, Noah. "Deep Time at the Dawn of the Anthropocene." *Representations* 129, no. 1 (February 1, 2015): 56–85. doi: 10.1525/rep.2015.129.1.56.

Higgins, Darren. "Words on Stone, Eggshells, Feathers, Etc.: Poems, Art and Interview with Jody Gladding." *Numéro Cinq*, August 14, 2014. http://numerocinqmagazine .com/2014/08/14/words-on-stone-eggshells-feathers-etc-poems-art-interview -with-jody-gladding-darren-higgins/.

Hume, Angela. "An Ecopoetics of the Limit: Myung Mi Kim's 'fell.'" *OmniVerse*, May 25, 2016. http://omniverse.us/angela-hume-an-ecopoetics-of-the-limit/.

Iijima, Brenda, ed. *Eco Language Reader.* Brooklyn, N.Y.: Portable Press at Yo-Yo Labs and Nightboat, 2010.

Johnson, Crockett. *Harold and the Purple Crayon.* New York: Harper and Brothers, 1955.

Keats, John. *Complete Poems.* Edited by Jack Stillinger. Cambridge, Mass.: Belknap Press, 1991.

Keller, Lynn. "The Ecopoetics of Hyperobjects: Evelyn Reilly's *Styrofoam*." *Interdisciplinary Studies in Literature and Environment* 22, no. 4 (November 25, 2015): 846–71. doi: 10.1093/isle/isv072.

————. *Thinking Poetry: Readings in Contemporary Women's Exploratory Poetics.* Iowa City: University of Iowa Press, 2010.

Keller, Lynn, and Steel Wagstaff. "An Interview with Ed Roberson." *Contemporary Literature* 52, no. 3 (2011): 397–429. doi: 10.1353/cli.2011.0032.

Killingsworth, Jamie M., and Jacqueline S. Palmer. "Millennial Ecology: The Apocalyptic Narrative from *Silent Spring* to Global Warming." In *Green Culture: Environmental Rhetoric in Contemporary America*, edited by Carl George Herndl and Stuart C. Brown, 21–45. Madison: University of Wisconsin Press, 1996.

Kim, Myung Mi. "Convolutions: The Precision, the Wild." In *American Poets in the 21st Century: The New Poetics*, edited by Claudia Rankine and Lisa Sewell, 251. Middletown: Wesleyan University Press, 2007.

————. *Penury.* Richmond, Calif.: Omnidawn, 2009.

Kimmerer, Robin Wall. *Braiding Sweetgrass: Indigenous Wisdom, Scientific Knowledge, and the Teachings of Plants.* Minneapolis: Milkweed Editions, 2013.

Knefel, John. "Apocalypse Soon: 9 Terrifying Signs of Environmental Doom." *Rolling*

Stone, August 18, 2015. http://www.rollingstone.com/culture/news/apocalyse-soon-9-terrifying-signs-of-environmental-doom-and-gloom-20150818.

Knickerbocker, Scott. *Ecopoetics: The Language of Nature, the Nature of Language*. Amherst: University of Massachusetts Press, 2012.

Kolbert, Elizabeth. *The Sixth Extinction: An Unnatural History*. New York: Henry Holt and Company, 2014.

Kumin, Maxine. "Intimations of Mortality: Review of *New and Selected Poems* by Mary Oliver." *Women's Review of Books* 10, no. 7 (1993): 19.

Kunkel, Benjamin. "Dystopia and the End of Politics." *Dissent Magazine*, Fall 2008. https://www.dissentmagazine.org/article/dystopia-and-the-end-of-politics.

Langston, Nancy. *Toxic Bodies: Hormone Disruptors and the Legacy of DES*. New Haven: Yale University Press, 2010.

Lewis, Simon L., and Mark A. Maslin. "Defining the Anthropocene." *Nature* 519, no. 7542 (March 12, 2015): 171–80. doi: 10.1038/nature14258.

"List of Coalition Military Operations of the Iraq War." *Wikipedia, the Free Encyclopedia*, July 19, 2016. https://en.wikipedia.org/w/index.php?title=List_of_coalition_military_operations_of_the_Iraq_War&oldid=730466634.

Little, Jake. "Jody Gladding, *Translations from Bark Beetle*." KMSU Weekly Reader. http://english.mnsu.edu/weeklyreader/author_pages/gladdingjody.html.

"Lux." *Wikipedia, the Free Encyclopedia*, June 9, 2016. https://en.wikipedia.org/w/index.php?title=Lux&oldid=724429895.

Magee, Paul. "Paul Magee Interviews Forrest Gander." *Cordite Poetry Review*, August 1, 2014. http://cordite.org.au/interviews/magee-gander/.

Manning, Maurice. Review of *Coal Mountain Elementary by Mark Nowak, with photographs by Ian Teh and Mark Nowak*, by Mark Nowak. *Bookforum*, July 24, 2009. http://www.bookforum.com/review/4016.

Martin, C. J. "On *Penury*." *Jacket2*, April 12, 2013. http://jacket2.org/article/penury.

Marx, Leo. "Pastoralism in America." In *Ideology and Classic American Literature*, edited by Sacvan Bercovitch and Myra Jehlen, 36–69. New York: Cambridge University Press, 1986.

Massey, Doreen B. *For Space*. London: SAGE, 2005.

———. "A Global Sense of Place." *Marxism Today*, June 1991, 24–29.

———. "Power-Geometry and a Progressive Sense of Place." In *Mapping the Futures: Local Cultures, Global Change*, edited by John Bird, Barry Curtis, Tim Putnam, and Lisa Tickner, 60–70. London: Routledge, 1993.

———. *Space, Place, and Gender*. Minneapolis: University of Minnesota Press, 1994.

Meeks, Raymond. *A Clearing*. Portland, Ore.: Nazraeli Press, 2008.

Melville, Herman. *Moby-Dick: Or, The Whale*. Indianapolis: Bobbs-Merrill, 1964.

Menely, Tobias. "Anthropocene Air." *Minnesota Review* 2014, no. 83 (January 1, 2014): 93–101. doi: 10.1215/00265667-2782279.

Moe, Aaron M. *Zoopoetics: Animals and the Making of Poetry*. Lanham, Md.: Lexington Books, 2014.

Moore, Jason W., ed. *Anthropocene or Capitalocene? Nature, History, and the Crisis of Capitalism*. Oakland: PM Press, 2016.

Morton, Timothy. *The Ecological Thought*. Cambridge, Mass.: Harvard University Press, 2010.

———. *Ecology without Nature: Rethinking Environmental Aesthetics*. Cambridge: Harvard University Press, 2009.

———. *Hyperobjects: Philosophy and Ecology after the End of the World*. Minneapolis: University of Minnesota Press, 2013.

Mukerjee, Madhusree. "Apocalypse Soon: Has Civilization Passed the Environmental Point of No Return?" *Scientific American*. May 23, 2012. http://www.scientificamerican.com/article/apocalypse-soon-has-civilization-passed-the-environmental-point-of-no-return/.

Nagel, Thomas. "What Is It Like to Be a Bat?" *Philosophical Review* 83, no. 4 (1974): 435–50. doi: 10.2307/2183914.

New American Standard Bible. Anaheim, Calif.: Lockman Foundation Publications, 1997.

Nixon, Rob. "Anthropocene 2." In *Fueling Culture: 101 Words for Energy and Environment*, edited by Imre Szeman, Jennifer Wenzel, and Patricia Yaeger, 43–46. New York: Fordham University Press, 2017.

———. "The Anthropocene and Environmental Justice." In *Curating the Future: Museums, Communities and Climate Change*, edited by Jennifer Newell, Libby Robin, and Kirsten Wehner, 23–31. New York: Routledge, 2016.

———. "The Anthropocene: Promise and Pitfalls of an Epochal Idea." *Edge Effects*, November 6, 2014. http://edgeeffects.net/anthropocene-promise-and-pitfalls/.

———. *Slow Violence and the Environmentalism of the Poor*. Cambridge: Harvard University Press, 2011.

Nordhaus, Ted, and Michael Shellenberger. "Apocalypse Fatigue: Losing the Public on Climate Change." *The Guardian*, November 17, 2009, sec. Environment. https://www.theguardian.com/environment/2009/nov/17/apocalypse-public-climate-change.

Nowak, Mark. "Coal Mountain." *Coal Mountain*. https://coalmountain.wordpress.com/.

———. *Coal Mountain Elementary*. Minneapolis: Coffee House Press, 2009.

Oliver, Mary. *House of Light*. Boston: Beacon Press, 1990.

Olivier, J. G. J., G. Janssens-Maenhout, M. Muntean, and J. A. H. W. Peters. "Trends in Global CO2 Emissions: 2015 Report." PBL Netherlands Environmental Assessment Agency, November 25, 2015. http://www.pbl.nl/en/publications/trends-in-global-co2-emissions-2015-report.

Osman, Jena. *The Network*. Albany, N.Y.: Fence Books, 2010.

Parker, Laura. "Ocean Trash: 5.25 Trillion Pieces and Counting, but Big Questions Remain." *National Geographic News*, January 11, 2015. http://news.nationalgeographic.com/news/2015/01/150109-oceans-plastic-sea-trash-science-marine-debris/.

People of Color Environmental Leadership Summit. "Principles of Environmental Justice." In *Sharing the Earth: An International Environmental Justice Reader*, edited by Elizabeth Ammons and Modhumita Roy, 279–80. Athens: University of Georgia Press, 2015.

"Plastics Foodservice Packaging Group (PFPG), The." *American Chemistry Council.* https://plastics.americanchemistry.com/Plastics-Foodservice-Packaging-Group/.

Plumwood, Val. *Environmental Culture: The Ecological Crisis of Reason.* London; New York: Routledge, 2002.

Pope Francis. *"Laudato Si':* Encyclical Letter of the Holy Father Francis on Care for Our Common Home." Papal encyclical. Rome: Catholic Church, May 24, 2015. http://w2.vatican.va/content/francesco/en/encyclicals/documents/papa-francesco_20150524_enciclica-laudato-si.html.

Purdy, Jedediah. "Losing Nature: Living in the Anthropocene." *Fieldwork,* April 3, 2013. http://jedfieldwork.blogspot.com/2013/04/font-face-font-family-font-face-font.html.

Queyras, Sina. "In Conversation: Sina Queyras and Adam Dickinson." *Lemon Hound,* September 27, 2013. http://lemonhound.com/2013/09/27/in-conversation-sina-queyras-adam-dickinson/.

Rasula, Jed. *This Compost: Ecological Imperatives in American Poetry.* Athens: University of Georgia Press, 2002.

Rawlings, Angela. "Coach House Books Asks a.rawlings a Few Things about *Wide Slumber for Lepidopterists.*" *Coach House Books.* http://www.chbooks.com/q-a/coach-house-books-asks-arawlings-few-things-about-wide-slumber-lepidopterists. Accessed January 12, 2011.

———. Email to Lynn Keller. "Wide Slumber for Lepidopterists." July 4, 2011.

———. *PennSound: a.rawlings.* PennSound. http://writing.upenn.edu/pennsound/x/Rawlings.php.

———. *Wide Slumber for Lepidopterists.* Toronto: Coach House Books, 2006.

Reed, Brian M. *Nobody's Business: Twenty-First Century Avant-Garde Poetics.* Ithaca: Cornell University Press, 2013.

Reilly, Evelyn. *Apocalypso.* New York: Roof Books, 2012.

———. "Eco-Noise and the Flux of Lux." In *Eco Language Reader,* edited by Brenda Iijima, 255–74. Brooklyn: Portable Press at Yo-Yo Labs and Nightboat, 2010.

———. "Environmental Dreamscapes and Ecopoetic Grief." *OmniVerse,* 2013. http://omniverse.us/evelyn-reilly-environmental-dreamscapes-and-ecopoetic-grief/.

———. "The Grief of Ecopoetics." *Interim* 29, no. 1–2 (2011): 320–23.

———. Interview by Sarah Dimick and Lynn Keller. September 11, 2014.

———. *Styrofoam.* New York: Roof Books, 2009.

Retallack, Joan. *The Poethical Wager.* Berkeley: University of California Press, 2003.

———. "What Is Experimental Poetry & Why Do We Need It?" *Jacket,* April 2007. http://jacketmagazine.com/32/p-retallack.shtml.

Roberson, Ed. *City Eclogue.* Berkeley, Calif.: Atelos, 2006.

———. *To See the Earth Before the End of the World.* Middletown: Wesleyan University Press, 2010.

———. "We Must Be Careful." In *Black Nature: Four Centuries of African American Nature Poetry*, edited by Camille T. Dungy, 3–5. Athens: University of Georgia Press, 2009.

Ronda, Margaret. "Mourning and Melancholia in the Anthropocene." *Post45*, June 10, 2013. http://post45.research.yale.edu/2013/06/mourning-and-melancholia-in-the-anthropocene/.

———. "'Not Much Left': Wageless Life in Millenial Poetry." *Post45*, October 9, 2011. http://post45.research.yale.edu/2011/10/not-much-left-wageless-life-in-millenial-poetry/.

Rowling, Megan. "One in Seven People Still Live without Electricity: World Bank." *Reuters*, May 18, 2015. http://www.reuters.com/article/us-energy-renewables-poverty-idUSKBN0O31SJ20150518.

Rukeyser, Muriel. *The Collected Poems of Muriel Rukeyser.* Pittsburgh: University of Pittsburgh Press, 2005.

Russill, Chris, and Zoe Nyssa. "The Tipping Point Trend in Climate Change Communication." *Global Environmental Change* 19, no. 3 (August 2009): 336–44. doi: 10.1016/j.gloenvcha.2009.04.001.

Schellnhuber, Hans Joachim, Paul J. Crutzen, William C. Clark, and Julian Hunt. "Earth System Analysis for Sustainability." *Environment: Science and Policy for Sustainable Development* 47, no. 8 (2005): 10–25.

Scigaj, Leonard M. *Sustainable Poetry: Four American Ecopoets.* Lexington: University Press of Kentucky, 1999.

Shakespeare, William. *The Riverside Shakespeare.* New York: Houghton Mifflin, 1974.

Shockley, Evie. "On the Nature of Ed Roberson's Poetics." *Callaloo* 33, no. 3 (2010): 728–47. doi: 10.1353/cal.2010.0047.

———. *Renegade Poetics: Black Aesthetics and Formal Innovation in African American Poetry.* Iowa City: University of Iowa Press, 2011.

Silliman, Ron, Carla Harryman, Lyn Hejinian, Steve Benson, Bob Perelman, and Barrett Watten. "Aesthetic Tendency and the Politics of Poetry: A Manifesto." *Social Text*, no. 19/20 (1988): 261–75. doi: 10.2307/466189.

Simms, Andrew. "Apocalypse? No. But Unless We Change Tack, the Planet Is Running Out of Time." *The Guardian*, March 1, 2013, sec. Environment. https://www.theguardian.com/environment/2013/mar/01/100-months-apocalypse-warnings.

Skinner, Jonathan. "Animal Transcriptions: Listening to the Lab of Ornithology." *Sounding Out!* March 21, 2013. https://soundstudiesblog.com/2013/03/21/skinner-podcast/.

———. *Birds of Tifft.* Buffalo, N.Y.: BlazeVOX Books, 2011.

———. "Blackbird Stanzas." In *Big Energy Poets: Ecopoetry Thinks Climate Change*, edited by Heidi Lynn Staples and Amy King. Buffalo, NY: BlazeVOX, 2017.

———. *Chip Calls.* Textile Series. Houston: Little Red Leaves, 2014.

———. "Countersong: Rising or Falling." *The Goose* 14, no. 1 (September 1, 2015). http://scholars.wlu.ca/thegoose/vol14/iss1/26.

————. "Editor's Statement." *Ecopoetics* 1 (2001): 5–8.

————. "Poetry Animal." *Boundary 2* 36, no. 3 (September 21, 2009): 97–103. doi: 10.1215/01903659-2009-022.

————. "Slow Listening." In *Big Energy Poets: Ecopoetry Thinks Climate Change,* edited by Heidi Lynn Staples and Amy King. Buffalo, NY: BlazeVOX, 2017.

Slovic, Scott. *Seeking Awareness in American Nature Writing: Henry Thoreau, Annie Dillard, Edward Abbey, Wendell Berry, Barry Lopez.* Salt Lake City: University of Utah Press, 1992.

Snyder, Gary. *The Back Country.* New York: New Directions, 1971.

————. *The Practice of the Wild.* Berkeley, Calif.: Counterpoint Press, 2010.

Soper, Kate. "Humans, Animals, Machines." *New Formations* 49, no. 1 (Spring 2003): 99–109.

Spahr, Juliana. *The Transformation.* Berkeley, Calif.: Atelos, 2007.

————. *Well Then There Now.* Boston: David R. Godine, 2011.

Steffen, Will, Paul J. Crutzen, and John R. McNeill. "The Anthropocene: Are Humans Now Overwhelming the Great Forces of Nature?" *AMBIO: A Journal of the Human Environment* 36, no. 8 (December 1, 2007): 614–21. doi: 10.1579/0044-7447(2007)3 6[614:TAAHNO]2.0.CO;2.

Stevens, Wallace. *The Collected Poems of Wallace Stevens.* New York: Knopf Doubleday, 2011.

————. *Collected Poetry and Prose.* New York: Library of America, 1997.

Stewart, Kathleen, and Susan Harding. "Bad Endings: American Apocalypse." *Annual Review of Anthropology* 28, no. 1 (1999): 285–310. doi: 10.1146/annurev.anthro.28.1.285.

"Stupid Facts—License Plate Slogans." *MIStupid.com.* http://mistupid.com/facts/page050.htm.

Tsing, Anna Lowenhaupt. *The Mushroom at the End of the World: On the Possibility of Life in Capitalist Ruins.* Princeton: Princeton University Press, 2015.

Tuan, Yi-Fu. *Space and Place: The Perspective of Experience.* Minneapolis: University of Minnesota Press, 1977.

University of Virginia Library Online Exhibits. "Red, White, Blue and Brimstone: New World Literature and the American Millennium," November 1999. http://explore.lib.virginia.edu/exhibits/show/brimstone.

Veldman, Robin Globus. "Narrating the Environmental Apocalypse: How Imagining the End Facilitates Moral Reasoning among Environmental Activists." *Ethics and the Environment* 17, no. 1 (2012): 1–23.

Wagstaff, Steel. "An Interview with Mark Nowak." *Contemporary Literature* 51, no. 3 (2010): 453–76. doi: 10.1353/cli.2010.0014.

Waldrop, Rosmarie. *A Key into the Language of America.* New York: New Directions, 1994.

Wengen, Deidre. "Imagining the Unimaginable: Jorie Graham in Conversation." 2008. http://www.phillyburbs.com/pb-dyn/news/351-04012008-1512367.html.

Wenzel, Jennifer. "Turning over a New Leaf: Fanonian Humanism and Environmental Justice." In *The Routledge Companion to the Environmental Humanities,* edited by Ursula Heise, Jon Christensen, and Michelle Niemann, 165–73. New York: Routledge, 2017.

Westra, Laura. *Environmental Justice and the Rights of Ecological Refugees.* London; Sterling, Va.: Earthscan, 2009. http://public.eblib.com/choice/publicfullrecord.aspx?p=471088.

Williams, Raymond. *Problems in Materialism and Culture: Selected Essays.* London: Verso, 1980.

Williams, Roger. *A Key into the Language of America.* Detroit: Wayne State University Press, 1973.

Wilson, Edward O. *Half-Earth: Our Planet's Fight for Life.* New York: Norton, 2016.

Woods, Derek. "Scale Critique for the Anthropocene." *Minnesota Review* 2014, no. 83 (January 1, 2014): 133–42. doi: 10.1215/00265667-2782327.

Wordsworth, William. *Wordsworth's Poetry and Prose.* Edited by Nicholas Halmi. New York: W. W. Norton and Company, 2013.

Worster, Donald. "Second Earth: Thinking about Environmental History on a Planetary Scale." Presented at the Division of History of Science, Technology and Environment Colloquium Series, KTH Royal Institute of Technology, Stockholm, January 27, 2014.

———. *Shrinking the Earth: The Rise and Decline of American Abundance.* New York: Oxford University Press, 2016.

Yang, Chun Z., Stuart I. Yaniger, V. Craig Jordan, Daniel J. Klein, and George D. Bittner. "Most Plastic Products Release Estrogenic Chemicals: A Potential Health Problem That Can Be Solved." *Environmental Health Perspectives* 119, no. 7 (July 1, 2011): 989–96. doi: 10.1289/ehp.1003220.

Zalasiewicz, Jan, Alejandro Cearreta, Paul J. Crutzen, Erle Ellis, Michael Ellis, Jacques Grinevald, John R. McNeill, et al. "Response to Autin and Holbrook on 'Is the Anthropocene an Issue of Stratigraphy or Pop Culture?'" *GSA Today* 22 (September 2012): e21–e22. doi: 10.1130/GSATG162C.1.

Zalasiewicz, Jan, Mark Williams, Will Steffen, and Paul Crutzen. "The New World of the Anthropocene." *Environmental Science and Technology* 44, no. 7 (April 1, 2010): 2228–31. doi: 10.1021/es903118j.

Index

"Burning the Small Dead" (Snyder), 175–77, 180
Butler, Judith, 41
butterflies. *See* Lepidoptera
Byron, George Gordon, Lord, 121

Cage, John, 152
Calarco, Matthew, 139–40, 141, 144, 145
California, 165, 182, 185
calypso, 99, 125–26, 134
Canada, 70, 72, 142, 154, 156
Canadian Charter of Rights and Freedoms, 69, 73
capitalism, 16, 78, 178, 211; and the Anthropocene, 7; and climate change, 35, 58; and coal mining, 225; corporate, 241; global, 43, 177, 180, 202; language of, 116
carbon, 27, 46–52, 94, 222; and the Anthropocene, 3–4; atoms, 68, 69; consumption, 75; footprint, 43, 96, 132–33, 198, 208; monoxide, 230–31; sequestration, 6, 19, 142. *See also* coal; fossil fuels; oil; petroleum
"Carboniferous and Ecopoetics, The" (Gander), 27, 47–53, 57, 58
Carson, Rachel, 8, 100, 116, 181
Cash, Johnny, 131
Ceolin, Matt, 150, 161
Chakrabarty, Dipesh, 34–39, 52, 59, 247n8, 258n38
charismatic megafauna, 95, 127, 142, 149
chemistry, 62, 71–72, 75, 85
Chen, Mel Y., 203, 254n26
Chile, 202, 206
China, 195–96, 201, 242; coal mining in, 209, 221–31, 226
Chisholm, Dianne, 248n21, 257n21
Christianity, 247n2; and apocalyptic discourse, 98, 99, 103, 109, 127, 129–32
City Eclogue (Roberson), 29, 180–82, 211–21, 240
civil rights, 218, 220
Clark, Nigel, 2
Clark, Timothy, 37–39, 43, 47

class (socioeconomic), 186, 192, 209, 213, 229, 258n5
climate change: and the Anthropocene, 34–38; and apocalyptic discourse, 104, 108, 114, 118, 120; and the coal industry, 222–23; collective versus individual responsibility for, 37, 43–44; and digital technology, 241–42; emotional responses to, 38–44, 46, 57–58, 111; and other planets, 258n38; and plastics, 66, 75, 86; politics of, 101; refugees, 58, 210, 234; and tipping points, 248n16
coal, 49–51, 205; exhaustion of, 50; formation of, 49–50; industry, 221–31; mining of, 50, 209, 221–31. *See also* carbon; fossil fuels; oil; petroleum
Coal Mountain Elementary (Nowak), 29, 221–31, 226, 236, 240
Coetzee, J. M., 140, 148
Coleridge, Samuel Taylor, 9, 79, 251n30
collage, 20, 23, 76–77, 82, 91, 250n24
colonialism, 7, 174, 177, 179, 194; in the United States, 182–93
colonization: of the Americas, 6, 180, 186
conservation, 46–47, 74, 127, 209, 214; and bark beetles, 142; and ideas of nature, 10, 29, 210, 211; and nature poetry, 19
constraints: poetic, 69, 168, 169–70
constructivism, 147
consumption, 37, 43, 78, 82, 122; of coal, 223; energy, 87; of fossil fuels, 50–51, 208, 241
Core Samples from the World (Gander), 29, 193–203, 199, 201
cornucopia, 91–92, 93–95
cosmopolitanism, 179, 196, 252n32; eco-, 179
Coultas, Brenda, 240–44
Creeley, Robert, 129–30
Cresswell, Tim, 174
crisis, 98–135, 252n22; dwelling in, 28, 98, 100–120, 122, 130, 135; —, and embodied embeddedness in damaged ecosystems, 106–7, 126

Sago mining disaster, 222, 223–24, 227–28, 230–31

scalar dissonance, 27, 32, 38, 39–47, 104; emotional responses to, 39, 45, 59–60

scale, 31–60, 63, 203, 239; of Anthropocene planetary change, 26–27, 32, 105; of coal mining, 225; effects, 36–39; of human attention, 41; of individual action versus collective impact, 37, 44; perception of, 26, 32, 56; and toxicity, 66

science, 32, 35, 39, 94, 96, 146; and animals, 137–38, 147, 150, 155, 158–60, 162; and apocalyptic discourse, 103; and art, 62–63, 68, 76, 88, 91, 95; and collection of insect specimens, 155, 158–60, 163; critique of, 87–91; and perception of risk, 62; and plastics, 73, 78, 93; and realism, 67–68, 75; translation of, 47–48, 92

Scigaj, Leonard M., 9, 11

sea. *See* oceans

Sea Change (Graham), 28, 98–99, 107–20, 134–35, 239

segregation, 148, 213; racial, 210, 211, 216, 218, 220–21

self, 194, 195, 203, 220; bounded, 187; human, 144; nonhuman, 164. *See also* subject

sense of place. *See* place, sense of

senses: and dwelling in crisis, 106–7, 111–12, 114, 125; and eating, 184; and embodiment, 148–49, 152–53, 157; human versus nonhuman, 138–39, 142, 143, 145, 170; pleasures of, 84, 99–100, 106–7, 112–15, 120, 134; and poesis, 255n33; and scale, 49, 53, 57, 59–60

settler colonial society, 183, 185, 187–88, 190

Shakespeare, William, 59

Shellenberger, Michael, 101, 105

Shockley, Evie, 259n15

Sierra Nevada, 175–76

Silent Spring (Carson), 8, 100, 181

Skinner, Jonathan, 28, 99, 136, 142, 239; on birdsong, 138–39, 143–44, 145; "Blackbird Stanzas," 168–73, *173; ecopoetics* (journal), 12

slow listening, 138–39, 170, 173

Snyder, Gary, 9, 168, 182, 192, 198; on bioregionalism, 15, 177; "Burning the Small Dead," 175–77, 180

social justice, 210, 230, 237

sociology, 102, 215

Soper, Kate, 141, 143, 144

sound: of machines, 181; in poetry, 152–54, 169–70, 172–73, 232, 255n38; recordings of animals, 169–72

space, 29, 174–75, 177–80, 183; globalized, 193; outer, 21, 31, 53, 54; of the page, 23, 29, 232; racialization of, 29, 211, 214–20; scales of, 27, 32, 33, 41, 48. *See also* place, sense of; places

Spahr, Juliana, 53, 59, 239, 257n21; on nature poetry, 20; on place, 174–75, 179, 194, 197, 207; "Unnamed Dragonfly Species," 32, 38–47, 182; *Well Then There Now,* 27, 29, 39–47, 182–93, 240, 248n22

species: bird, 168, 171; chordate, 124; companion, 138; disparaged, 127–28, 134; endangered, 27, 39–47, 114; evolution of, 48; extinction, 3, 7, 20–22, 39, 57, 114, 138; global movement of, 6, 174, 188; humanity as, 2, 6–7, 33, 35–37, 208; humility, 34; impact of humans on other, 8, 20, 59, 137, 169; interdependence of human and nonhuman, 28, 99, 113, 126–27; intersubjectivity between human and nonhuman, 137–62; native, 19, 186; nonmammalian, 28; nonnative, 186–87, 190; not threatened, 142; not yet named, 45; subjective experiences of different, 140–41, 144–45, 153, 186

Spivak, Gayatri, 160

Steffen, Will, 4

Stein, Gertrude, 26, 183

Stevens, Wallace, 56, 114, 125, 170, 181

Stingel, Rudolf, 82–84, *83,* 86, 87, 96

Stoermer, Eugene, 2, 8

CPSIA information can be obtained
at www.ICGtesting.com
Printed in the USA
LVOW03s1006180218
567025LV00001B/131/P